To my good friend Robert,
With all best wishes,
Stuart

JĪVA GOSVĀMIN'S

TATTVASANDARBHA

JĪVA GOSVĀMIN'S

TATTVASANDARBHA

A Study on the Philosophical and Sectarian Development of the Gauḍīya Vaiṣṇava Movement

Stuart Mark Elkman

MOTILAL BANARSIDASS
Delhi Varanasi Patna Madras

First Edition: Delhi 1986

MOTILAL BANARSIDASS
Bungalow Road, Jawahar Nagar, Delhi 110 007
Branches
Chowk, Varanasi 221 001
Ashok Rajpath, Patna 800 004
120 Royapettah High Road, Mylapore, Madras 600 004

ISBN: 81-208-0187-3

PRINTED IN INDIA
BY JAINENDRA PRAKASH JAIN AT SHRI JAINENDRA PRESS, A-45 NARAINA INDUSTRIAL AREA, PHASE I, NEW DELHI 110 028 AND PUBLISHED BY NARENDRA PRAKASH JAIN FOR MOTILAL BANARSIDASS, DELHI 110 007

TO MY MOTHER, FATHER AND S.P.

for their unselfish love and unfailing support

ACKNOWLEDGEMENTS

It gives me great pleasure to finally be able to offer my sincere thanks to all of those who have so generously devoted their time and services in the creation of this book. I say "finally" because the few changes and finishing touches which I reluctantly made in order to get the manuscript ready for publication, have taken nearly as much time as the writing of the text, initially a doctoral dissertation for the University of Pennsylvania in 1981, accomplished with the luxury of ample time no longer so available.

First I would like to mention those who made my research time in India so profitable and personally rewarding: the AIIS and its Calcutta director, Mr. Tarun Mitra, for their funding and good company, respectively; my Indian advisor, Prof. Narayan Chandra Goswami, an embodiment of scholarship, simplicity, and humility; Prof. Govinda Gopal Mukherjee, for his invaluable help in the translation portion of this work, for his hospitality, and for his kindness; the Caitanya Prema Sansthana, for presenting me with an extremely useful and rare edition of the *Tattva-sandarbha*; and the sadhus and staff of the Ramakrishna Mission Institute of Culture, both for their academic help and for providing me with a spiritual haven during my year in Calcutta—my debt to them is especially immense and will not soon be forgotten.

I would also like to express my gratitude to all those members of the South Asia and Oriental Studies Departments of the University of Pennsylvania with whom I have worked through the years: Prof. Ludo Rocher, for patiently going through the original manuscript of my dissertation, for providing constant moral support throughout the course of my studies, and for introducing me to one of my great loves, the Sanskrit language; Prof. Rosane Rocher, for the privilege of working with her as the teaching assistant in her first-year Sanskrit class; Prof. Peter Gaeffke, for his many valuable suggestions and keen interest in this project; Ms. Tan Wen, for introducing me to another of my great loves, the Bengali language; Dr. Richard Cohen, for reading some of the Brajabhāṣā texts of the Vallabha school with me; Ms. Kanta Bhatia, for her help in arranging xerox and microfilm copies of important texts; and Ms. Teresa Torelli, for submitting an application for funding on my behalf while I was in India, oblivious to such details.

I am also indebted to Brahmacari Nitya Caitanya and Swami Viprananda of the Vedanta Society of Southern California for their great help in editing and proof-reading, respectively. Without their valuable aid, I am afraid my already flagging enthusiasm might have given way to inertia altogether.

Finally, my heartfelt thanks go out to my advisor, Prof. Wilhelm Halbfass, whose breadth of knowledge and sympathy for Indian thought have been a constant source of wonderment and inspiration for me. For the many happy hours spent together in the study of Indian philosophy, for his ceaseless interest and aid in this project from its inception to its conclusion, for his encouragement, and for his friendship, I am ever grateful.

CONTENTS

		page
ACKNOWLEDGEMENTS		vii
ABBREVIATIONS		x
INTRODUCTION		xi
	PART I	
I.	Caitanya	1
II.	Jīva	21
III.	Baladeva	25
IV.	Rādhāmohana	51
	PART II	
V.	*Tattvasandarbha*: Preliminary Remarks	57
VI.	*Tattvasandarbha*: Text, Translation, and Notes	66
CONCLUSION		179
GLOSSARY		189
BIBLIOGRAPHY		197
INDEX		201

ABBREVIATIONS

Ag.P.	*Agni Purāṇa*
Bh.P.	*Bhāgavata Purāṇa*
Br.S.	*Brahmasūtra*
Bṛ.U.	*Bṛhadāraṇyaka Upaniṣad*
C.C.	*Caitanya Caritāmṛta*
ā.	*ādilīlā*
m.	*madhyalīlā*
a.	*antyalīlā*
Ch.U.	*Chāndogya Upaniṣad*
Ka.U.	*Kaṭha Upaniṣad*
Ma.P.	*Matsya Purāṇa*
M.Bh.	*Mahābhārata*
Pa.P.	*Padma Purāṇa*
Śi.P.	*Śiva Purāṇa*
Sk.P.	*Skanda Purāṇa*
S.S.	*Sarvasaṃvādinī*
Tai.U.	*Taittirīya Upaniṣad*
T.S.	*Tattvasandarbha*
Vā.P.	*Vāyu Purāṇa*
Vi.P.	*Viṣṇu Purāṇa*
B.D.	Baladeva
K.K.	Kṛṣṇadāsa Kavirāja
R.M.	Rādhāmohana

INTRODUCTION

The birth of Caitanya in 1486 was, in many respects, one of the most significant events in the history of Bengal. In his short lifetime of 48 years, only half of which were spent in his native Bengal, Caitanya initiated one of India's most vigorous *bhakti* movements, the effects of which have been felt not only in the field of religion, but also in the fields of social reform, literature, and philosophy.

Caitanya's birthplace, Navadvīpa, 75 miles north of Calcutta, was an important trading center, and famed throughout India for its developments in the field of Navya Nyāya; and despite the Muslim dominance of Bengal, Navadvīpa was still a great center of Sanskrit learning at the time of Caitanya's birth. Nevertheless, as Jadunath Sarkar explains:

> ...if we may believe the biographers of Caitanya, the atmosphere of the town was sceptical and unspiritual. There was a lack of true religious fervour and sincere devotion. Proud of their intellectuality, proud of the vast wealth they acquired by gifts from rich Hindus, the local *pandits* despised *bhakti* or devotion as weak and vulgar, and engaged in idle ceremonies or idler amusements. Vedantism formed the topic of conversation of the cultured few; wine and goat's meat were taken to kindly by the majority of the people, and such *Shākta* rites as were accompanied by the offering of this drink and food to the goddess and their subsequent consumption by her votaries, were performed with zeal and enthusiasm. (Sarkar: 1932: 7)

Although social reform was not Caitanya's primary interest, his life, as portrayed in the biographies, was such as to combat and resolve many of the social ills and historical problems of his time. While not disregarding the social institutions of caste rigidly adhered to by the orthodox Hindu community of Navadvīpa, Caitanya stressed the equality of all with regard to spiritual questions, emphasizing the practice of *saṅkīrtana*, or congregational singing of devotional songs, to which all were welcome. Though an accomplished Sanskrit scholar, Caitanya disdained dry speculation and vain argumentation; and while later generations of Gauḍīya Vaiṣṇavas adopted certain erotic tantric practices as means to experience the love between Rādhā and Kṛṣṇa, Caitanya himself placed great emphasis on chastity and other moral and ethical virtues.

Caitanya's life gave rise to an unusually rich and varied literature, and may even be considered one of the chief factors in the emergence of the Bengali language as an important literary medium. The most common theme of this literature was, naturally, Caitanya's life itself, and a large number of biographies were composed, first in Sanskrit and later in Bengali. As a result of the widespread practice of *saṅkīrtana*, a great many lyrics were also written in Bengali, either on traditional Rādhā/Kṛṣṇa motifs, or on incidents from the lives of Caitanya and his associates.

Caitanya left behind no writings on philosophical or theological questions. Instead, he entrusted the formulation of the doctrines of the school to a small group of scholarly followers, known as the six Gosvāmins, all of whom passed their days in Vṛndāvana, a small town just north of the Muslim stronghold of Agra, where they devoted their lives to their Sanskrit compositions, spiritual practices, and the re-establishment of the fabled site of Kṛṣṇa's youth, Vṛndāvana. Of the six Gosvāmins, Raghunātha Bhaṭṭa, Raghunātha Dāsa, Gopāla Bhaṭṭa, Rūpa, Sanātana, and Jīva, only the first left behind no writings, and only Jīva did not receive personal instruction from Caitanya, joining the group, presumably, just after Caitanya's death.

Among the greatest contributions of the six Gosvāmins are the theological writings of Rūpa. In his two principal works, the *Bhaktirasāmṛtasindhu* and *Ujjvalanīlamaṇi*, Rūpa categorizes and illustrates the different stages of devotion from ritualistic practice to passionate love of God, the physical and psychological changes which accompany the different stages of devotion, and the various attitudes, or *rasas*, an aspirant may assume in relationship to God, such as that of a servant to his master, a lover to his beloved, etc. Rūpa also composed dramas of high literary value, such as the *Vidagdhamādhava* and *Lalitamādhava*.

The Smṛti scripture of the school, the *Haribhaktivilāsa*, is attributed by some to Sanātana and by others to Gopāla Bhaṭṭa; probably it represents some sort of collaboration between the two. This work contains prescriptions for the daily behavior of Gauḍīya Vaiṣṇavas, as well as for their ritualistic worship, observance of religious festivals, initiation, founding of temples, etc. The text shows signs of influence from the Śrī Sampradāya of Rāmānuja, a fact which is usually taken as evidence that Gopāla Bhaṭṭa, a native of South India and descendant of Śrī Vaiṣṇavas, had a hand in its authorship. Sanātana also wrote one of the school's several *Bhāgavata* commentaries, the *Vaiṣṇavatoṣiṇī*.

Raghunātha Dāsa's contribution was mainly in the field of poetry and drama, while Jīva was almost single-handedly responsible for the philosophical writings of the school, chief of which is his six-volume *Bhāgavatasandarbha*. Jīva was also the most prolific and versatile of the Gosvāmins, writing on such varied topics as grammar, literature, theology, and philosophy.

As was the case with other Vaiṣṇava *bhakti* movements of the 16th and 17th centuries, questions of self-image and legitimacy began to take on added importance for the Gauḍīya Vaiṣṇavas of Vṛndāvana with the influx of other Vaiṣṇava sects to the area, especially since the Gauḍīyas had neither a formal affiliation with one of the recognized Vaiṣṇava *sampradāyas* as, for example, the Rāmānandins had with the Śrī Sampradāya, nor an independent commentary on Vedānta as, for example, the Vallabhācārins had. An early tradition did exist linking Caitanya to the Brahma Sampradāya of Madhva, although this was not recognized by either the Gosvāmins of Vṛndāvana or the orthodox biographers. However, when the status of the Gauḍīya school was formally called into question in the early 18th century, Baladeva Vidyābhūṣaṇa, the second great name in the history of Gauḍīya Vaiṣṇava philosophy, made an official declaration on behalf of the school acknowledging its affiliation with the Mādhva Sampradāya. Baladeva also provided the Gauḍīya Vaiṣṇavas with their first and only commentary on the *Brahmasūtra*, and made repeated attempts to show the dependence of Gauḍīya Vaiṣṇava thought on the philosophical views of Madhva.

As a result of Baladeva's writings and sectarian activities, a rift was created within the Gauḍīya Vaiṣṇava community on the question of sectarian allegiance which exists to this day, one section defending the position of an independent Caitanya Sampradāya, and the other claiming allegiance to the Mādhva Sampradāya. The extent to which these two groups differ is clearly seen in the statements of their respective proponents. Janardan Chakravarti, representing the former position, states: "Valadeva Vidyābhūṣaṇa of *Govinda-Bhāṣya*-fame showed a leaning towards affiliating Chaitanyism to the Mādhva-sect. But this has been stoutly opposed by the devout and scholarly followers of Sri Chaitanya." (Chakravarti: 1975: 11) And Bhaktivinod Ṭhākur, a champion of the latter position, writes: "What doubt can there be that those who reject the line of gurus [tracing Caitanya to Madhva] are the chief enemies of Caitanya's followers?" (Bhaktivinod, *Śrīmanmahāprabhur Śikṣā*, quoted in Baladeva: 1968: 16)

Scholarly interest in the social and literary aspects of the Gauḍīya Vaiṣṇava movement and, to a somewhat lesser degree, in their philosophical doctrines has been great, and it may safely be said that no other Vaiṣṇava movement can claim such an abundance of secondary literature. The interest of Western scholars dates back to the early 19th century with the work of H. H. Wilson on the different Hindu sects (*Religious Sects of the Hindus*, first published as articles in 1828 and 1832, and later in two volumes in 1861 and 1862). J. N. Farquhar continued the work of Wilson with *An Outline of the Religious Literature of India* in 1920, and Melville Kennedy provided the first important work by a Western scholar devoted wholly to the Gauḍīya Vaiṣṇava movement with his *Caitanya Movement* in 1925, still one of the best works on the subject. It is significant to note, however, that neither Kennedy nor his predecessors, Wilson and Farquhar, make any reference to the sectarian disputes within the Gauḍīya school, the latter two accepting the association with the Mādhvas as a historical fact. Present-day interest in Gauḍīya Vaiṣṇava studies in the West, under the leadership of Edward Dimock, is mainly in the field of Bengali literature, although several religious and social questions have been discussed by Friedhelm Hardy in his article, "Mādhavendra Purī: A Link Between Bengal Vaiṣṇavism and South Indian *Bhakti*", and Joseph O'Connell in his 1970 dissertation, entitled *Social Implications of the Gauḍīya Vaiṣṇava Movement.*

The belief in the Mādhva affiliation of the Gauḍīya Vaiṣṇavas was fostered to a large extent by the writings of Dinesh Chandra Sen in the early decades of this century. He writes, for example, "It was to the Māddhi (sic) sect that Bengal owes her great Vaiṣṇava faith, the culminating point of which was reached in the life of Chaitanya." (Sen: 1917b: 297) This contention was not seriously challenged by Indian scholars until S. K. De wrote his monumental *Early History of the Vaiṣṇava Faith and Movement in Bengal* in 1942. Both De and A. K. Majumdar, in his scholarly work *Caitanya: His Life and Doctrine*, 1969, argue vigorously against the historical accuracy of the *guruparamparā* linking Caitanya to the Mādhva Sampradāya, relying heavily on the Bengali work of Bipan Bihari Majumdar, *Caitanyacariter Upādāna*, 1939, by far the most comprehensive study on the biographical accounts of Caitanya's life.

Interest in the philosophical writings of the Gauḍīya Vaiṣṇavas is almost totally absent in Western scholarship, and not one of Jīva's works, unquestionably the most important and authoritative philosophical texts of the school, has been translated into English. Baladeva's *Brahmasūtra* commentary, the *Govindabhāṣya*, and his *Prameyaratnāvali* both appear in English translation in the *Sacred Books of the Hindus*, Vol. V (1912), a fact which in itself is an indication of the sectarian views of the school in the early part of this century. Bengali authors, most notably Sudhindra Chandra Chakravarti (*Philosophical Foundations of Bengali Vaiṣṇavism*, 1969), have given good summaries of the major philosophical doctrines of the school, and have pointed out the special contributions of Baladeva, as well as the differences between him and Jīva, but, not surprisingly, have placed little emphasis on the historical circumstances surrounding the philosophical developments or on the effects these developments have had on the sectarian evolution of the school.

The present study will thus serve a double purpose. On the one hand, it will make available for the first time an English translation of Jīva's *Tattvasandarbha*, the introductory volume of his *Bhāgavatasandarbha*, the single most important and authoritative philosophical writing of the Gauḍīya Vaiṣṇava school and the only work of Jīva's to be commented on by Baladeva. In addition to the text and translation, extensive notes will be given from Jīva's *Sarvasaṃvādinī*, an appendix to the *Bhāgavatasandarbha*, and the commentaries of Baladeva and Rādhāmohana, a junior contemporary of Baladeva and critic of his views on Mādhva affiliation.

The second intention will be to show the development of the Gauḍīya Vaiṣṇava school along philosophical and sectarian lines on the basis of the evidence of the *Tattvasandarbha* and its commentaries. This latter task will include analyses of: 1) the relationship between the life and teachings of Caitanya as portrayed in his biographies and the philosophical doctrines of Jīva; 2) the relationship between the sectarian and philosophical views of Baladeva and those of Jīva; and 3) the orthodox reaction to the views of Baladeva, as represented by the *Tattvasandarbha* commentary of Rādhāmohana.

Due to the historical nature of this latter study, a certain familiarity with the major figures and events concerned will be helpful in order to appreciate the full significance of the philosophical texts being dealt with. For this reason, the translation and notes of the *Tattvasandarbha* will be prefaced by a short study on the lives of Caitanya, Jīva, Baladeva, and Rādhāmohana, in which the points briefly outlined here will be more fully discussed. It is hoped that at the end of this study, the philosophical developments which so profoundly affected the direction of the Gauḍīya Vaiṣṇava movement as well as the self-image of its adherents will be seen in a clearer light, and that the *Tattvasandarbha* and commentaries by Baladeva and Rādhāmohana will be more fully appreciated, not only for their philosophical interest, but also as important documents concerning the sectarian development of the Gauḍīya Vaiṣṇava school.

Chapter I

CAITANYA

Shortly after the death of Caitanya in 1533, a considerable number of biographies began to appear, first in Sanskrit and later in Bengali. Although discrepancies over details are found in the various biographies, and reports of miraculous events are commonplace, the biographies are, for the most part, unusually good historical accounts considering the period in which they were written and the lack of any real historical tradition at the time.[1]

The earliest of these works seems to be the Sanskrit composition of Murāri Gupta, entitled *Śrīkṛṣṇacaitanyacaritāmṛta*. The author was a close companion of Caitanya in Navadvīpa, and later biographers have relied heavily on his work as source material for Caitanya's first 24 years, that is, up until his initiation into *sannyāsa* and subsequent departure from Navadvīpa. The next Sanskrit biography was written by Dāmodara Svarūpa, one of Caitanya's closest companions in Puri, and although no longer available, has been referred to by later biographers as a chief source of information for Caitanya's later years. Kavi Karṇapūra, the next Sanskrit biographer, wrote three important compositions: a poem entitled *Caitanyacaritāmṛtamahākāvya*; the drama *Caitanyacandrodaya*; and a rather controversial and, for the purposes of this study, important work entitled *Gauragaṇoddeśadīpikā*, in which the *guruparamparā* linking Caitanya to Madhva is first found. Although the works of Karṇapūra are of high literary value—D. C. Sen calls them "by far the greatest books written in Bengal about Chaitanya" (Sen: 1917b: 71)—they do not seem to have enjoyed much popularity, probably due to a reluctance on the part of the Vṛndāvana Gosvāmins to acknowledge them as authoritative.[2] As the works of Kavi Karṇapūra are of special interest to this study, there will be occasion to discuss them more fully in subsequent sections.

Among the Bengali biographies, two stand out in particular, both for their own special merits and the extraordinarily high esteem in which they are held by the Gauḍīya Vaiṣṇavas. The earlier of the two, the *Caitanya Bhāgavata*, was witten by Vṛndāvanadāsa at the request of Nityānanda, the most highly venerated of Caitanya's companions and chief propagator of the movement in Bengal. Vṛndāvanadāsa never met Caitanya, and presumably relied heavily on Nityānanda's reminiscences of Caitanya's Navadvīpa days for source material. Consequently, his *Caitanya Bhāgavata* is devoted chiefly to the early part of Caitanya's life. The work, probably written within two or three decades of Caitanya's death, was very well received by the Vṛndāvana Gosvāmins, and may be said to represent the authoritative version of Caitanya's Navadvīpa period.

The second great Bengali biography, the *Caitanya Caritāmṛta* of Kṛṣṇadāsa Kavirāja, is by far the most authoritative biography for the Gauḍīya Vaiṣṇava school, although probably not as popular as the *Caitanya Bhāgavata*. Its author, a disciple of Raghunātha Dāsa and intimate companion of the other Gosvāmins of Vṛndāvana as well, was himself an accomplished Sanskrit scholar, and received a thorough education from the Gosvāmins in theology and philosophy. Kṛṣṇadāsa undertook the writing of his biography towards the end of his life at the request of the Vaiṣṇava community of Vṛndāvana, unsatisfied with the sketchy treatment Caitanya's later years had received at the hands of Vṛndāvanadāsa, completing the work, according to tradition, in 1581. Kṛṣṇadāsa consequently devotes most of his attention to Caitanya's life as a *sannyāsin*, referring his reader to the *Caitanya Bhāgavata* for accounts of Caitanya's early years. Like his predecessor Vṛndāvanadāsa, Kṛṣṇadāsa relies to a large extent on the early Sanskrit biographies; it is almost certain that he made use of the personal reminiscences of the Gosvāmins as well.

The speciality of the *Caitanya Caritāmṛta* lies less in its literary value than in its exhaustive and scholarly treatment of the theological doctrines of the Gosvāmins, presented as the teachings of Caitanya. Kṛṣṇadāsa's work thus serves the valuable function of making the subtle and intricate doctrines of the school known to those followers who lack the erudition or knowledge of Sanskrit necessary to read the works of the Gosvāmins.

Kṛṣṇadāsa's extreme faithfulness to the writings of the Gosvāmins has, understandably, led to a somewhat skeptical attitude on the part of some scholars. S. K. De, for example, writes:

> It is indeed difficult to say how much of the elaborate theologising which is piously put in his [Caitanya's] mouth was actually uttered by him, for these reported utterances of his are in fact faithful summaries of the highly scholastic works of the six Vṛndāvana Gosvāmins themselves, who as leisured recluses could devote their keen and highly trained minds to the construction of elaborate systems of speculation. (De: 1974: 73)

Kṛṣṇadāsa has also been criticized for his credulous acceptance of miraculous events, his inclusion of incidents not found in earlier biographies, and his somewhat sectarian attitude. Nevertheless, the *Caitanya Caritāmṛta* is an extremely valuable source of information, especially as it represents the most authoritative version of Caitanya's life and teachings within the Gauḍīya Vaiṣṇava school; and we will base the following account of Caitanya's life mainly on this work. Other biographies will be occasionally referred to, particularly with regard to certain early incidents in his life, such as his taking of *sannyāsa*, etc.

In utilizing the *Caitanya Caritāmṛta* as our chief source, it will be necessary to distinguish as far as possible which of Kṛṣṇadāsa's accounts represent actual fact, and which represent either later traditional beliefs concerning Caitanya, the distinctive teachings of the Gosvāmins, or Kṛṣṇadāsa's own sectarian biases. The criteria for these decisions will necessarily vary from case to case, but as a general rule, some kind of verification will be sought from other sources, such as the early biographies, independent historical accounts, etc. In defense of Kṛṣṇadāsa it should be added that there is no reason to suspect him of deliberately falsifying the facts of Caitanya's life, and that if there are inacccuracies in his accounts, they are the result of the Kavirāja's great faith in the divinity of Caitanya, and in his belief that the Gosvāmins were merely the faithful recorders of Caitanya's own teachings.

Caitanya was born in 1486 in the town of Navadvīpa, West Bengal, then a great center of Sanskrit learning and a place of considerable political importance. He was given the name Viśvambhara and affectionately called "Nimāi" until his initiation into *sannyāsa* in 1510.

All the biographers agree that Nimāi led an extremely mischievous childhood, and developed into a proud young scholar with a reputation for his skill in Sanskrit grammar. At that time, a small community of Vaiṣṇavas lived in Navadvīpa, who would meet under the leadership of Advaita, a resident of nearby Śāntipur and disciple of Mādhavendra Purī[3], and hold *saṅkīrtana* sessions. Many members of the group were well-known to Nimāi who, like most of the orthodox community of Navadvīpa, had little respect for their devotional practices.

One day Īśvara Purī, also a disciple of Mādhavendra Purī, came to Navadvīpa, where he was warmly received by the local Vaiṣṇavas. In the course of his stay, he visited the home of Nimāi and took his meal there. Īśvara was highly impressed with Nimāi, and thereafter made repeated attempts to attract him to the views of the Vaiṣṇavas. While Nimāi, then 21 years old and a married householder, showed Īśvara Purī the respect due a *sannyāsin*, there is no indication that any intimate relationship arose between them at that time to account for the radical change which Nimāi underwent at their later meeting in Gayā. It is even recorded that when Īśvara sought Nimāi's opinion on a book he had written, *Kṛṣṇalīlāmṛta*, the young paṇḍit gave it a critical review, pointing out various errors in grammar.

After a trip to East Bengal, during which his first wife died of snake-bite, followed by his subsequent marriage to Viṣṇupriyā, Nimāi set off for Gayā in 1508 to perform the Śrāddha ceremony for his deceased father. While in the Viṣṇu temple, Nimāi chanced to meet Īśvara Purī again. Their meeting this time was highly emotional, due in part to the effect of the holy city of Gayā on Nimāi. Subsequent meetings with the Purī in Gayā culminated in Nimāi's initiation with him in the ten-syllabled Gopāla mantra. The effect of this on Nimāi was so great that he felt a total aversion for his earlier worldly pursuits, and would not have returned to Navadvīpa at all were it not for the urging of a divine voice commanding him to do so.

Nimāi returned to Navadvīpa, no longer the proud scholar he had been before his trip to Gayā. The news of his conversion was received with great joy by the Vaiṣṇavas of Navadvīpa, and Nimāi soon became the central figure of their group and the object of their veneration and worship. As a result of his now frequent ecstasies and constant absorption in spiritual moods, it soon became impossible for him to continue his teaching career, and he began to spend most of his time with his new companions, often passing whole nights with them in *saṅkīrtana* sessions rather than return home.

Nimāi's growing aversion for worldly life and his longing for spiritual fulfillment were, no doubt, the key ingredients in his ultimate decision to formally take to a life of *sannyāsa*. The catalyst, however, was a particular incident, which is of special interest insofar as it clearly shows the vision which Nimāi then had of his future mission.

According to Kṛṣṇadāsa's account, Nimāi was sitting quietly one day, deeply absorbed in the mood of the milkmaids of Vṛndāvana and uttering the word *gopī* again and again. One of his students interrupted him and suggested that he would do better to repeat the name of Kṛṣṇa instead. Disturbed in his mood Nimāi rushed at the student with a stick in his hand. The student fled safely, but the incident caused a great commotion in the city, leading Nimāi to reflect:

> I was born to bring salvation to the world, but just the opposite is happening. I have not been able to bestow the gift of *bhakti*; my enemies curse me and are not able to accept it. Therefore, I must become a *sannyāsin*. Then the very ones who curse me and show me disrespect will ultimately be saved. Then all will make respectful obeisance to me, their sins will be destroyed, and devotion will blossom in their pure hearts. There is no other way to save these sinners. (C. C. ā. 17/261-7)

About this time, a *sannyāsin* by the name of Keśava Bhāratī came to Navadvīpa. Nimāi approached him respectfully and invited him to take his meal at Nimāi's home, at which time Nimāi requested Keśava to initiate him into *sannyāsa*. Keśava agreed, and within a few days Nimāi set off for nearby Katwa where Keśava stayed, accompanied by Nityānanda and a few others.

According to Vṛndāvanadāsa, after Nimāi had reached Keśava's place, he informed Keśava that he had been visited by a holy man in a dream who whispered a *sannyāsa* mantra into his ear. Nimāi whispered the same mantra to Keśava to see if he would consent to initiating him with it. Keśava was amazed to hear the mantra, and proceeded to initiate him accordingly.

Vṛndāvanadāsa explains Nimāi's uttering of the mantra as a ploy on his part, by virtue of which he actually initiated Keśava, thereby making the guru his disciple. Keśava remarked that it was by the grace of Kṛṣṇa that Nimāi had received the mantra, giving the impression that the mantra in question was a Vaiṣṇava mantra. (C. Bh.m. 26/197-201) This assumption is also made by A.K. Majumdar, who writes:

> [The initiation of Caitanya with such a mantra] was most unusual, and if Caitanya had not intervened, Keśava Bhāratī would have initiated him with a *mahāvākya* with its monistic implications to which Caitanya had the greatest possible objection. (Majumdar: 1969: 262)

However, if we look at the account of this incident as reported by Murāri Gupta, a close companion of Caitanya and the earliest of all biographers, we get a quite different impression. He writes:

> The master said to us one day, "A noble *brāhmaṇa* appeared to me in a dream and, smiling, uttered the *sannyāsa* mantra in my ear. Ever since hearing it, I have been sick at heart and cry day and night. How can I desert my beloved Lord Hari for something else?" (*Kaḍacā* 2/18/1-3)[4]

Although Caitanya did not divulge the mantra to his companions, it is clear from Murāri's reply that all present assumed it to be the *mahāvākya, tat tvam asi* ("You are That"). Murāri said, "O Master, think of the words [*tat* and *tvam*] as forming a genitive compound [meaning "You are His"] and be at ease." (2/18/3-4)[5] Caitanya is reported to have accepted Murāri's interpretation, but to have still felt sad at heart since the mere hearing of the words *tat* and *tvam* brought to his mind the idea of non-duality. A similar description of this incident is given by Kavi Karṇapūra in his *Mahākāvya* (11/41-42) with the difference that Murāri's reply is there said to have removed Caitanya's grief.

Murāri also describes Caitanya as having whispered the mantra into Keśava's ear for verification. He writes:

> Caitanya uttered the purified *sannyāsa* mantra three times into his ear. Keśava remarked, "This is the supreme, pure *sannyāsa* mantra of Hari." Then Caitanya, the eternal guru and Lord of men, having craftily initiated his [soon-to-be] guru, stood with folded hands and requested his own initiation. (*Kaḍacā* 3/2/8-9)[6]

The reason for Keśava's designation of the mantra as the "pure *sannyāsa* mantra of Hari" is then explained in terms of Keśava's new understanding of the *mahāvākya, tat tvam asi* as meaning "You are His", its "purified" meaning, consistent with the Gauḍīya Vaiṣṇava doctrine that the *jīva* represents a portion of *brahman.*

Caitanya's initiation with a *mahāvākya* signifies at least a formal entrance into the Advaitic Bhāratī order of his guru, Keśava, a fact which was never denied by Caitanya who, according to the *Caitanya Caritāmṛta,* often referred to himself, though somewhat disparagingly, as a "Māyāvādī sannyāsī". The early Sanskrit biographies, including Kavi Karṇapūra's *Caitanyacandrodaya,* also describe Caitanya as having received the *mahāvākya* from Keśava and belonging to the Bhāratī Sampradāya. No mention is made of Keśava either prior to or after this event, and it does not seem that he had any special influence on Caitanya's spiritual outlook. Kṛṣṇadāsa lists Keśava as one of Mādhavendra Purī's disciples, but this seems most unlikely, both because of Keśava's Bhāratī title and because of his lack of contact with Mādhavendra's other disciples, such as Advaita, who lived nearby.

A. K. Majumdar also suggests that Caitanya was never formally initiated into *sannyāsa* by Keśava. This suggestion is based on the fact that the Caitanya title (the full name given was Kṛṣṇa Caitanya) is normally given in the Bhāratī order at the time of *brahmacarya,* not *sannyāsa.* He corroborates this by mentioning the case of Dāmodara Svarūpa who is also said to have taken *sannyāsa* initiation, but was given the title Svarūpa, also a *brahmacārin* designation.

The fact that Caitanya did not take the Bhāratī title did not go unnoticed by the biographers. According to Vṛndāvanadāsa, Keśava explained:

> Technically, the disciple of a Bhāratī should also be a Bhāratī. But in your case it's not fitting. Since you have inspired so

many to take the name of Kṛṣṇa, and have awakened their hearts by the spreading of *saṅkīrtana*, your name will be Kṛṣṇa Caitanya, "he by whose grace the lives of all will become blessed". (C.Bh.m. 26/216-7)

Vṛndāvanadāsa's explanation is not fully satisfying, although it seems clear that Caitanya did receive initiation into *sannyāsa* that day, because he put on the ochre robes of a monk immediately after the ceremony.[7] In the case of Dāmodara Svarūpa, Majumdar is probably correct that he never took formal *sannyāsa*, since Kṛṣṇadāsa specifically states that he did not assume the dress of a *sannyāsin*.[8] It should also be noted that Dāmodara took his initiation in Benares, where the practice of not giving *sannyāsa* initiation before *brahmacarya* was probably more strictly followed. It is possible that Keśava's giving of a Caitanya name represented a desire on his part to adhere to the established customs, at least in a formal way, and that because of its appealing meaning, the name Kṛṣṇa Caitanya, often shortened to Caitanya, somehow stuck.

After his initiation into *sannyāsa*, Caitanya gradually made his way to Puri, the home of the famous Jagannātha temple, in the neighbouring state of Orissa, where he was to spend nearly all of his remaining years. Upon reaching the Jagannātha temple, he entered, attempted to embrace the image, and fell down unconscious, overcome with emotion. As the angered temple guards were about to forcibly evict him from the temple, the well-known Advaitin and Navya Nyāya scholar, Vāsudeva Sārvabhauma, came to his rescue and had Caitanya brought to his home. Later, when Caitanya's companions discovered his whereabouts, Sārvabhauma made inquiries about Caitanya's background. He is reported by Kṛṣṇadāsa to have asked, "Into which *sampradāya* has he taken *sannyāsa*, and what is his name?" (C.C.m. 6/70) Sārvabhauma's brother-in-law, Gopīnātha, replied, "His name is Śrī Kṛṣṇa Caitanya, and his guru is the blessed Keśava Bhāratī." (6/71) Sārvabhauma said, "His name is first class but the Bhāratī Sampradāya is only mediocre."[9] (6-72) Gopīnātha replied that Caitanya paid no attention to such superficialities and didn't care one way or the other about the status of his *sampradāya*. (6-73)

Nevertheless, Sārvabhauma felt it his duty to see that the young *sannyāsin* honor the traditions of his calling, and undertook to instruct him in the philosophy of Advaita. According to Kṛṣṇadāsa, Sārvabhauma lectured Caitanya for seven consecutive days on the *Brahmasūtra* with Śaṅkara's commentary, possibly explaining later Advaita doctrines as well. On the eighth day, Sārvabhauma asked Caitanya, who had listened in silence the whole time, if he understood what he had heard. Caitanya replied, "The meaning of the *Sūtras* is perfectly clear; but listening to your explanations has confused my mind." (C.C.m. 6/130)

Caitanya continued with a lengthy reply, in the course of which he outlined many of the beliefs which later became standard Gauḍīya Vaiṣṇava doctrines as formulated by the Vṛndāvana Gosvāmins, such as: the supremacy of *śabda pramāṇa*; the idea that Purāṇas clarify the meaning of the Vedas; the three-fold *śakti* theory elucidated in the *Viṣṇu Purāṇa*; the distinction between *iśvara* and *jīva* based on their respective dominance over and subordinance to *māyā*; the refutation of Vivartavāda and defense of Śaktipariṇāmavāda; and the establishment of *bhagavat* as the object of all the scriptures, *preman* as the highest goal of life, and *bhakti* as the means of attaining that goal. (C.C.m. 6/130-180)

All of the doctrines referred to by Caitanya in this section can be found in Jīva's *Tattvasandarbha*, and there is no question that Kṛṣṇadāsa relied heavily on that work for his exposition of the views stated here. While this does not prove that Caitanya did not also hold such views, it certainly casts some doubt on the question, and it must ultimately be admitted that the exact relationship between the teachings of Caitanya, the philosophy of Jīva, and the accounts of Kṛṣṇadāsa in cases such as this is extremely difficult to determine. We might only mention that due to the discrepancies between Kṛṣṇadāsa's version of this incident and Vṛndāvanadāsa's, the sophistication of Caitanya's arguments, and the numerous Sanskrit quotations uttered by Caitanya, indicating a knowledge of the scriptures which some feel to be exaggerated, some scholars have expressed doubts regarding the historicity of this incident.[10]

Within a few months of his arrival in Puri, Caitanya decided to make an extensive pilgrimage to South India. According to Kṛṣṇadāsa, Caitanya was accompanied by a *brāhmaṇa* attendant, also named Kṛṣṇadāsa. However, according to the *Kaḍacā* of Govindadāsa, a highly controversial work dealing solely with this

South India tour, Caitanya and Kṛṣṇadāsa parted ways shortly after starting out, and Govindadāsa, said to have been a former attendant of Īśvara Purī, accompanied Caitanya for the remainder of his tour. As Govindadāsa's accounts of the tour differ substantially from other accounts, his *Kaḍacā* has not been traditionally accepted, although D. C. Sen argues strongly for its authenticity, and suggests that it was not favorably received by the Vṛndāvana Gosvāmins because of its unusually human treatment of Caitanya and its depiction of him in a non-sectarian light. As an example, Sen mentions Caitanya's ecstasy in a temple dedicated to Kālī in Padmakota, the worship of whom has always been held in great contempt by orthodox Vaiṣṇavas. (Sen: 1917a: 237-8, 248) In any event, as none of Caitanya's intimate companions or early biographers was eye-witness to this part of Caitanya's life, the accounts of the Southern tour cannot be considered as reliable as those of Caitanya's Navadvīpa or Puri periods.

Caitanya's first stop was Vidyānagara where, at the request of Sārvabhauma, he met the local governor of the province, a great devotee by the name of Rāmānanda Rāya. This meeting proved to be of special importance, since it was here that Caitanya first heard detailed accounts of the *rasa* doctrine, later systematized by Rūpa, which posits the love of Rādhā for Kṛṣṇa as the highest devotional sentiment. Caitanya found Rāmānanda's words so attuned to his own natural mood and experiences that he requested Rāmānanda to meet him again in Puri. Soon after this meeting, Rāmānanda did in fact retire from service and move permanently to Puri, where he remained one of Caitanya's closest companions throughout the latter's life.

In the course of the continuing South Indian tour, Caitanya visited nearly all of the important pilgrimage sites, converting, according to Kṛṣṇadāsa, virtually all who saw him to Vaiṣṇavism. It was on this trip that he had copies made of the Sanskrit works *Brahmasaṃhitā* and *Kṛṣṇakarṇāmṛta*, which later became standard texts for the Gauḍīya school, the former being commented on by Jīva, and the latter by Kṛṣṇadāsa Kavirāja, among others. Caitanya is also reported to have visited the Śaṅkarācārya Monastery at Śṛṅgeri on this trip, and it is interesting to note that while Caitanya is said to have entered into debate with nearly all of the different sects of South India, he is not reported to have done so here. It is possible, assuming Kṛṣṇadāsa's account to be reliable, that Caitanya refrained from any verbal attack out of respect for his guru Keśava, whose Bhāratī Sampradāya recognizes the Śṛṅgeri Monastery as its headquarters. It is also likely that Caitanya was cordially received there when it was learned that he was also a *sannyāsin* of the Bhāratī order.

In sharp contrast to Caitanya's visit to Śṛṅgeri is his reported confrontation with the monks of the Mādhva Monastery in Uḍipī. As described by Kṛṣṇadāsa:

When the master saw the image of Kṛṣṇa (at Uḍipī), he was filled with joy, and, overcome with divine love, began to sing and dance. The Tattvavādins at first took the master for a Māyāvādin, and refused to talk to him. Later, when they saw him overcome with divine love, they were awe-struck and, realizing him to be a Vaiṣṇava, received him respectfully. Caitanya could see their vanity at being Vaiṣṇavas, and smilingly engaged them in conversation. As the Tattvavādin *ācārya* was well-versed in the scriptures, the master assumed a humble attitude and said, "I do not understand what is meant by *sādhya* and *sādhana* (the goal of life and the means of attainment). Please explain them to me."

The *ācārya* replied, "The offering of one's caste and *āśrama* duties to Kṛṣṇa is the highest *sādhana* for a devotee of Kṛṣṇa, while the attainment of Vaikuṇṭha and enjoyment of the five kinds of *mukti*[11] are the ultimate *sādhya*. This is the opinion of the scriptures."

To this the master replied, "According to the scriptures, the chief *sādhana* is the listening to and singing of Kṛṣṇa's praises, culminating in love for and service of Kṛṣṇa. By means of these practices, one attains the highest aim of all human endeavors, the fifth *puruṣārtha*.[12] All the scriptures condemn *karman* and recommend its abandonment. No one achieves love and devotion for Kṛṣṇa by means of *karman*. True devotees renounce the five kinds of *mukti* and consider them no better than hell. *Mukti* and *karman*, the two things which you call *sādhya* and *sādhana*, are the very things which real devotees reject. It must be that, taking me for a (Māyāvādin) *sannyāsin*, you have decided to dupe me, and have not truly described the nature of *sādhya* and *sādhana*."

> Hearing this, the *ācārya* felt shamed at heart and, seeing the master's true Vaiṣṇava spirit, was struck with wonder. The *ācārya* replied, "All that you have said is true; this is the sure conclusion of all the Vaiṣṇava scriptures. Still, our *sampradāya* is bound to honor the views set forth by Mādhva."
>
> The master then said, "Both *karmins* and *jñānins* are devoid of devotion; these are the very two signs visible in your *sampradāya.* The only virtue I see in your *sampradāya* is that you accept the true form of the Lord." (C.C.m. 9/249-77)

It is difficult to assess the accuracy of Kṛṣṇadāsa's account of this incident. For one thing, the views attributed to the Mādhva *ācārya* do not seem to have much in common with the traditional teachings of their school. B. N. K. Sharma remarks, "...the criticisms *said to have been made by Caitanya on the doctrines of Mādhva* [his italics] suffer from a serious misunderstanding and misrepresentation of the true and actual position taken up by Mādhva on the relative positions of Karma, Jñāna and Bhakti, in the scheme of Sādhanas." (Sharma: 1961a: 330)

The incident with the Mādhvas at Uḍipī is not found in the *Kaḍacā* of Govindadāsa. Kṛṣṇadāsa does, however, express his indebtedness to the *Kaḍacā* of Dāmodara Svarūpa (no longer available) for his accounts of the Southern tour, and according to S. K. De, he also relied heavily on the accounts of Murāri Gupta and Kavi Karṇapūra. (De: 1961: 91) Regardless of the trustworthiness of Kṛṣṇadāsa's account, however, it is clear that within the first several decades after Caitanya's passing away, the orthodox tradition recognized no connection between Caitanya and the Mādhva Sampradāya, nor did it recognize any doctrinal similarities.

Soon after his return to Puri, Caitanya was met by his Bengali followers, who thereafter made annual pilgrimages to Puri during the four months of the rainy season to witness the Car Festival of Jagannātha and to have the company of Caitanya. It was here that Caitanya gave explicit instructions to Nityānanda and Advaita to propagate his message throughout Bengal. In fact, Caitanya was so anxious that Nityānanda devote himself to this project full time that he requested him not to make subsequent trips to Puri, a request which Nityānanda was not, however, able to honor.

Within two years of his pilgrimage to South India, Caitanya again felt the urge to travel, and made arrangements to visit the holy city of Vṛndāvana in North India. His first attempt to reach his destination was unsuccessful due to his large retinue and the consequent commotion caused by their presence wherever they went. The trip was not a total loss, however, since as they were proceeding through Bengal, Caitanya made the acquaintance of two high officials of the Muslim court, later to become two of his most intimate companions and establishers of the Gauḍīya Vaiṣṇava school, Rūpa and Sanātana Gosvāmin. Caitanya then returned to Puri and within a few months started out again for Vṛndāvana, this time with a single attendant and by less-travelled roads.

Caitanya's Northern pilgrimage is notable for several reasons. Aside from seeing all of the spots around Vṛndāvana associated with the life of Kṛṣṇa, Caitanya also had the opportunity of meeting Rūpa and Sanātana again, instructing the former for ten days at Prayāga (and later for ten months in Puri) and his brother Sanātana for two months in Benares. The accounts given of these meetings in the *Caitanya Caritāmṛta* describe Caitanya as giving very detailed teachings to both Rūpa and Sanātana, containing all of the essential points later incorporated in their writings.

While in Benares, Caitanya entered into dialogue with the renowned *sannyāsin* and Advaitin, Prakāśānanda. It seems that Prakāśānanda's opinion of Caitanya was not very high because of the latter's emotional behavior and failure to devote his time to the study of Vedānta. When the two of them met, Prakāśānanda requested Caitanya to explain his interpretation of the *Brahmasūtra* and his refutation of Māyāvāda. Caitanya's reply was similar to the one he had given to Sārvabhauma in Puri, with one significant difference. Earlier he had criticized Śaṅkara on the grounds that his commentary did not reflect the primary meaning of the *sūtras*. Now he made the claim that no commentary which was composed by an ordinary person could claim to adequately explain the meaning of the *Brahmasūtra*. According to Kṛṣṇadāsa, Caitanya explained:

> The meaning of Vyāsa's *sūtras* is extremely deep. Vyāsa was *bhagavat* himself (i.e. an *avatāra* of *bhagavat*). As no mere mor-

tal is capable of understanding the meaning of his *sūtras*, he himself has explained them. Now, when the author himself explains his own *sūtras*, their true meaning can be understood. The meaning of the syllable *om* is contained in the *Gāyatrī*, and the meaning of the *Gāyatrī* is explained in the *Catuḥślokī*, the four *Bhāgavata* verses (2/9/30-33) which were handed down from *īśvara* to Brahmā, from Brahmā to Nārada, and from Nārada to Vyāsa. When Vyāsa first heard these verses, he thought, "This is indeed the correct interpretation of my *sūtras*. I will compose the *Bhāgavata* to serve as a commentary on these *sūtras*."

Vyāsa then gathered together all of the doctrines found in the four Vedas and Upaniṣads. Each verse which forms the subject of a particular *sūtra* was made into a verse of the *Bhāgavata*. Thus the *Bhāgavata* represents the (true) commentary on the *Brahmasūtra*. The *Bhāgavata* and the Upaniṣads speak with one voice. (C.C.m. 25/89-98)

The significance of these views concerning both the *Brahmasūtra* and the *Bhāgavata Purāṇa* cannot be overestimated. Whether or not the actual dialogue between Caitanya and Prakāśānanda ever took place—and because of the fact that Kṛṣṇadāsa is the sole biographer to mention it, there is room for some doubt—there can be little question that the views expressed therein represent some of Caitanya's firmest beliefs, and provide the only plausible explanation why not a single commentary was written on the *Brahmasūtra* by any of the Gosvāmins, especially when Jīva, of all of them, was so eminently qualified to do so.

Caitanya returned to Puri shortly after his meeting with Prakāśānanda, and remained there until his death in 1533. While in Prayāga on his earlier visit to North India, Caitanya had met the great Vaiṣṇava *ācārya*, Vallabha.[13] Now Vallabha came to Puri boasting of a commentary he had written on the *Bhāgavata Purāṇa* which he wanted Caitanya to hear. Caitanya noted his smug attitude and repeatedly put him off. After a few days, Vallabha approached Caitanya and his companions, and said, "I do not accept the views of Śrīdhara on the *Bhāgavata* and have refuted his interpretation. He has not been consistent in his commentary, so I have not followed it." (C.C.a. 7/110)

Caitanya smiled and said, "Whoever does not honor one's

svāmin[14] is no better than a harlot." (7/111) Vallabha was reportedly humbled by this reply and decided to leave Puri as soon as was possible. When he came to take leave of Caitanya before starting on his journey, Caitanya said to him:

> You have the vanity to write your own commentary without showing respect to Śrīdhara, and have even criticized him! It is by the grace of Śrīdhara that I have understood the *Bhāgavata*. He is a world teacher; I consider him to be my very own guru. Whatever you have written out of pride against Śrīdhara is wasted effort; no one will accept it. Give up your false pride and follow Śrīdhara in your commentary. Whatever you write in accordance with Śrīdhara will be honored and accepted by all. (C.C.a. 7/128-32)

Although the historicity of this incident has also been disputed, and the identity of this Vallabha questioned, it seems clear that the sentiments expressed here represent Caitanya's own beliefs, and that he had a profound respect for Śrīdhara who, though an avowed Advaitin and follower of Śaṅkara, was an ardent proponent of *bhakti*.[15] Perhaps the most persuasive evidence that Caitanya held such views concerning Śrīdhara is the fact that all of the Gosvāmins who wrote full or partial commentaries on the *Bhāgavata* are unanimous in their praise of Śrīdhara, even though their interpretations are often at variance with his. Jīva, for example, writes at the commencement of his *Bhāgavata* commentary, the *Kramasandarbha*: "I salute the venerable Śrīdhara, the sole guardian of *bhakti*. This commentary, bearing the name *Kramasandarbha*, should be understood to function as clarifying what was not clearly stated by the Svāmin, or mentioning what was occasionally left unsaid."[16]

Of all the information available to us of Caitanya's beliefs from the various biographies, S. K. De seems to place the gereatest emphasis on this single reference to Śrīdhara. He writes:

> It is our impression that Caitanya could not have been such an anti-Śaṃkara as depicted by Kṛṣṇadāsa Kavirāja. The Kavirāja, however, is careless enough to give us a rough idea as to what Caitanya's metaphysics could possibly have been when he makes Caitanya ridicule Vallabha Bhaṭṭa for differ-

> ing from Śrīdhara's commentary on the *Bhāgavata*, and says that Śrīdhara was 'Jagad-guru'... Possibly Caitanya was a Śaṃkarite Saṃnyāsin of the Śrīdhara type, although he was far ahead of Śrīdhara in what he understood to be the implications of Bhakti, and the Bhakti which he practiced may have been very much like what Rūpa and Jīva say about it. (De: 1961: 151)

Even accepting the truth of Caitanya's remarks concerning Śrīdhara, they are nevertheless somewhat surprising. For one thing, from the time of his initiation in Gayā, Caitanya seemed to have lost all interest in intellectual or metaphysical questions, and reportedly gave up reading almost entirely, preferring to let some of his intimate associates recite to him such devotional compositions as the lyrics of Caṇḍīdāsa and Vidyāpati, Jayadeva's *Gītagovinda*, or the tenth *skandha* of the *Bhāgavata* describing Kṛṣṇa's *līlā* with the Gopīs. It is unlikely that he ever studied Śrīdhara's commentary during his later years at Puri, although he must have had occasion to hear recitations of it either in his early stay in Puri or while still in Navadvīpa. It is significant to note also that whereas the Gauḍīya Vaiṣṇavas base their Rādhā/Kṛṣṇa doctrine almost entirely on the tenth *skandha* of the *Bhāgavata*, Śrīdhara does not mention the name of Rādhā even once.

It thus seems likely that Caitanya's admiration for Śrīdhara represents more than a simple intellectual preference, although De is probably correct that Caitanya was not as antagonistic to Advaita as his biographers made him out to be; and it may even be possible that a direct link existed between Caitanya and Śrīdhara through Īśvara Purī and his guru, Mādhavendra.

According to D. C. Sen, the *Bhāgavata Purāṇa* first became popular in Bengal through the *Bhaktiratnāvalī*, an anthology of *Bhāgavata* verses selected and arranged by Viṣṇu Purī, and translated into Bengali in the beginning of the 15th century. (Sen: 1917a: 297) Viṣṇu Purī's dates are not easily fixed, but as he refers to Śrīdhara, usually assigned to the middle of the 14th century, he probably completed his *Bhaktiratnāvalī* towards the end of that century. Since Śrīdhara, like Viṣṇu Purī, was also a *sannyāsin* of the Advaitic Purī order, it is possible that the devotional brand of Advaita epitomized in Śrīdhara's writings and the emphasis on the *Bhāgavata Purāṇa* were distinguishing features of the Purī Sampradāya. Rādhāmohana, in his commentary on *Tattvasandarbha* 28, refers to a division within the Śaṅkarācārya order, designating followers of the path of *bhakti*, such as Śrīdhara, "Bhāgavatas", and those who follow the path of *jñāna*, "Smārtas". It is conceivable that Mādhavendra Purī belonged to this very branch of Bhāgavata *sannyāsins*.[17]

Had Mādhavendra indeed been a member of this Bhāgavata Sampradāya, it would help explain not only the great respect which Śrīdhara commands within the Gauḍīya Vaiṣṇava school, but also the popularity of the *Viṣṇu Purāṇa*, the only Purāṇa other than the *Bhāgavata* to be commented on by Śrīdhara. It would also help to explain Caitanya's apparent lack of interest in Vedānta, an attitude also seen in Śrīdhara, whose extant writings are limited to commentaries on the *Bhāgavata Purāṇa*, *Viṣṇu Purāṇa* and *Bhagavadgītā*.

Although such a link between Caitanya and Śrīdhara may have existed, it should be remembered that neither Kṛṣṇadāsa nor any of the Vṛndāvana Gosvāmins ever looked beyond Mādhavendra, whose own guru is never mentioned, for the original roots of the Gauḍīya Vaiṣṇava movement. As Kṛṣṇadāsa writes, "Mādhava Purī was the initial sprout of the wish-fulfilling tree of *bhakti*; Īśvara Purī was the seedling; and Caitanya, though himself the gardener, was, by his inscrutable power, the sturdy tree." (C. C. ā. 9/10-12)

Thus, despite the fact that Caitanya was formally a member of the Bhāratī Sampradāya of his *sannyāsa* guru Keśava, he has traditionally been linked to the *bhakti* movement associated with Mādhavendra, not only because of the similarities between Caitanya and Mādhavendra, but also because of the minimal role which Keśava played in Caitanya's spiritual development. Whether or not Caitanya's great reverence for the *Bhāgavata Purāṇa* and his profound respect for its commentator, Śrīdhara Svāmin, can be traced directly to Mādhavendra, and from him to Śrīdhara himself, is a matter of speculation, though it is clear that these two elements rank among the most important and distinctive beliefs of the early Gauḍīya Vaiṣṇava school, and may, as S. K. De suggests, provide us with one of our best clues in evaluating both the teachings of Caitanya and the tradition to which he belonged.

NOTES

1. The best critical account of the biographies of Caitanya is the Bengali *Caitanyacariter Upādāna* of Biman Bihari Majumdar. Shorter, but reliable, English accounts may be found in S. K. De's *Early History of the Vaiṣṇava Faith and Movement in Bengal* and A. K. Majumdar's *Caitanya: His Life and Doctrine*.

2. The power which the Vṛndāvana Gosvāmins enjoyed in this respect was apparently quite considerable. D. C. Sen writes, "No book that did not bear the stamp and seal of the six Gosvāmīs of Vṛndāvana was recognized as a standard authority in the 16th century." (Sen: 1917b: 10)

3. Mādhavendra was also the guru of Caitanya's mantra-guru, Īśvara Purī, and it is through him that Kavi Karṇapūra and, later, Baladeva attempt to associate Caitanya with the Mādhva Sampradāya. As Mādhavendra's sectarian affiliation is one of the key issues of this study, it will be discussed in some depth in subsequent portions of this chapter, and in the chapter on Baladeva.

4. *tataḥ kiyaddine prāha bhagavān kāryamānuṣaḥ |*
svapne dṛṣṭo mayā kaścid āgatya brāhmaṇottamaḥ ||
sannyāsamantraṃ matkarṇe kathayām āsa susmitaḥ |
tat śrutvā vyathito rātrau divā cāhaṃ virodiṣi ||
kathaṃ priyaṃ hariṃ nāthaṃ tyaktvānyad ucitaṃ mama |

5. *murāriḥ prāha tat śrutvā tanmantre bhagavan svayam ||*
ṣaṣṭhīsamāsaṃ manasā vicintya tvaṃ sukhī bhava |

It should be noted that the *mahāvākya* traditionally associated with the Śṛṅgeri Maṭha is not *tat tvam asi* but *ahaṃ brahmāsmi* (I am *brahman*).

6. *vāratrayaṃ tatśravaṇāntikaṃ svayaṃ*
provāca sannyāsamantraṃ viśuddham |
śrutvāvadat so 'pi harer idaṃ syāt
sannyāsamantraṃ paramaṃ pavitram ||
vyājena dīkṣāṃ gurave sa dattvā
lokaikanātho gurur avyayātmā |
guro dadasvādya manīṣitaṃ me
sannyāsam ity āha puṭāñjaliḥ prabhuḥ ||

7. *parilen aruṇavasana manohara |*

8. *yogapaṭṭa nā nile nāma haila svarūpa |*

The term *yogapaṭṭa* is also used in the Daśanāmin tradition to indicate the title which one assumes at the time of *sannyāsa*, such as Bhāratī, Purī, etc. (Cf. *Vāsudevāśrama Yatidharmaprakāśa* 8/24, 53/30, 66/1-24)

9. The tradition of a hierarchy within the Śaṅkarācārya order has been explained in terms of a certain incident said to have occurred between Śaṅkara and certain of his disciples. According to this tradition, Śaṅkara became angry with certain of his disciples who were heads of the various *sampradāyas* and either broke their staffs or took them away. The *sampradāyas* under the former *ācāryas* were then considered mediocre, while those under

the latter were considered low. The remaining *sampradāyas,* namely Tīrtha, Āśrama, and Sarasvatī, were considered high. A. K. Majumdar also refers to this tradition, but maintains that the Bhāratī Sampradāya was one of the low orders, based on a reference to it by Caitanya as *hīna* (inferior). (Majumdar : 1969 : 262) The editor of the Sādhanā Prakāśanī edition of the C. C. states, however, that of the three orders associated with the Śṛṅgeri Maṭha, the Purī is lowest, the Sarasvatī is highest, and, as Sārvabhauma states, the Bhāratī is mediocre. (Kṛṣṇadāsa : 1963 : 246) It is difficult to say just how factual this tradition is. Probably the distinction between the various orders, if observed at all, is based on the fact that some restrict their membership to *brāhmaṇas,* while the others are either non-*brahmaṇa* or mixed.

10. Cf. Majumdar: 1969 : 172-5 for a defence of the accuracy of Kṛṣṇadāsa's account of this incident.

11. The five kinds of *mukti* are: 1) *sālokya*—attainment of the same abode as the deity worshipped; 2) *sārṣṭi*—attainment of a similar condition or capacities; 3) *sārūpya*—attainment of a similar form; 4) *sāmīpya*—attainment of proximity to the deity; and 5) *sāyujya*—attainment of union with the deity, usually applicable to worshippers of the unconditioned *brahman* and considered to be the least acceptable to a devotee.

12. That is, *preman,* or love of God, the other four being: *kāma*—the fulfillment of worldly desires; *artha*—striving for wealth ; *dharma*—performance of duties; and *mokṣa*—the seeking of liberation.

13. S. K. De argues strongly against the view that the Vallabha Bhaṭṭa mentioned here is the same as the famous Vallabhācārya. However, as A. K. Majumdar points out (1969: 236), the literature of the Vallabha school also mentions Caitanya's meeting with Vallabha, both in the village of Adel near Prayāga and in Puri, although the accounts of the two rival schools differ substantially in content. (Cf. Parekh : 1943: 90-100 for a discussion on the relationship between Caitanya and Vallabha from the point of view of the Vallabha school.)

14. There is a pun on the word *svāmin* which means "husband" in Bengali, in addition to referring to Śrīdhara Svāmin.

15. Śrīdhara acknowledges his debt to Śaṅkara at the beginning of his commentary on the *Bhagavadgītā.* He writes, "After studying, according to my own light, the interyretation of the commentator (Śaṅkara) and the writings of his sub-commentators, I begin this commentary on the *Gītā.*"

(*bhāṣyakāramataṃ samyak tadvyākhyātṛgiras tathā* /
yathāmati samālocya gītāvyākhyāṃ samārabhe //)

It should be noted, however, that Śrīdhara does not always follow Śaṅkara's interpretations very closely, placing greater emphasis on *bhakti,* often speaking of the *jīva* as a portion of *brahman,* and giving a more realistic interpretation to the concept of *śakti.* According to tradition, there was considerable objection to his *Gītā* commentary by the orthodox Advaitins of Benares, and it was only through divine intervention that his commentary was ultimately accepted. (Vireswarananda: 1948: ii)

16. *śrīdharasvāmipādāṃs tān vande bhaktyekarakṣakān |*
svāmipādair na yad vyaktaṃ yad vyaktaṃ cāsphuṭaṃ kvacit ||
tatra tatra ca vijñeyaḥ sandarbhaḥ kramanāmakaḥ |

17. Friedhelm Hardy also refers to a devotional tradition within the Purī Sampradāya, with roots in South Indian *bhakti*, dating back to Śrīdhara and including Māhavendra. Hardy mentions the fact that Viṣṇu Purī is listed in C.C. (a. 9/11-12) as one of Mādhavendra's disciples. However, if the dates D. C. Sen gives for the writing of the Bengali translation of Viṣṇu Purī's *Bhaktiratnāvalī* are correct, Mādhavendra was probably not yet born when Viṣṇu Purī compiled his work on the *Bhāgavata Purāṇa*. (Cf. Hardy : 1974 : 31-41)

Chapter II

JĪVA

Reliable information on any of the Gosvāmins is difficult to come by, and especially so in the case of Jīva who, as the last of the Gosvāmins to reach Vṛndāvana and the only one not to have had personal contact with Caitanya, is not mentioned in any of the biographies, with the exception of an occasional reference in the *Caitanya Caritāmṛta*. The little that we do know about Jīva seems to be based mainly on accounts from the Bengali works, the *Premavilāsa* and the *Bhaktiratnākara*.[1]

Jīva's dates are not definitely known. Jadunath Sarkar places his date of birth at 1511 (Sarkar: 1932:3), and on the basis of our knowledge of Jīva's father's early death, we may assume that this date is more or less correct. Jīva's father, Anupama (also known as Vallabha), was the younger brother of Rūpa and Sanātana, and also a devout follower of Caitanya. Anupama first met Caitanya in his village of Rāmkeli when Caitanya stopped there on his aborted trip to Vṛndāvana in 1513, and left home shortly thereafter in the company of Rūpa. The two brothers met Caitanya again in Prayāga, and later, as they were on their way to Puri to meet Caitanya again, Anupama died. This means that Jīva could not have been born later than 1514, and if the accounts of the *Bhaktiratnākara* are correct, that Jīva was already a young boy when Caitanya passed through his village, then the date of Jīva's birth must be pushed back another few years at least. At any rate, the placing of his birth "between 1530 and 1540", as Mahanama Brahmachari has done (Mahanama: 1974: 57), is certainly not tenable.

With his father dead and his two uncles now settled in Vṛndāvana, Jīva reportedly lost all interest in worldly pursuits, hoping only to join his two uncles in Vṛndāvana one day. By the time he had reached the age of twenty, his mother was also dead, and he resolved to lead the life of a Vaiṣṇava recluse[2] in the company of Rūpa and Sanātana.

Before heading for Vṛndāvana, Jīva first visited the town of Navadvīpa, where he was met by Nityānanda and taken to all of the places associated with Caitanya's youth. At the bidding of Nityānanda, Jīva proceeded to Benares to complete his studies in Sanskrit learning. There Jīva studied with a scholar by the name of Madhusūdana Vācaspati who, according to S. K. De, was "an accomplished grammarian, Smārta and Vedāntist" (De: 1961: 150), not to be confused with the Madhusūdana Sarasvatī of *Advaitasiddhi* fame. A. K. Majumdar, however, disagrees. He writes, "Jīva Gosvāmin studied under a Madhusūdana Sarasvatī at Vārāṇasī, and it is quite likely that this teacher was none other than this great *advaita* scholar." (Majumdar: 1969: 89) Dulal Chandra Ghosh identifies Jīva's teacher as a disciple of Vāsudeva Sārvabhauma, which is not unlikely, since this would mean that he was probably a Bengali and well-versed in both Vedānta and logic, two subjects which Jīva obviously studied while in Benares.

Regardless of the identity of his teacher, Jīva clearly received a thorough education in Benares, and became well-versed in all branches of Vedānta, as well as in other fields such as Pūrva Mīmāṃsā and Nyāya. He is reported to have acquired a considerable reputation for his learning in Benares, which is not surprising when we consider the versatility he displays in his writings, particularly in his *Sarvasaṃvādinī*, where he refers to such divergent *Brahmasūtra* commentators as Madhva, Rāmānuja, Śaṅkara, and Vācaspati.

After completing his studies, Jīva joined the Gosvāmins in Vṛndāvana, where he took initiation with Rūpa and engaged himself in the study of the *Bhāgavata* and other Vaiṣṇava scriptures with Sanātana and the other Gosvāmins. Very little is known of Jīva's life in Vṛndāvana, with the exception of a single incident regarding a debate which took place between him and one Vallabha Bhaṭṭa.

It seems that Vallabha had earlier challenged Rūpa to a debate, and that Rūpa had refused, conceding victory by default. Jīva, pained at this slight to his guru, sought out Vallabha and soundly defeated him in argument, only to be chastized by Rūpa and expelled from the Vaiṣṇava community on the grounds that he had succumbed to pride, one of the cardinal sins for a Vaiṣṇava. Ultimately, Rūpa forgave his nephew at the intercession of Sanātana, and Jīva was readmitted to the community.[3]

As the last surviving member of the six Gosvāmins, the responsibility for the organization of the movement fell squarely on Jīva's shoulders. S. K. De writes, "Jīva became the highest court of appeal in doctrinal matters as long as he lived." (De: 1961: 150) It was also due to Jīva that the theology of Vṛndāvana made its way into Bengal and Orissa, spread by his three eminent proteges, Śrīnivāsa, Narottama, and Śyāmānanda. Jīva was likewise a major force in making Vṛndāvana an important center of learning and religion, devoting his time and efforts to the construction of new temples as well as a library of Sanskrit religious literature. Jīva is said to have lived beyond eighty, and Jadunath Sarkar places his date of death at 1596. (Sarkar: 1932: 3)

Jīva was an unusually versatile and prolific writer, having to his credit 25 different works, according to the *Bhaktiratnākara* (1/833-51), although some of these are actually parts of larger works, and not all are currently available. His wiritings include: three works on Sanskrit grammar, *Harināmāmṛtavyākaraṇa*, *Sūtramālikā*, and *Dhātusaṅgraha*; commentaries on the *Bhāgavata Purāṇa* (the *Kramasandarbha*), *Gopālatāpinī Upaniṣad*, *Brahmasaṃhitā*, the *Yogasārastava* of the *Padma Purāṇa*, the *Gāyatrīnirvāṇakathana* of the *Agni Purāṇa*, and Rūpa's *Bhaktirasāmṛtasindhu* and *Ujjvalanīlamaṇi*; literary works such as the *Gopālacampū* (*Pūrva* and *Uttara*), *Gopālavirudāvalī*, *Mādhavamahotsava*, *Saṅkalpakalpavṛkṣa*, *and Bhāvārthasūcakacampū*; and theological and philosophical works such as the *Bhaktirasāmṛtaśeṣa*, *Kṛṣṇārcanadīpikā*, *Kṛṣṇapadacihna*, *Rādhikākarapadacihna*, *Sarvasaṃvādinī*, and the six-part *Bhāgavatasandarbha*.[4]

Notes

1. The *Premavilāsa* was written by Nityānandadāsa, a student of Nityānanda's son Vīrabhadra, and friend of Śrīnivāsa, one of the most important leaders of the movement in the 17th century, probably some time between 1630 and 1650. D. C. Sen calls it "one of the most trusted historical works of the Vaiṣṇavas in the 16th and the early part of the 17th century" (Sen: 1917a: 221), but S. K. De writes that it "must be taken with extreme caution" regarding the earlier phase of the movement (De: 1961: 66). The *Bhaktiratnā-*

kara was written probably in the second or third decade of the 18th century by Narahari Cakravartin, a Vṛndāvana recluse and Sanskrit scholar who is said to have spent time as a cook in the Vṛndāvana Govindadeva temple. (Kennedy: 1925: 134)

2. Although the Vṛndāvana Gosvāmins all led lives of extreme renunciation, it is not known whether or not any of them ever took formal initiation into *sannyāsa*. To continue the tradition of Caitanya would have meant taking initiation into the Advaitic Bhāratī order, a step which they would not have been anxious to take and which was probably not something Caitanya would have been in favor of. In any case, it seems that Caitanya preferred to have the traditions of the school handed down hereditarily, through the offspring of Advaita and others, and even persuaded Nityānanda to marry late in life for this purpose. Even today, the gurus of the school are generally direct descendants of Advaita, Nityānanda, and a few of Caitanya's other intimate associates, all of whom add the title "Gosvāmī" to their names, despite the existence of a loosely structured ascetic order of Vairāgins, probably initiated by Nityānanda's son, Vīrabhadra. (Cf. Kennedy: 1925: 148-79 for a good discussion of this topic.)

3. It is difficult to say whether or not this is the famous Vallabhācārya, although mention is also made in the literature of the Vallabha Sampradāya of a debate between Jīva and Vallabha. While the details and conclusion of this incident vary greatly in the accounts of the two schools—the Vallabhas claim that Caitanya was also present—it is possible that a meeting of some sort actually took place between the two of them, especially if the accounts of Vallabha's visit to Puri are correct, in which case he might have sought to vindicate his humiliating experience there at the expense of the Vṛndāvana Gosvāmins. If a meeting did in fact take place between Jīva and Vallabhācārya, Jīva's date of birth would have to be pushed back another few years, since Vallabha is said to have died in 1531, and Jiva was probably at least 22 when he reached Vṛndāvana. It would also mean that Caitanya was still alive when Jīva reached Vṛndāvana, which, though not impossible, contradicts the tradition of the school and raises the question why Jīva did not seek a visit with Caitanya before joining the Gosvāmins in Vṛndāvana. (Cf. Parekh 1969: 96 for the Vallabha school's description of this incident.)

4. Cf. Chakravarti: 1975: 65-67 for a more or less complete list and description of Jīva's writings.

Chapter III

BALADEVA

There is a fair amount of information on the life of Baladeva, and most biographers are in general agreement concerning the details of his early years, that is, up until the time of his arrival in Jaipur, where he made his claim of Mādhva affiliation on behalf of the Gauḍīya Vaiṣṇavas of Vṛndāvana and wrote his commentary on the *Brahmasūtra*, the *Govindabhāṣya*. It is at this point that the accounts begin to differ significantly, both because of the lack of reliable information regarding the events which led to the incident in Jaipur, and because of the different sectarian interests of the various biographers.

Baladeva was born some time around 1700 in a family of Khaṇḍayat Vaiśyas, his birthplace being a small village near Remunā in the Baleśvara district of Orissa. Baladeva reportedly left home at an early age and joined a community of *paṇḍits* living on the bank of the Cilkāhrada with whom he studied grammar, rhetoric, and logic. He later travelled to Mysore, where he studied Vedānta according to the systems of Śaṅkara and Madhva, eventually taking *sannyāsa* with the Mādhva Sampradāya. After returning to Orissa, Baladeva settled down in a Tattvavāda Monastery in Puri and began to participate in debates with the local *Paṇḍits* of the city.

The Gauḍīya Vaiṣṇavas of Puri could not help noticing Baladeva's intelligence and other good qualities. One of the leaders of their community, a Kānyakubja *brāhmaṇa* by the name of Rādhādāmodara Dāsa,[1] began to hold philosophical discussions with Baladeva. Baladeva's interest in Gauḍīya Vaiṣṇava doctrine was aroused, and he requested Rādhādāmodara to instruct him in Jīva's *Bhāgavatasandarbha*. As a result of these studies, Baladeva's reverence for Rādhādāmodara also increased, and after a friendly debate in which Rādhādāmodara was victorious, Baladeva accepted him as his guru.

The actual significance of Baladeva's initiation with Rādhādāmodara is not entirely clear. Bhaktivinod Ṭhākur maintains that Baladeva retained his sense of identity with the Mādhva

Sampradāya, and that his initiation with Rādhādāmodara represented more an acceptance of the divinity of Caitanya than a change in philosophical outlook. (Baladeva: 1970: xlv) Bhaktivinod also cites this as the beginning of the Gauḍīya Mādhva Sampradāya, although it does not seem that this designation was used before the beginning of the present century, when it become current largely through the efforts of Bhaktivinod himself. Still, judging from Baladeva's writings, it is evident that his early training in Mādhva philosophy had left an indelible mark on him, and that his affiliation with the Mādhva Sampradāya was something which he was not only anxious to maintain, but which he wished to confer on the Gauḍīya Vaiṣṇava school as well.

After his initiation, Baladeva proceeded to Vṛndāvana by way of Navadvīpa. Shortly after his arrival in Vṛndāvana, news came of a dispute involving the Gauḍīya Vaiṣṇavas in Jaipur. As Viśvanātha Cakravartin,[2] then head of the Gauḍīya community of Vṛndāvana, was too old to make the trip to Jaipur himself, he began to look for a suitable replacement. Baladeva was brought before Viśvanātha, and after proper examination, was deputed to settle affairs there.

Unfortunately for students of the Gauḍīya Vaiṣṇava movement, the exact nature of the Jaipur dispute is not known, the various accounts of it all differing on important points. As a proper understanding of this incident is necessary in order to evaluate Baladeva's actual motives for making the claim of Mādhva affiliation in Jaipur and for writing his *Brahmasūtra* commentary, the *Govindabhāṣya*, we will give a brief survey of the different accounts, and on the basis of available historical information and the evidence of Baladeva's own writings, attempt to come up with a plausible version of this incident.

1) According to the "Śrīsajjanatoṣaṇī", a periodical published by Bhaktivinod Ṭhākur (Baladeva: 1970: xlv-xlvi), a group of *mahantas* of the Śrī Sampradāya who had recently come to Jaipur objected to the fact that the Gauḍīya Vaiṣṇava custom of conducting the worship of Govinda prior to that of Nārāyaṇa was being followed in the temples. One of the Jaipur Rājās, Sadācārī Rājā, was disturbed by the attempts of these *mahantas* to reverse the order of worship, and made arrangements for a Vaiṣṇava paṇḍit to come to Jaipur from Vṛndāvana to debate the issue.

When Viśvanātha was informed of the situation, he sent Baladeva to Jaipur. Upon seeing Baladeva, the Śrī Vaiṣṇavas asked him which *Brahmasūtra* commentary he was prepared to base his case on. Baladeva replied that, as he was affiliated with the Mādhva Sampradāya, he would thus rely on Madhva's commentary. The Śrī Vaiṣṇavas remarked that Madhva's commentary established Kṛṣṇa alone, and asked if he was prepared to consent to the worship of Kṛṣṇa without Rādhā, an arrangement contrary to the standard practice of the Gauḍīya Vaiṣṇavas.

Baladeva realized the predicament he was in and begged a short leave of absence from the assembly. He then retired to the Govinda temple where, at the command of Govinda himself, he began to write his own commentary on the *Brahmasūtra* (the *Govindabhāṣya*), together with commentaries on the *Bhagavadgītā*, *Viṣṇusahasranāma*, and Upaniṣads. Upon completion of these works, Baladeva returned to the assembly and defeated the Śrī Vaiṣṇavas on the strength of his own commentaries, thereby keeping intact the Gauḍīya traditions regarding the priority of the worship of Govinda and his consort Rādhā. As a result of his success, the assembly conferred on Baladeva the title "Vidyābhūṣaṇa" ("Adorned with knowledge"), by which he has been known ever since.

2) According to Haridās Dās (1956: 1292), news came to Vṛndāvana at about the time of Baladeva's arrival there that the Bengali priests had been removed from their positions in the temples of Jaipur on the grounds that they did not belong to a recognized *sampradāya*. Viśvanātha, then at an advanced age, sent Baladeva and one Kṛṣṇadāsa Sārvabhauma to Jaipur, where the pair defeated their opponents in a debate. They then re-established a Gauḍīya center on top of a hill by the Galta Valley, and installed the image of Vijaya Gopāla, which remains there to this day. Baladeva also brought great glory to the Gauḍīya Vaiṣṇavas at this time by composing his *Govindabhāṣya*.

3) The account found in the introduction to the Bengali edition of the *Govindabhāṣya* (Baladeva: 1968: 18-19) represents a partial synthesis of the two previous accounts. According to this version, the dispute centered around the Govindadeva temple in Jaipur, the image of which had been earlier discovered by Rūpa Gosvāmin in Vṛndāvana. It seems that the Bengali priests who conducted the worship in the temple were accused by the local

Rāmānandins of not representing a legitimate *sampradāya* since they had no *Brahmasūtra* commentary of their own. Ultimately, the Rāmānandins lodged a formal complaint with the Mahārāja of Jaipur against the Gauḍīya Vaiṣṇavas. As a result of these charges, the image of Rādhā was removed from the temple and installed in its own temple where it was worshipped separately. When the Rāmānandins also demanded that the worship of Nārāyaṇa precede that of Govinda, the Mahārāja decided to convene a meeting of *paṇḍits* to resolve the various disputed questions. Baladeva was sent by Viśvanātha to attend this meeting and, defeating the opposition in debate, succeeded in keeping the Bengali priests in office and in having the worship performed according to Gauḍīya Vaiṣṇava custom. When the *paṇḍits* asked to see the *Brahmasūtra* commentary on which Baladeva had based his arguments, he took a seven day's respite and returned with his *Govindabhāṣya*.

4) According to an article by S. Das entitled "Govinda-Bhāṣya—History of its Composition" (Das: 1960: 57-60), the Gauḍīya Vaiṣṇavas had been accused by the rival Rāmānandins of Galta of not representing a legitimate *sampradāya*, and were called upon either to accept Madhva's *Brahmasūtra* commentary and be considered members of his *sampradāya*, or to establish themselves as an independent *sampradāya* by writing their own commentary. Baladeva accepted the challenge and completed his *Govindabhāṣya* within 18 days.

5) A. K. Majumdar writes:

> In the middle of the 18th century a controversy arose in Jaipur where Caitanya's followers were asked to stand in line behind the Mādhvas when *prasāda* (food) was distributed in the temple. They, however, wanted to form a separate row like the other four sects, claiming that they were an independent sect. In order to prove this claim Baladeva Vidyābhūṣaṇa wrote the *Govinda-bhāṣya* on the Br. S. which was considered by a learned assembly which decided on the basis of the G. Bh. that Caitanya's sect was not affiliated to the Mādhva sect. (Majumdar: 1969: 269)

Majumdar then explains Baladeva's *guruparamparā* linking Caitanya to Madhva as a mere expedient without which his case would not have been considered, since it was necessary for him to first show that Caitanya had been initiated in a recognized *sampradāya* before he could claim the independence of the Caitanya Sampradāya. As a precedent, Majumdar cites the case of Madhva, who took initiation with the Advaitic Tīrtha order, only to break away and found his own *sampradāya*.

6) To give a final example of the confusion surrounding the incident in Jaipur, we will cite the statement of Ashim Kumar Roy. After writing that the Gauḍīya Vaiṣṇavas had been accused by the Rāmānandins of being *asampradāyin* and not qualified to perform the temple worship, Roy concludes:

> It is difficult to say how far this story of the religious debate in Galta is true. *Govinda-Bhashya* as the Gaudiya Vaishnava commentary of the Brahma Sutra does no doubt exist, but there is no memory of this religious debate in Jaipur, not even in the family of the priests of the Govindadeva temple. (Roy: 1978: 171)

The differences between the various accounts are of the greatest significance regarding Baladeva's views on the sectarian affiliation of the Gauḍīya Vaiṣṇavas. On the one hand, Baladeva is portrayed as a champion of an independent Gauḍīya Vaiṣṇava Sampradāya, forced to admit a formal association with the Mādhva Sampradāya only to demonstrate his school's independent status, which he accomplished through the writing of his *Govindabhāṣya*. On the other hand, he is depicted as a proponent of Mādhva philosophical views, who helped restore the Bengali priests of Jaipur to their temple duties by proving their affiliation to the Mādhva Sampradāya. According to this latter view, the *Govindabhāṣya* was written either after the dispute had already been settled, or because of the relatively insignificant point regarding procedures of worship in the temples, while according to the former view, the writing of the *Govindabhāṣya* was a necessary prerequisite for establishing the Gauḍīya Vaiṣṇavas as an independent *sampradāya*.

In order to evaluate the accuracy of these various accounts and to determine which of the two above-mentioned views more accurately reflects Baladeva's own motives for writing his *Govindabhāṣya*, it will be necessary to examine three types of evidence: 1) the controversial *guruparamparā* from the introduction to Baladeva's *Govindabhāṣya* which links Caitanya to Madhva; 2) the philosophical stance adopted by Baladeva in the body of his *Govindabhāṣya* and allied works; and 3) the political situation at that time in the Jaipur and Vṛndāvana areas.

The *guruparamparā*, found both in Baladeva's *Govindabhāṣya* and *Prameyaratnāvalī*, is preceded in each case by the following verses, said to belong to the *Padma Purāṇa*:

> Those mantras which do not belong to any *sampradāya* are considered fruitless. Thus, in the Kali Yuga, there will be four founders of *sampradāyas*, Śrī, Brahmā, Rudra, and Sanaka, all world-purifying devotees of Viṣṇu. These four will emerge in the Kali Yuga from Puruṣottama (Jagannātha) in Utkala (Puri). Śrī chose Rāmānuja (to establish her *sampradāya*); the four-faced Brahmā chose Madhva. Rudra chose Viṣṇusvāmin, while the four "Sanas" (Sanaka, Sanatkumāra, Sanānda, and Sanātana) chose Nimbārka.[3]

Baladeva then gives Caitanya's *guruparamparā* as follows: Kṛṣṇa to Brahmā; Brahmā to Bādarāyaṇa (Vyāsa); Bādarāyaṇa to Madhva; Madhva to Padmanābha; Padmanābha to Nṛhari; Nṛhari to Mādhava; Mādhava to Akṣobhya; Akṣobhya to Jaya Tīrtha; Jaya Tīrtha to Jñānasindhu; Jñānasindhu to Dayānidhi (or Mahānidhi); Dayānidhi to Vidyānidhi; Vidyānidhi to Rājendra; Rājendra to Jayadharma; Jayadharma to Puruṣottama; Puruṣottama to Brahmaṇya; Brahmaṇya to Vyāsa Tīrtha; Vyāsa Tīrtha to Lakṣmīpati; Lakṣmīpati to Mādhavendra; Mādhavendra to Īśvara, Advaita, and Nityānanda; and Īśvara to Caitanya.

S. K. De and A. K. Majumdar are two of the more virulent critics of this *guruparamparā*, both regarding its historical accuracy and its origin. De writes:

> As the time of some of these Mādhva gurus is well-known, the historical accuracy of the list can be easily challenged, and there can be no doubt that the list was made up for the occasion [i.e. the debate in Jaipur] mainly from hearsay or imagination. (De: 1961: 15)

Majumdar also questions the fact that three gurus are said to intervene between Caitanya and Vyāsa Tīrtha, a contemporary of Caitanya, and terms the affiliation of Caitanya with Madhva an "invention" on the part of Baladeva. (Majumdar: 1969: 266)

There is no doubt that there are certain difficulties with the *guruparamparā* given by Baladeva. For one thing, Padmanābha, Nṛhari (Narahari), Mādhava, and Akṣobhya were all direct disciples of Madhva, and not successive disciples as Baladeva states. In addition, the names of Jñānasindhu and Dayānidhi are not found in the lists of Mādhva gurus. Aside from these differences, however, Baladeva's *guruparamparā* corresponds perfectly with the *guruparamparā* of the Vyāsarāya Maṭha, one of the three Mūla Maṭhas of the Mādhva Sampradāya, at least as far as Vyāsa Tīrtha. The names of Lakṣmīpati, Mādhavendra's purported guru, and of those after him are not found in any of the Mādhva *guruparamparās*, but this is probably because, unlike the other gurus, none of these was ever a *mahanta* of the order.

We may therefore assume that Lakṣmīpati was a wandering *sādhu*, free to give initiation at any time, as opposed to the *sādhus* living in the various monasteries who could only give initiation during their tenures as *mahanta*. It is thus not unlikely that within a very short period of time the line of his disciples could have multiplied rapidly. Moreover, if we assume that Lakṣmīpati's own initiation took place towards the beginning of Vyāsa Tīrtha's tenure as *mahanta* in 1478, and that he initiated Mādhavendra shortly thereafter, there is no reason why Mādhavendra's disciple, Īśvara, could not have taken initiation from Mādhavendra and also initiated Caitanya by 1510, as the biographies claim.

The real difficulty with this *guruparamparā* comes when we try to explain how Mādhavendra and Īśvara could both have had Purī designations when Mādhva *sannyāsins* invariably take the Tīrtha designation. If Mādhavendra had indeed been a disciple of Lakṣmīpati, it was probably only on the basis of mantra initiation, his *sannyāsa* initiation coming from the Advaitic Purī order. This would of course mean that Mādhavendra was not formally a Mādhva. However, given Baladeva's statement that only Vaiṣṇava *sampradāyas* are to be considered authentic, he probably felt justified in considering Mādhavendra a member of the Mādhva Sampradāya, just as he felt justified in tracing

Caitanya's lineage through his mantra guru, Īśvara, rather than through his *sannyāsa* guru, Keśava, even though none of the orthodox biographers took such a liberty.

A further difficulty comes when we consider that there was nothing in Mādhavendra's demeanor or in the traditions handed down by him to indicate any association with the Mādhvas. His emotional behavior was radically different from that of the Mādhva gurus, who were generally analytical in nature; and as mentioned earlier, it is more likely that Mādhavendra was influenced by the devotional Advaita of Śrīdhara and Viṣṇu Purī than by the doctrines of the Mādhva school. The *Caitanya Bhāgavata* (3/3) states that Mādhavendra took *sannyāsa* at an advanced age, so it is possible that between the time of his mantra initiation and *sannyāsa* initiation, his views underwent a significant change, leading him to feel a greater affinity for the Purī order of Śāṅkara *sannyāsins* than for the Mādhvas. The possibility must also be considered that, when the time came for Mādhavendra to take *sannyāsa*, he simply looked for a qualified *sannyāsin* to perform the ceremony, just as Caitanya apparently did many years later. This would also help explain why no mention is ever made of Mādhavendra's *sannyāsa* guru, although, assuming he were an Advaitin, it is not likely that the Gauḍīya Vaiṣṇavas would have emphasized his influence on Mādhavendra even had they known about him.

As a final thought regarding Mādhavendra's Purī designation, we may mention the statement of B. B. Majumdar that in the 16th century, titles such as Purī and Bhāratī were also used as family names, and did not necessarily imply association with the Śāṅkara Sampradāya. (Majumdar: 1959. 549) While this may have been true for householders, however, it certainly could not have been the case with Mādhavendra who, as a *sannyāsin*, would have discarded his family name at the time of initiation. It therefore must be concluded that Mādhavendra's formal affiliation was with the Purī order which, as suggested earlier, may have been influenced by the devotional Advaita of Śrīdhara, and that his association with the Mādhva Sampradāya, if it existed at all, was through his purported (mantra) guru, Lakṣmīpati.

It is now necessary to consider the origin of the *guruparamparā* given by Baladeva. B. B. Majumdar cites six different Gauḍīya

Vaiṣṇava works in addition to Baladeva's *Govindabhāṣya* and *Prameyaratnāvalī* which affirm Caitanya's affiliation with the Mādhva Sampradāya. (Majumdar: 1959: 544) Of these, the most important and probably the earliest is Kavi Karṇapūra's *Gauragaṇoddeśadīpikā*, written no later than 1576 and possibly as early as 1544. The work contains a *guruparamparā* virtually identical with the one given by Baladeva; but the authenticity of the work as a whole has been questioned. S. K. De writes:

> ...but interpolation into the text may be suspected. As an instance, one may point out that this work expressly affiliates the Caitanya Sampradāya to the Madhva, but Karṇapūra's [earlier] drama testifies to Caitanya's dislike of Mādhva doctrine and his being an Advaita Saṃnyāsin! In style and treatment the work is pedestrian, and its theology is clearly of later development; it is difficult to say if it is really a genuine work of Kavikarṇapūra's. (De: 1961: 46)

B. B. Majumdar also mentions that some scholars have even speculated that the *Gauragaṇoddeśadīpikā* was written by Baladeva under Karṇapūra's name, which is probably what De is hinting at when he writes that the *guruparamparā* of this work "looks suspiciously similar to a list given by Baladeva". (De: 1961: 14) Such accusations, however, are clearly based on sectarian interest and have little evidence to back them up. Karṇapūra's *guruparamparā* is quoted both in the *Bhaktiratnākara* (5/2149-62), probably written around the time of Baladeva's arrival in Vṛndāvana, and in Viśvanātha's *Gauragaṇatattvasvarūpacandrikā*, a work dealing specifically with Karṇapūra's *Gauragaṇoddeśadīpikā*.

Of perhaps equal importance to Karṇapūra's *guruparamparā* is a second and identical list in Sanskrit verse, also found in the *Bhaktiratnākara* (5/2169-72), and attributed to Gopālaguru, a disciple of Vakreśvara Paṇḍit. This evidence is not nearly as convincing as Karṇapūra's list since the work in which Gopālaguru presented this *guruparamparā* is no longer available. However, if the latter list actually represents the work of Gopālaguru, it could conceivably predate Karṇapūra's *Gauragaṇoddeśadīpikā* and help explain the change in attitude regarding Caitanya's sectarian affiliation seen in Karṇapūra's later work. Vakreśvara, Gopālaguru's guru, was a contemporary of Caitanya and one of his close associates in Puri. It is thus possible that Gopālaguru either composed a larger work containing this *guruparamparā*, or simply the *guruparamparā* within a very short time of Caitanya's death in 1533.

Gopālaguru was a resident of Orissa and the founder of the Rādhākānta Maṭha in Puri, a fact which may provide an important clue in discovering the origin of the Caitanya *guruparamparā*. According to Prabhat Mukherjee, the local Vaiṣṇava community of Orissa was held in very low esteem at the time of Caitanya's residence in Puri. (Mukherjee: 1940: 122) Although the majority of Caitanya's companions in Puri were Bengali, he did have Orissan followers as well, and even those Vaiṣṇavas who were not directly associated with Caitanya sought to identify themselves with his popular movement in order to legitimize themselves in the eyes of their peers. Consequently, a series of *guruparamparās* began to appear after the death of Caitanya affiliating various Orissan authors with Caitanya. Mukherjee lists four such *guruparamparās*, all of which trace Caitan-ya's lineage back to Nārāyaṇa, in most cases through Mādhavendra Purī and Madhva, although one list shows Mādhavendra to be a direct disciple of Vyāsa. (Mukherjee: 1940: 120)

Perhaps the earliest instance of such a *guruaprramparā* is the one found in Acyutānanda Dāsa's *Bhaktijñānabrahmayoga*. Acyutānanda was said to have been a close companion of Caitanya's in Puri, and to have been present in the Jagannātha temple when Caitanya passed away. He was reportedly given a plot of land in Puri by the king of Orissa, Pratāpa Rudra, on which he built a monastery known as the Gopāla Maṭha.

In his *guruparamparā*, Acyutānanda traces Caitanya's lineage as follows: Nārāyaṇa to Brahmā, Brahmā to Nārada, Nārada to Madhva, Madhva to Padmanābha, Padmanābha to Mādhavendra, Mādhavendra to Keśava Bhāratī, and Keśava to Caitanya. Although this list is unquestionably inaccurate, it does represent the skeleton of the *guruparamparā* of Karṇapūra and Gopālaguru, and it is possible that one of them, more likely the resident of Puri, Gopālaguru, came across Acyutānanda's list, accepted it as genuine but incomplete, and filled it in as best he could with the help of the *guruparamparā* from the Mādhva Vyāsarāya Maṭha.

Although Mukherjee labels the Orissan *guruparamparās* "ficticious", he nevertheless believes that the idea of Caitanya's Mādhva affiliation predates the writings of the Orissan authors. He writes:

> The reference in Acyutānanda's book shows that the Māddha (sic) parentage was accepted shortly after the passing away of the master. It is evident that the Oriya writers could not follow it clearly. (Mukherjee: 1940: 120)

While it is difficult to say to what extent this belief was accepted in Puri and whether or not the Orissan Vaiṣṇavas were themselves responsible for either its origin or popularity, it is clear that an early tradition of Mādhva affiliation did exist in Puri, and it is quite possible that Baladeva, being a native of Orissa, was familiar with this tradition, although it is almost certain that he based his own *guruparamparā* on Bengali sources.

A third possibility exists regarding the origin of the belief in Mādhva affiliation which, unlike the others, does not directly relate to the Gauḍīya Vaiṣṇava movement, but rather to the traditions of the Vallabha Sampradāya, although once again, the key figure is Caitanya's *paramaguru*, Mādhavendra. According to the *Do Sau Bāvan Vaiṣṇava kī Vārtā*, written in Vrajabhāṣā and attributed to Vallabha's grandson, Gokulanātha, Mādhavendra at one time lived in the village of Adel, Vallabha's dwelling place near Prayāga, where he would come to Vallabha's home and instruct him in devotional scriptures. (Gokulanātha: 1931: 504) M. C. Parekh writes that Mādhavendra was Vallabha's teacher when the Ācārya was just a boy in Benares (Parekh: 1969: 44), and J. G. Shah claims that it was Mādhavendra who initiated Vallabha into *sannyāsa* at the end of the latter's life in 1531 (Shah: 1969: 50), although the latter claim is certainly false as Mādhavendra probably did not live past the year 1500.

The account of the *Do Sau Bāvan* opens with the statement that Mādhavendra was a *sannyāsin* of the Mādhva Sampradāya, and goes on to relate the story of his association with the Govardhananātha temple of Vṛndāvana. According to this account, Mādhavendra discovered the image of Govardhananātha hidden in a woods near Vṛndāvana; and after Vallabha himself installed the image in a temple, Mādhavendra was appointed by him to preside over the worship with the help of some priests from Bengal. After being commanded by the deity to worship him with sandalwood from the South, Mādhavendra set off for the Malaya Mountains where, having obtained the sandalwood, he again had the vision of the deity, who this time commanded him to offer the sandalwood in the temple of Himagopāla. Mādhavendra did as bidden, and remained there until his death. (Gokulanātha: 1931: 505-7)

A similar account is found in the *Caitanya Caritāmṛta*, leaving little doubt that the Mādhavendra mentioned in the Vallabha literature and Caitanya's *paramaguru* are one and the same individual. The Bengali account, however, makes no mention of Vallabha's connection with the Vṛndāvana temple, and claims that Mādhavendra got the sandalwood from the priests of the Jagannātha temple in Puri. Kṛṣṇadāsa also writes that Mādhavendra offered the sandalwood, again at the bidding of Govinda, at the Gopīnātha temple in Remunā, just north of Puri. The *Caitanya Caritāmṛta* makes no mention of Mādhavendra's death, but Mukherjee writes that he passed away at Remunā, his sandals and burial ground being worshipped at the Gopīnātha temple to this day. (Mukherjee: 1940: 66) D. C. Sen speculates that Mādhavendra died either before Caitanya's birth or shortly thereafter (Sen: 1922: 45), and judging from the fact that no mention is made of Mādhavendra in the biographies aside from the above account or with reference to Mādhavendra's disciples, we may accept Sen's estimate as more or less accurate.

It is difficult to say whether the accounts of the Vallabha school represent an independent tradition or were based on the Gauḍīya Vaiṣṇava accounts. J. G. Shah sets Gokulanātha's dates at 1552-1641 (Shah: 1969: 343), and if he indeed authored the *Do Sau Bāvan*, it is likely that it is a later work than Kṛṣṇadāsa's *Caitanya Caritāmṛta*. The two schools were in close contact in Vṛndāvana and must have been familiar with the literature and traditions of each other. It is also important to note that both had ample reason to emphasize their association with Mādhavendra, since the temple associated with him later became the focus of an unfortunate power struggle between the two schools. According to the *Caurāsī Vaiṣṇava kī Vārtā*, also attributed to Gokulanātha, the Vallabhas had accused the priests of the temple, who were clearly Gauḍīya Vaiṣṇavas, of hoarding the temple offerings and turning them over to their gurus, the Vṛndāvana Gosvāmins. In order to gain control of the temple, the Vallabhas one day set fire to the huts of the priests, and occupied the temple when the Bengalis rushed out to extinguish the fires. (Gokulanātha: 1970: 530-5) According to A. K. Majumdar, this incident took place in 1573. (Majumdar: 1969: 236)

Regardless of the accuracy of this account and its possible influence on the Vallabha traditions concerning Mādhavendra, what is interesting for our purpose is the fact that the Vallabhas speak of Mādhavendra as a Mādhva *sannyāsin*. For one thing, the Vallabhas had nothing to gain by making such a claim since, due to Vallabha's real or supposed connection with the Rudra Sampradāya of Viṣṇusvāmin, and also because of his *Brahmasūtra* commentary, the Vallabhācārins did not face the same sectarian problems as did Caitanya's followers. Also, if the writings of Kṛṣṇadāsa and the Gosvāmins may be considered representative of the views of the Vṛndāvana Gauḍīya community in the 16th century, it cannot be assumed that the Vallabhas borrowed the idea of Mādhavendra's sectarian affiliation from the Gauḍīya Vaiṣṇavas. As mentioned earlier, neither Kṛṣṇadāsa nor any of the Gosvāmins ever mention the *sampradāya* to which Mādhavendra belonged, and it seems clear that Kavi Karṇapūra's *guruparamparā* linking Caitanya to the Mādhva Sampradāya was one of the principal reasons why his *Gauragaṇoddeśadīpikā* was not recognized by the Gosvāmins as an authoritative work.[4]

There is thus good reason to believe that the Vallabha tradition regarding Mādhavendra was an independent one, unless, of course, either the tradition is not as old as suspected, or Karṇapūra's *Gauragaṇoddeśadīpikā* did attain some measure of popularity in Vṛndāvana in the 16th century, despite the apparent opposition of Kṛṣṇadāsa and the Gosvāmins. That it did eventually come to be accepted as a legitimate work by the Gauḍīya community of Vṛndāvana is evidenced by the fact that Viśvanātha Cakravartin devoted an entire work, the

Gauragaṇatattvasvarūpacandrikā, to the theme of Karṇapūra's composition, including within the work the controversial *guru-paramparā*.

Even if the Vallabha tradition concerning Mādhavendra's ties with the Mādhva Sampradāya was not an independent tradition, there can be little doubt that it helped pave the way for the positive response which Baladeva's claims evoked, both in Vṛndāvana and Jaipur. Viśvanātha's own acceptance of Karṇapūra's *guruparamparā* and the fact that he himself authorized Baladeva to settle affairs in Jaipur also had to have been important factors in the subsequent success of Baladeva's campaign since, as the acknowledged leader of the Gauḍīya Vaiṣṇava community at that time, Viśvanātha's full support would have been absolutely necessary for Baladeva's claims to have been recognized as representative of the Gauḍīya Vaiṣṇava position, especially as Baladeva was then a very recent member of the Vṛndāvana Gauḍīya community.

It may thus be concluded that, despite the historical difficulties surrounding Baladeva's *guruparamparā*, the confusion concerning its origin, and the lack of corroboration in the orthodox literature of the school, it nevertheless represented a tradition which had its beginnings in the early years of the Gauḍīya Vaiṣṇava movement, and which, for various reasons, gained in strength and respectability as time wore on. Baladeva's official declaration of Mādhva affiliation in Jaipur, though unquestionably a radical departure from the orthodox 16th century tradition, nevertheless represented the logical fulfillment of certain strong historical tendencies, waiting, as it were, for the proper time to manifest themselves. The sectarian dispute in Jaipur was the propitious time for their manifestation; the stage was perfectly set with the assembly in Jaipur; and Baladeva was the right person at the right time.

It is important to remember, however, that even those who accepted the sectarian affiliation with the Mādhva Sampradāya, Viśvanātha included, never looked upon the writings of Madhva as authoritative literature. Caitanya's life and teachings, the writings of the Gosvāmins, and the *Bhāgavata Purāṇa* were still the unquestioned authorities of the school, at least until Baladeva wrote his *Govindabhāṣya* in Jaipur. It is only when we examine the nature of Baladeva's philosophical views that we can fully appreciate how radically they differ from traditional Gauḍīya Vaiṣṇava doctrine, and can gain a clearer insight into Baladeva's actual motives for claiming Mādhva affiliation for the Gauḍīya Vaiṣṇava school.

Baladeva's attempt to identify Gauḍīya Vaiṣṇava doctrine with the teachings of Madhva is nowhere more clearly seen than in his *Prameyaratnāvalī*, a sort of appendix to his *Govinda-bhāṣya*, in which he summarizes the major tenets of the school in a series of nine *prameyas*, or propositions. Baladeva opens the work with a series of *maṅgala* verses, one to Govinda, one to Caitanya, Nityānanda, and Advaita, and one to Madhva, followed by the same *Padma Purāṇa* verses and *guruparamparā* as found in his *Govindabhāṣya*. Baladeva then enumerates the nine propositions, introducing them with the words "Madhva declared", and closing with the phrase "thus is it taught by the Lord, Kṛṣṇa Caitanya".

Despite Baladeva's claim that the propositions were first declared by Madhva, many of the doctrines found in the text are peculiar to the teachings of the Gauḍīya Vaiṣṇavas, such as the three-fold *śakti* theory from the *Viṣṇu Purāṇa* (6/7/60), the belief that Kṛṣṇa is the source of all *avatāras*, the deification of Rādhā, the *pañcabhāva* doctrine, and the distinction between *vaidhībhakti* (preliminary devotional practices according to scriptural injunction) and *rucibhakti* (the mature, spontaneous stage of devotion). However, while the subject matter of the nine propositions is, for the most part, consistent with Gauḍīya Vaiṣṇava doctrine, the treatment is often significantly different, the most important difference centering around Baladeva's adoption of the Mādhva concept of *viśeṣa*.

In section 16 of the first *prameya*, Baladeva defines *viśeṣa* as "that by virtue of which a distinction between an object and its attributes appears to exist, when in reality none exists at all".[5] It is this phenomenon which lets us speak of the waves as distinct from the ocean, for example, when in ontological terms, no real distinction can be maintained. It is also this phenomenon which allows us to speak of *brahman* as possessing the attributes, existence, knowledge, and bliss, when in reality they represent not his attributes but his very being. In sharp distinction to this is the doctrine of Acintyabhedābhedavāda, developed by Jīva, which maintains that an entity is ontologically both identical with and distinct from its attributes, in a relationship which transcends the traditional bounds of logic. Thus, according to Jīva, *brahman* (more properly, *bhagavat*) is not only pure awareness, but the possessor of awareness, not only pure bliss, but a blissful being.

The distinction between these two doctrines seems almost trivial at first, until we realize that according to the Gauḍīya Vaiṣṇavas, both living beings and the phenomenal universe represent *śaktis*, or powers, of the divine, and hence may be considered attributes of *brahman* (here Jīva uses the term *paramātman*), while according to Madhva, the three categories, *brahman*, *jīva*, and *prakṛti*, are ontologically distinct. Thus, the application of the category of *viśeṣa* to the dualistic model of the Mādhvas in no way affects the radical dualism of their system, while the same application to the Gauḍīya Vaiṣṇava model results in a non-dualism equally as radical as Śaṅkara's Advaitavāda.

Baladeva, unwilling to abandon completely the Gauḍīya doctrine that the universe and living beings represent *śaktis* of *paramātman*, and unable to accept the consequences of applying the category of *viśeṣa* to the *māyāśakti* and *jīvaśakti* of *paramātman*, resorts to a partial application of *viśeṣa* in which only the essential *śaktis* of the divine, such as being, knowledge, and bliss, are identified with him. Thus, while Baladeva claims to accept the *śakti* theory of the Gauḍīya Vaiṣṇavas, due to his discriminating application of *viśeṣa*, the result is an ontology logically equivalent to the pure dualism of Madhva and in sharp contrast to the closely related Gauḍīya doctrines of Saktipariṇāmavāda and Acintyabhedābhedavāda.[6] This acceptance of dualism by Baladeva finds explicit expression in the fourth of the nine *prameyas*, designated "the reality of difference" and introduced by the words "Now (we will demonstrate) the difference between *jīvas* and Viṣṇu."[7]

A second significant departure from the traditional Gauḍīya standpoint is found in the ninth *prameya* of the same work, and concerns the question of *pramāṇas*, or the means of acquiring right knowledge. Here Baladeva follows Madhva, accepting only *pratyakṣa* (sense-perception), *anumāna* (inference), and *śabda* (revelation) as valid means of knowledge, as opposed to Jīva, who accepts all ten of the so-called *paurāṇika pramāṇas*.[8] Baladeva argues for the supremacy of *śabda pramāṇa*, as does Jīva, but restricts his definition of *śabda* to the Vedas and Upaniṣads, thus contradicting the important Gauḍīya Vaiṣṇava belief in the authoritative nature of Purāṇas, particularly the *Bhāgavata Purāṇa*.

The question of Baladeva's loyalty to Madhva in his *Govindabhāṣya* is somewhat more complex. Obviously, it would not have been possible for Baladeva to have accepted the whole of Madhva's *Brahmasūtra* commentary and still expect his *Govindabhāṣya* to be recognized as an original work. Thus, certain differences do exist between the two commentators, again, based primarily on Baladeva's partial acceptance of Śaktipariṇāmavāda. Still, as B.N.K. Sharma explains:

> Baladeva has drawn heavily upon Madhva's B.S.B. and incorporated many of his special and peculiar interpretations of the Sūtras that differ completely from those of Śaṁkara and Rāmānuja...Baladeva is virtually in agreement with Madhva on all the fundamental points of his system. (Sharma: 1961: 403, 407)

Despite Baladeva's obvious indebtedness to Madhva, attempts have been made to downplay his influence on Baladeva. A.K. Majumdar, for example, writes:

> It is usually held that Baladeva borrowed the category of *viśeṣa* from Mādhva system, but it is apparent that he got the idea of *viśeṣa* through his teacher Rādhā-Dāmodara the author of the *Vedānta-Syamantaka*. (Majumdar: 1969: 271)

Such claims are, however, open to serious question. For one thing, the authorship of the *Vedāntasyamantaka* is itself a disputed issue, some scholars attributing the work not to Rādhādāmodara but to Baladeva himself. The Punjab Oriental Series edition of the text, based on only two manuscripts, closes with a colophon identifying Rādhādāmodara as the author. Haridās Dās, however, obviously working with different manuscripts, writes that according to the final verse of the work, the text was written by Baladeva, at the urging of Rādhādāmodara. (Dās: 1956: 1334) Also, considering that the *Vedāntasyamantaka* contains many of the ideas found in Baladeva's writings, such as the *viśeṣa* doctrine, the five *tattva* theory,[9] the acceptance of three *pramāṇas*, and the restriction of *śabda* to the Vedas and Upaniṣads, etc., it seems more logical to credit the work directly to Baladeva with his early training in Mādhva doctrine, than to the *Bhāgavatasandarbha* specialist, Rādhādāmodara, especially since not a single reference to any of the works of Jīva is found in the text.

In any event, Baladeva's explicit statements regarding Madhva in the *Prameyaratnāvalī*, his great reliance on Madhva's *Brahmasūtra* commentary in his *Govindabhāṣya*, and the various *maṅgala* verses to Madhva with which Baladeva opens most of his works all testify to his extreme regard for Madhva and the doctrines of his school. Also, the fact that Baladeva prefaces his *guruparamparā* with verses restricting the number of authentic *sampradāyas* to four indicates that he had no intention of establishing the Gauḍīya Vaiṣṇavas as an independent *sampradāya*. In fact, far from feeling compelled to declare the Gauḍīya Vaiṣṇavas affiliated with the Mādhvas by the circumstances in Jaipur, Baladeva probably saw the situation as a golden opportunity to make certain claims which were perfectly consistent with his own beliefs and philosophical standpoint, and to have those claims wield an influence over the Gauḍīya Vaiṣṇava community which otherwise might not have been possible.

Having thus gained a certain insight into the nature of Baladeva's activities in Jaipur, we may now turn to the political situation in North India at the time of this incident before coming to any definite conclusions regarding the sectarian problems which faced the Gauḍīya community at that time, and which culminated in the assembly in Jaipur.

It is generally agreed that Viśvanātha was quite old at the time of Baladeva's arrival in Vṛndāvana. Viśvanātha's date of birth is traditionally set at either 1654 or 1664, and given the fact that his *Śrīkṛṣṇabhāvanāmṛta* was written in 1679, we may take the earlier date as the more likely of the two. If we assume that Viśvanātha was beyond the age of 65 at the time Baladeva reached Vṛndāvana, then the Jaipur incident probably did not take place prior to 1720; and for reasons which we will mention shortly, it is unlikely that the incident took place later than 1723. This also makes sense from Baladeva's side, since his only dated work, a late commentary on Rūpa's *Stavamālā*, is said to have been written in 1764. It is thus probable that Baladeva was born around 1700, was still in his early twenties when he went to Jaipur, and continued his literary career well into the final years of his reportedly long life.

During the period in question, Sawai Jai Singh, the founder of the modern city of Jaipur, held the position of Mahārāja of Amer. He was known as a devout Vaiṣṇava and devotee of the Govindadeva temple, the image of which had been earlier installed in Vṛndāvana by Rūpa Gosvāmin, although it does not seem that he was affiliated with any particular Vaiṣṇava sect. A. K. Roy writes that "he was acknowledged as the most important and learned Hindu chief in the country" and "was invited to arbiter in matters of religious disputes even up to Bengal". (Roy: 1978: 19)

In 1722, the government of the district of Agra was placed under the control of Jai Singh in Amer as the result of incidents related to the Jāt rebellion. According to Richard Haynes (1970: 121), one of the Rājā's immediate concerns was to somehow control the rapidly multiplying number of sects in Vṛndāvana, which, according to Growse (1978: 264), he made his occasional residence during the period of 1721-8. Consequently, one of Jai Singh's first acts was the passing of an ordinance requiring all the sects to provide evidence of formal affiliation with one of the four recognized *sampradāyas*.[10]

There is evidence of one sect, in particular, having been directly affected by this policy. According to Haynes, the Haridāsī sect prepared a *guruparamparā* on this occasion, affiliating its members with the Nimbārka Sampradāya. This affiliation, initiated by the *sādhu* branch of the school, was not very well received by the other members of the sect and once Jai Singh's ten-year period of rule came to an end, was no longer maintained. (Haynes: 1970: 122-3)

Since there is no record of the Gauḍīya Vaiṣṇavas of Vṛndāvana having been similarly affected by Jai Singh's ordinance, we may assume that the debate in Jaipur came prior to the edict in Vṛndāvana, and that by the time of Jai Singh's campaign, the position of the Gauḍīya Vaiṣṇavas had already been secured. It may even be speculated that the happy solution to the sectarian dispute in Jaipur, presided over, perhaps, by Jai Singh himself, was an important factor in his decision to take similar steps in Vṛndāvana.

There is also good reason to believe that the Rāmānandins were somehow involved in the Jaipur dispute. A. K. Roy writes:

> ...the *Rama Bhakti* or the *Ramavat* school had established itself quite early in Galta near Jaipur...Payohari Krishnadas, a great *Ramanandi* sadhu came to Galta early in the 16th century...Galta later became one of the most important centres of the *Ramanandi* sect and came to be known as *Uttar Todari* or Todari of the north. (Roy: 1978: 24)

It may also be mentioned that, though they had no *Brahmasūtra* commentary of their own, due to their alleged connection with the Śrī Vaiṣṇavas, the Rāmānandins were in a position to make sectarian charges against the Gauḍīya Vaiṣṇavas without fear of their own status being questioned.

It also seems likely that the dispute centered around the Jaipur Govindadeva temple. As mentioned earlier, the image of Govinda worshipped there had been discovered many years prior to that by Rūpa Gosvāmin in Vṛndāvana, and had been removed to Jaipur out of fear of desecration by Aurangzīb. Consequently, the temple was the most important of the Jaipur temples for the Gauḍīya Vaiṣṇavas, although it was apparently frequented by members of all the local Vaiṣṇava sects. A. K. Roy writes:

> The worship of Govinda is carried on here in the Gauḍīya Vaishnava manner since the priests of the temple belong to that sect. However, so far as the devotees are concerned there is no sectarian bias and this temple is the most popular temple in the city. (Roy: 1978: 168)

Whether or not the dispute grew out of any specific charges by the Rāmānandins regarding the Gauḍīya Vaiṣṇava methods of worship is not known, and is probably of secondary importance. The Rāmānandans generally worship Sītā and Rāma together, and it is unlikely that they would have objected to the joint worship of Rādhā and Kṛṣṇa, although it is possible that they would have preferred the worship of Nārāyaṇa to take precedence over the worship of Rādhā and Kṛṣṇa (see pp. 26-30). In any event, it seems likely that the Rāmānandins sought to solve their disputes with the Gauḍīya Vaiṣṇava priests by having them expelled from the temple on the grounds of not belonging to a recognized *sampradāya*.

The theory, held by A. K. Majumdar and others, that Baladeva was trying to establish the Gauḍīya Vaiṣṇavas as an independent *sampradāya* is not tenable for several reasons. For one thing, the tradition of there being only four legitimate Vaiṣṇava *sampradāyas* was already well-established at that time in North India—Farquhar (1967: 327) speculates that it is as old as 1500—and it is certain that an orthodox Vaiṣṇava like Jai Singh would have been well aware of it. The same tradition was not only accepted by Baladeva, but explicitly mentioned by him in his *Govindabhāṣya* and *Prameyaratnāvalī*. Furthermore, although Baladeva does not follow Madhva's *Brahmasūtrabhāṣya* in all cases, there is little in the *Govindabhāṣya* to indicate that he was attempting to refute Madhva's conclusions or establish an independent philosophical system. And even in later works, such as his *Tattvasandarbha* commentary, when it would no longer have been necessary to maintain the affiliation to Madhva, Baladeva repeatedly expresses the fact that their tradition goes directly back to Madhva.

The question may thus legitimately be asked: If Baladeva had been merely trying to show that the Gauḍīya Vaiṣṇavas were affiliated with the Mādhva Sampradāya, why then did he bother to write his own commentary on the *Brahmasūtra* ? Presumably the *guruparamparā* linking Caitanya to Madhva would have been sufficient proof of affiliation with the Mādhva Sampradāya, as was the case with the Haridāsīs and their affiliation with the Sanakādi, or Haṃsa, Sampradāya of Nimbārka.

A. K. Majumdar makes much of this line of reasoning, and indeed, the fact of Baladeva's *Govindabhāṣya* is the most convincing piece of evidence in support of the view that Baladeva was trying to establish the Gauḍīya Vaiṣṇavas as an independent, *sampradāya*.

In reply, we would first of all suggest that the writing of the *Govindabhāṣya* was not directly related to the solution of the Jaipur dispute, as attested to by several accounts of this incident. Very likely, the happy conclusion to the dispute turned on the Caitanya *guruparampā* alone as argued for by Baladeva in the assembly at Jaipur. If, in addition to the *guruparamparā*, Baladeva had been required to submit something in writing proving the Gauḍīya Vaiṣṇava affiliation with the Mādhvas, there is no reason to assume that it had to have taken the form of a *Brahmasūtra bhāṣya*, especially when the Haridāsīs, under similar circumstances, established the legitimacy of their school without such a commentary.

Baladeva's reasons for writing his *Govindabhāṣya* at this time can probably be traced to his belief in the authority of the *prasthānatraya* of Vedānta (i.e. the *Brahmasūtra*, Upaniṣads, and the *Bhagavadgītā*) and to his desire to enhance the legitimacy of the Gauḍīya Vaiṣṇavas by placing their school within the accepted bounds of Vedānta. It may also be the case that Baladeva, being familiar with his school's long-standing bias against *Brahmasūtra* commentaries, saw this as a perfect opportunity to have his commentary accepted by the Gauḍīya Vaiṣṇava community due to the special circumstances in Jaipur, without having them feel they were compromising the teachings of Caitanya. The desire to have his *Govindabhāṣya* well-received by the Gauḍīya Vaiṣṇavas may also have been at the root of the tradition that Govinda himself had commanded Baladeva to write such a commentary.[11] In any event, the traditions linking the writing of the *Govindabhāṣya* to the dispute in Jaipur and to the command of Govinda were advantageous to both Baladeva and later generations of Gauḍīya Vaiṣṇavas, especially to those who were not anxious to admit their school's affiliation with the Mādhvas or to compromise the teachings of Caitanya, but who nevertheless recognized the prestige which Baladeva's commentary brought to the school.

While it thus seems clear that Baladeva was strongly in favor of Mādhva affiliation, it should not be assumed that he sought to obliterate completely the distinction between the Gauḍīya Vaiṣṇavas and the Mādhvas. Such an attempt would have been not only impossible, considering the many differences between the two schools regarding ritual, mantras, sectarian marks, etc., but also unacceptable to the Gauḍīya Vaiṣṇavas. As the Mādhvas were then almost entirely restricted to South India, it is more likely that Baladeva wanted to establish the Gauḍīya Vaiṣṇavas as the North Indian representatives of Madhva's Brahma Sampradāya, much in the same way that the Rāmānandins and Vallabhācārins were representatives of the Śrī and Rudra Sampradāyas, respectively. However, while Vallabha did not acknowledge his debt to Viṣṇusvāmin, the founder of the Rudra Sampradāya, in his *Brahmasūtra bhāṣya*, leading his followers to ultimately repudiate their connection with Viṣṇusvāmin, Baladeva clearly wished to stress both the philosophical and sectarian association of the Gauḍīya Vaiṣṇavas with the Mādhvas. The radically different traditions regarding the Jaipur incident and Baladeva's motives for writing his *Govindabhāṣya* testify to the mixed emotions which this position must have evoked, not only within the Gauḍīya Vaiṣṇava community of the day, but also for later generations of Gauḍīya Vaiṣṇavas; and it is clear that the present-day disputes within the school regarding the question of sectarian affiliation can be directly traced to the overall confusion surrounding Baladeva's role in the resolution of the dispute in Jaipur.

Virtually nothing is known of Baladeva's life after his return to Vṛndāvana from Jaipur. It seems that he spent the remainder of his life in Vṛndāvana, devoting his time to his Sanskrit writings and spiritual practices, and it is likely that he assumed the role of leader of the Gauḍīya Vaiṣṇava community after the death of Viśvanātha. He is credited with several original works as well as many commentaries, although neither their dates nor the order of their composition is known, with the exception of his commentary on Rūpa's *Stavamālā*, written in 1764.

Baladeva's works include: a commentary on the *Brahmasūtra* entitled *Govindabhāṣya*, and sub-commentary entitled *Sūkṣmā*; a commentary on the *Bhagavadgītā* entitled *Gītābhūṣaṇa*; a commentary on the *Bhāgavata Purāṇa* entitled *Vaiṣṇavānandinī*; commentaries on the *Īśā Upaniṣad*, *Sahasranāma*, and *Gopālatāpinī*; and commentaries on Jīva's *Tattvasandarbha*, Rūpa's *Stavamālā*, *Laghubhāgavatāmṛta*, and *Nāṭakacandrikā*, and Jayadeva's *Candrāloka*; original works on Vedānta entitled *Siddhāntaratna*, with commentary, *Vedāntasyamantaka* (also attributed to Rādhādāmodara), *Prameyaratnāvalī*, and *Siddhāntadarpaṇa*; two works on poetics entitled *Sāhityakaumudī* and *Kāvyakaustubha*; and a work of fiction entitled *Aiśvaryakādambinī*.

It is interesting to note that Baladeva's *Govindabhāṣya* and *Prameyaratnāvalī* both appear in English translation in the *Sacred Books of the Hindus*, a series which also features some of the important works of Madhva. The other important publisher of the works of Baladeva is the Sārasvata Gauḍīya Āsana and Mission, whose editions of Baladeva's works contain not only Bengali translations, but, in the case of Baladeva's *Īśā Upaniṣad* commentary, the commentary of Madhva as well.

Aside from the above organization, the works of Baladeva do not seem to occupy the same place of importance within the Gauḍīya Vaiṣṇava community as do the works of the Gosvāmins, and while Baladeva's *Govindabhāṣya* is no doubt recognized as the Gauḍīya Vaiṣṇava commentary on Vedānta, it is difficult to say to what extent it is actually studied and what influence it has had on the thought of the Gauḍīya Vaiṣṇava community as a whole.

NOTES

1. Rādhādāmodara's own *guruparamparā* is as follows: Nityānanda, Gaurīdāsa Paṇḍit, Hṛdaya Caitanya, Śyāmānanda, Rasikānanda Murāri, Nayanānanda, and Rādhādāmodara.

2. Viśvanātha was one of the school's most important authors and spiritual leaders, composing many original works, as well as summaries and commentaries on some of the more important writings of the Gosvāmins. He also composed commentaries on the *Bhāgavata Purāṇa* and *Bhagavadgītā*, among others. (Cf. Chakravarti : 1975: 75-76, for a list and description of Viśvanātha's writings.) Jadunath Sinha describes Viśvanātha as a faithful representative of the teachings of Caitanya, Rūpa, and Jīva, who repudiates both the non-dualism of Śaṅkara and the dualism of Mādhva. (Sinha: 1976: 87, 89)

3. *yad uktaṃ padmapurāṇe*

sampradāyavihīnā ye mantrās te viphalā matāḥ |
ataḥ kalau bhaviṣyanti catvāraḥ sampradāyinaḥ ||
śrībrahmarudrasanakā vaiṣṇavā kṣitipāvanāḥ |
catvāras te kalau bhāvyā hy utkale puruṣottamāḥ ||
rāmānujaṃ śrīḥ svīcakre madnvācāryaṃ caturmukhaḥ |
śrīviṣṇusvāmiṇaṃ rudro nimbādityaṃ catuḥsanaḥ ||

H. H. Wilson cites the first two of these verses, with some variation, as belonging to the *Padma Purāṇa*, but, like Baladeva, does not give verse numbers. (Wilson: 1976: 34) If these verses are found in the *Padma Purāṇa* at all, they may be assumed to be relatively recent interpolations, probably not written prior to the fourteenth century.

4. B. B. Majumdar expresses surprise at the fact that Karṇapūra, despite his many scholarly and poetical Sanskrit writings, was never considered qualified to be called a Gosvāmin like his counterparts in Vṛndāvana, and suggests that some ill-will might have existed between him and the Gosvāmins. As evidence of this, Majumdar points out that Karṇapūra wrote a *Bhāgavata* commentary which was never circulated among the Gauḍīya Vaiṣṇavas, as well as several works which paralleled those of the Gosvāmins, but which emphasized the worship of Caitanya over Kṛṣṇa. (For example, Karṇapūra's *Gauragaṇoddesadīpikā* was clearly some kind of reply to Rūpa's *Kṛṣṇagaṇoddesadīpikā.*) According to Majumdar, the emphasis on the worship of Caitanya as an end in itself, an attitude typical of Bengal, and the fact that Karṇapūra did not join the Gosvāmins in Vṛndāvana were the major reasons for the tension which apparently existed between him and the Gosvāmins. It may also be assumed that Karṇapūra's attempt to link Caitanya to the Mādhvas only worsened matters, and may have had something to do with Kṛṣṇadāsa's highly unflattering description of the Mādhvas in his *Caitanya Caritāmṛta.*

5. *na bhinnā dharmiṇo dharmā bhedabhānaṃ viśeṣataḥ* /

6. According to Śaktipariṇāmavāda, the universe and living beings represent transformations of the divine power, and according to Acintyabhedābhedavāda, the universe and living beings, being powers of the divine, are both identical with and distinct from the divine.

7. *atha viṣṇuto jīvānāṃ bhedaḥ* /

8. Cf. footnote 4 on *Tattvasandarbha* 9 of this work for a list and description of these ten *pramāṇas.*

9. The five *tattvas*, or ontological categories, are *īśvara, jīva, māyā, kāla* (time), and *karman.* Cf. footnote 1 on *Tattvasandarbha* 34 of this work for Baladeva's description of the five *tattvas.*

10. Richard Haynes writes that the sanctioned groups were the Gauḍīya Sampradāya, the Nimbārka Sampradāya, the Viṣṇusvāmin Sampradāya, and the Śrī Vaiṣṇavas, and that the criteria for their recognition were commentaries on the Upaniṣads, *Brahmasūtras*, and the *Bhāgavata Purāṇa.* The sources which Haynes cites, however, do not bear out his claims, and it may be assumed that the Brahma, or Mādhva, Sampradāya was one of the four sanctioned groups, and not the Gauḍīya Vaiṣṇavas. The reference to the *Bhāgavata Purāṇa* is also probably an error for the *Bhagavadgītā*, the third member of the *prasthānatraya* of Vedānta.

11. Baladeva writes at the end of his *Siddhāntaratna* :

vidyārūpaṃ bhūṣaṇam me pradāya
khyātiṃ ninye tena yo mām udāraḥ /
śrīgovindaḥ svapnanirdiṣṭabhāṣyo
rādhābandhur bandhurāṅgaḥ sa jīyāt //

"May the illustrious Govinda reign supreme, who bestowed upon me the ornament of knowledge, bringing me great renown, who is the beloved of Rādhā and of enchanting features, and who came to me in a dream and instructed me to write my (*Govinda*) *bhāṣya*." (*Siddhāntaratna* 8/31)

CHAPTER IV

RĀDHĀMOHANA

Although the most recent of the four main figures featured in this study, virtually nothing is known of the life of Rādhāmohana. Haridās Dās (1956: 1334) places his time of birth some time in the fourth decade of the 18th century, based on the date of a gift of land from the Rājā of Navadvīpa. We know from the colophon to his *Tattvasandarbha* commentary[1] that Rādhāmohana was a descendant of Advaita; and Dās informs us that he was the chief *paṇḍit* of Śāntipur, Bengal, the main center for the Gosvāmins of the Advaita line. P. V. Kane writes that Rādhāmohana was a friend of H. T. Colebrooke (Kane: 1930: 523), although no mention is made of him in the biography written by Colebrooke's son (Colebrooke: 1873).

From his commentary on Jīva's *Tattvasandarbha*, it seems clear that Rādhāmohana was opposed to any attempt at affiliating the Gauḍīya Vaiṣṇavas with the Mādhva Sampradāya, either on sectarian or philosophical grounds; and it may be speculated that he wrote his commentary specifically to counter Baladeva's attempt to interpret the *Tattvasandarbha* from a Mādhva point of view. Rādhāmohana's own views regarding the relationship between the Gauḍīya Vaiṣṇava position and that of the various other Vaiṣṇava schools are best seen in his remarks on *Tattvasandarbha* 28, the major portion of which is given below:

> After grouping together the various different view-points found in the doctrines of Śrīdhara and other respected philosophers, Jīva presents his own viewpoint, making it clear that he does not belong to the tradition (*sampradāya*) of any one of them.
>
> Here, the system of Śaṅkara known as Māyāvāda, which deals with the unqualified *brahman*, is not considered, since it contradicts the *bhakti* scriptures of Jīva's school. Śaṅkara,

however, also demonstrated the significance of the *Bhāgavata* by describing [in his poetry] such events as Kṛṣṇa's theft of the Gopīs' clothes, etc. There consequently developed a split within Śaṅkara's school on account of the *bhakti*-oriented doctrines which he passed on to his disciples, the [devotional] group of Advaitins being known as "Bhāgavatas", and the other as "Smārtas".

Of these, Śrīdhara is an adherent of the "Bhāgavata" tradition. However, since he places special emphasis on Nārāyaṇa, even in his *Bhāgavata* commentary, Jīva only follows him when he stresses that form of *bhagavat* which is taught in the *Bhāgavata*, and shows special devotion to him; Jīva does not accept Śrīdhara's doctrines in their entirety.

The same is the case with the qualified non-dualist and devotee of Nārāyaṇa (Lakṣmīnātha), Rāmānuja, who considers Nārāyaṇa to be *bhagavat* himself. Rāmānuja also considers the universe to be a transformation of the insentient portion of the Lord, but denies that *prakṛti* is the material cause of the universe. The whole of Rāmānuja's doctrines are also not consistent with the significance of the *Bhāgavata*. However, by accepting certain portions of his views in this text, such as his refutation of Māyāvāda, his conception of the *jīva*, his belief in the reality of the universe, etc., Jīva has strengthened Rāmānuja's own position.

Similarly, the doctrines of the dualist, Madhva, are not accepted in their entirety. According to Madhva, Viṣṇu is *bhagavat* himself. Furthermore, since Madhva accepts Lakṣmī as Viṣṇu's principal *śakti*, he cannot consider the Gopīs to represent the highest *śaktis*. Consequently we find in his *bhāṣya* that knowledge is the chief means to liberation, and that liberation is the highest goal of life. Jīva does, however, accept certain of Madhva's doctrines, such as the belief that *bhagavat* possesses attributes, that *prakṛti* is eternal, that the universe is a transformation of *prakṛti* and, thus, real, and that the *jīva*, being a peripheral portion of *brahman*, is distinct from *brahman*. The major difference between Jīva and Madhva lies in the fact that Madhva does not consider *prakṛti* to partake of the nature of *brahman*.

The Dvaitādvaitavāda of Bhāskara, on the other hand, which maintains that the universe is a transformation of the *śaktī* inherent in *brahman*, and that this *śakti* is identical with *prakṛti*, composed of the three *guṇas*, is consistent with Jīva's own position.

All of these are noble doctrines, since it is said, "They worship *bhagavat*, following a variety of different teachers." But the doctrines of Mahāprabhu Caitanya are superior to all since they represent an assemblage of the essential features of all the other schools. Thus, just as Madhva, though a disciple of Śaṅkara,[2] initiated his own independent *sampradāya* by writing commentaries on the *Brahmasūtra*, etc., after joining the Brahma Sampradāya, so also Kṛṣṇa Caitanya, though himself an *avatāra* of *bhagavat*, accepted the indispensability of having a guru and belonging to his *sampradāya*,[3] and initiated his own school through Advaitācārya and other intimate associates. At his own command, his doctrines were put into concrete form by the Gosvāmins; but in the case of Jīva, rather than compose a new *Brahmasūtra* commentary, he chose to interpret that commentary which the Lord Nārāyaṇa himself taught to Brahmā, namely the *Bhāgavata Purāṇa*.[4]

It is difficult to say anything specific about Rādhāmohana's own philosophical views based on his *Tattvasandarbha* commentary. For the most part, Rādhāmohana limits himself to the task of elucidating the text, which he does in a clear and straightforward manner. His commentary reveals a thorough familiarity with the Upaniṣads and the doctrines of Advaita Vedānta, as well as with the Purāṇas of his school, and is written in a lucid and sensitive fashion, sharply contrasted to the ironic, polemical style of Baladeva.

Considering the many merits of Rādhāmohana's *Tattvasandarbha* commentary, it is not a little surprising that it has achieved such a meagre popularity. None of the early editions of the text includes his commentary, and in the edition of Nityasvarūpa Brahmacārī which contains the commentaries of both Baladeva and Rādhāmohana, the interpretations of Baladeva are almost exclusively followed in the Bengali translation of the text, and no mention is made of any contradictions between the two commentators.

The explanation for Rādhāmohana's relative lack of importance, both within the Gauḍīya Vaiṣṇava school and without, can probably be traced to the continuing role of Vṛndāvana to dictate the official doctrine of the school through the 18th century. It is not known how many years passed between Baladeva's *Govindabhāṣya* and his *Tattvasandarbha* commentary, but it may be assumed that by the time he wrote the latter work, he had already attained the enviable position of leadership within the Vṛndāvana Gauḍīya community, and that his writings were then unquestionably accepted as authoritative statements of Gauḍīya Vaiṣṇava doctrine.

Rādhāmohana's *Tattvasandarbha* commentary, written probably within half a century of Baladeva's, thus had little chance of wide-spread acceptance, despite the fact that his views on the independence of the Caitanya tradition must have been well-appreciated by many Gauḍīya Vaiṣṇavas, particularly those living in Bengal, far from the sectarian squabbles of Vṛndāvana and Jaipur. It is a matter of regret that, as a result of his attempt to defend a tradition based on the writings of the Vṛndāvana Gosvāmins and on the traditional biographies of Caitanya, Rādhāmohana has suffered the fate of being almost wholly ignored as a philosopher of any merit within the Gauḍīya Vaiṣṇava school. As a result, his commentary on the *Tattvasandarbha* occupies a place of very little importance within the present-day school, and next to nothing is known about Rādhāmohana himself.

In addition to his *Tattvasandarbha* commentary, Rādhāmohana also wrote a commentary on the *Bhāgavata Purāṇa*, entitled *Dīpanī*, which is allegedly based on the commentary of Śrīdhara, as well as a commentary on Raghunandana's *Ekādaśītattva*. Umesh Mishra calls Rādhāmohana a "19th century Naiyāyika" and credits him with a work on Nyāya entitled *Tattvadīpikā*, a *Nyāyasūtravivaraṇa*[5], and a sub-commentary on Haridāsa's commentary on Udayana's *Kusumāñjuli*, entitled *Vyākhyāprakāśa*. (Mishra: 1966: 450)

Notes

1. *kaliyugapāvanāvatāraśrīmadadvaitakulodbhavaśrīrādhāmohanagosvāmibhaṭṭācāryakṛtā tattvasandarbhaṭippanī sampūrṇā|*

2. The reference to Madhva's discipleship with Śaṅkara is based on Jīva's own statements in *Tattvasandarbha* 24 and 28. (Cf. section 24, footnotes 4, 5, and 8 of this work for a discussion of this controversial point.)

3. The reference here is almost certainly to Caitanya's *sannyāsa* initiation with Keśava Bhāratī, although some maintain that it isto his mantra initiation with Mādhavendra Purī. (Cf. T. S. 28, footnote 4 for a discussion of this question.)

4. Many of the points raised by Rādhāmohana in this portion of his commentary have specific reference to Jīva's own remarks in the text of the *Tattvasandarbha*, and their full significance will be better appreciated when read in their proper context. The Sanskrit for this portion of Rādhāmohana's commentary may be found in the Acyutagranthamālā edition of the *Tattvasandarbha*, pp. 79-80.

5. First published serially in the periodical, "Pandit", between the years 1901-1903, and reprinted in Benares in 1903.

CHAPTER V

TATTVASANDARBHA : PRELIMINARY REMARKS

Jīva's *Tattvasandarbha* forms the first volume of his six-part *Bhāgavatasandarbha*, or *Ṣaṭsandarbha*. As the title of the work suggests, the *Bhāgavatasandarbha* is a compilation (literally, a "stringing together") of carefully selected verses from the *Bhāgavata Purāṇa*, arranged and interpreted in such a fashion as to constitute a comprehensive philosophical system. As the first volume of this work, the *Tattvasandarbha* serves as an introduction to the work as a whole, and also contains a brief summary of the doctrines found in the other five volumes.

The *Tattvasandarbha* may be broken down into two main segments: a *pramāṇakhaṇḍa*, in which Jīva ascertains the standards of knowledge to be used in the text; and a *prameyakhaṇḍa*, in which these standards are employed to determine the philosophical questions under discussion.

Jīva opens the work with a series of *maṅgala* verses to Caitanya, Rūpa, and Sanātana, and then explains the circumstances which led to the writing of the *Bhāgavatasandarbha*. Jīva writes that the original version of these *sandarbhas* had been composed earlier by "a certain Bhaṭṭa from South India", presumably Gopāla Bhaṭṭa, one of the six Gosvāmins, and that Rūpa and Sanātana had urged Jīva to make some revisions and additions to the original text. Since Jīva acknowledges his debt to Gopāla Bhaṭṭa at the commencement of each of the six *sandarbhas*,[1] it is likely that an earlier version, or at least outline, of the text did exist, although it is almost certain that Jīva, out of a sense of humility, has significantly de-emphasized his role in the authorship of this work. Jīva also makes the first of several statements here acknowledging his debt to the earlier Vaiṣṇava *ācāryas*, whom he identifies in *Sarvasaṃvādinī* as Rāmānuja, Madhva, Śrīdhara, and others.

Section 8 of the text is composed of what appears to be a simple *maṅgala* verse dedicated to Kṛṣṇa, but which, as Jīva himself notes, represents a concise statement of the essence of the *Bhāgavatasandarbha*. The verse is based on the famous lines from the *Bhāgavata* (1/2/11): "That non-dual consciousness which the knowers of truth (*tattva*) consider truth is designated *brahman*, *paramātman*, and *bhagavat*."[2] The *tattva* which forms the subject of this first *sandarbha* and after which it takes its name is none other than the non-dual consciousness mentioned in the first line of this verse, and the following three *sandarbhas*, the *Bhagavat*, *Paramātma*, and *Kṛṣṇa sandarbhas*, are all elucidations of this same *tattva* from different points of view.

Section 9 contains a statement of the *anubandhas*, the preliminary questions which are considered necessary prerequisites for works of this kind, namely: 1) the subject matter of the text (the *sambandha*), which is the *tattva* mentioned above; 2) the purpose of the text (the *prayojana*), which is to instill love of God in the aspirant who reads it; and 3) the means of attaining this aim (the *abhidheya*), which is devotional practices as set forth in the *Bhāgavata*.[3] Thus, the first four *sandarbhas*, as previously mentioned, deal with the *sambandha*, the fifth, or *Bhaktisandarbha*, deals with the *abhidheya*, and the sixth, or *Prītisandarbha*, deals with the *prayojana*.

Jīva then begins his investigation of the question of *pramāṇa* in order to discover the authority on which these questions may be determined. After first ruling out the possibility that sense-perception, inference, or related means of knowledge can be relied upon in deciding metaphysical questions, Jīva turns his attention to *śabdapramāṇa* (valid testimony or revelation). According to Jīva, the authority of the Vedas stems from the fact of their divine origin. Since, he maintains, the Purāṇas and Itihāsa are also divine in origin, their authority is to be considered equal to that of the Vedas. Jīva supports this proposition with numerous quotations, mostly from the Purāṇas themselves, but also from the Upaniṣads.

Having established the authoritative nature of the Purāṇas and Itihāsa, Jīva proceeds to point out the advantages which they enjoy over the Vedas, namely that they are easier to comprehend, are available in their entirety, and are better suited to the present age. And of all the Purāṇas and Itihāsa, the *Bhāgavata Purāṇa*, Jīva claims, is best able to determine metaphysical or spiritual questions. Jīva's arguments in favor of the pre-eminence of the *Bhāgavata* are based mainly on some unidentified verses from the *Garuḍa Purāṇa* which describe the *Bhāgavata* as representing a commentary on the *Brahmasūtra*, demonstrating the significance of the *Mahābhārata*, explaining the *Gāyatrī*, and supplementing (or fortifying) the Vedas.[4] Jīva thus justifies his decision to rely on the *Bhāgavata* not only as his sole authority for this work, but also for its subject matter. As he explains in section 27, his own words are meant to introduce and explain the words of the *Bhāgavata*, just as the various *sūtras* of the *Brahmasūtra* serve the purpose of introducing the different Upaniṣadic verses indicated by them.

Towards the end of the *pramāṇākhaṇḍa* (secs. 23-28), Jīva discusses the origin of the *Bhāgavata* commentary tradition and the procedures to be followed by him in his own interpretations of the *Bhāgavata* verses. According to sections 23 and 24, Śaṅkara knowingly expounded the false doctrine of Māyāvāda at the express command of Viṣṇu, so that beings would remain deluded and the present cycle of creation would continue. Śaṅkara, being an *avatāra* of Śiva and a devotee of Viṣṇu, could not, however, bring himself to apply the same distorted interpretation to the *Bhāgavata*, the most beloved text of Viṣṇu, and thus refrained from writing a commentary on it. Some of Śaṅkara's disciples, however, understood the doctrine of Māyāvāda to represent Śaṅkara's actual beliefs, and composed commentaries on the *Bhāgavata* from the Advaitic point of view. Madhva, characterized by Jīva as one of Śaṅkara's disciples, realized the mistake his fellow disciples had made, and wrote a commentary of his own representing the actual import of the *Bhāgavata* as understood by Śaṅkara.

In addition to crediting Madhva with originating an authentic commentary tradition on the *Bhāgavata*, Jīva also claims to have cited certain scriptural verses from the writings of Madhva which he was unable to see in their original form.[5] However, when it comes time to acknowledge the earlier philosophers who have influenced Jīva, only the names of Śrīdhara and Rāmānuja[6] are explicitly stated. Jīva writes in section 27 that he will follow the *Bhāgavata* commentary of Śrīdhara, but only when it represents the purely "Vaiṣṇava" point of view. Otherwise, he claims to follow the views of Rāmānuja or, if necessary, to give new interpretations based on the natural sense of the *Bhāgavata*.

After completing the introductory portion, Jīva opens the text proper with a handful of verses from the *Bhāgavata* describing the origin of that Purāṇa. According to Bh. P. 1/7/4-11, Vyāsa, while seated for meditation one day, attained the state of perfect concentration of mind known as *samādhi*,[7] and had the vision of the supreme *puruṣa* and *māyā*. He also realized that the individual, suffering because of the deluding power of *māyā*, can put an end to his misery by developing devotion for Kṛṣṇa. Vyāsa then composed the *Bhāgavata* in order to teach this truth to mankind. Later, he taught the *Bhāgavata* to his all-renouncing son, Śuka, who thereafter studied it daily.

Jīva discusses these eight *Bhāgavata* verses in sections 29-49, in terms of the categories, *sambandha*, *abhidheya*, and *prayojana*. In the course of this discussion, Jīva offers refutations of the Advaitic doctrines of Pratibimbavāda and Paricchedavāda, and states his own position of Acintyabhedābhedavāda which attempts to reconcile both the dualistic and non-dualistic standpoints. This section also represents a brief summary of the ideas found in the remaining *sandarbhas*.

Jīva then begins his treatment of the *tattva*, or philosophical principle, which is the actual subject matter of this first *sandarbha*. The *tattva*, described in section 51 as non-dual consciousness, is first considered from the individual, or *vyaṣṭi*, point of view as representing the essential nature of the individual soul, and then from the aggregate, or *samaṣṭi*, point of view as representing the ground of the universe (the *āśraya*).

Since the *āśraya* principle is described in the *Bhāgavata* as the tenth and final characteristic of a Mahāpurāṇa, Jīva next discusses all ten topics one after the other, in order to show that the first nine ultimately serve the purpose of clarifying the meaning of the tenth, which represents the true import of the *Bhāgavata*. Finally, Jīva returns to the individual point of view to show that the same *āśraya* principle which constitutes the ground for the universe is also the ground for the individual souls, dwelling within all beings as the inner controller.

The *Tattvasandarbha* has been edited several times, either by itself or together with the five other *sandarbhas* which collectively constitute the complete *Bhāgavatasandarbha*. A chronological list and description of these various editions is given below, based in part on the list given by Sitanath Goswami in the introduction to his edition of the *Tattvasandarbha* (1967: xxiii):

1) *Ṣaṭsandarbha*: Edited and translated into Bengali by Rāmanārāyaṇa Vidyāratna, with Baladeva's commentary; printed in Berhampur, Bengal in 1882 and reissued in 1956, also in Berhampur, published by Śyāmasundara Miśra.

2) *Śrībhāgavatasandarbha*: Edited by Śyāmalāla Gosvāmī, Calcutta, 1900; includes Baladeva's commentary.

3) *Tattvasandarbha*: Edited, published, and translated into Bengali by Satyānanda Gosvāmī, Calcutta, 1912; also includes Baladeva's commentary.

4) *Tattvasandarbha*: Edited and translated into Bengali by Nityasvarūpa Brahmacārī and Kṛṣṇacandra Gosvāmī, published by Sacīndramohana Ghoṣa, Calcutta, 1919; contains commentaries of Baladeva and Rādhāmohana, as well as the corresponding portions of Jīva's *Sarvasaṃvādinī*.

5) *Tattvasandarbha*: Edited by Gaurkisor Gosvami, Calcutta, 1938; includes the editor's own Sanskrit commentary, the *Svarṇalatā*,[8] as well as an English introduction.

6) *Tattvasandarbha*: Edited by Purīdāsa Mahāśaya, Calcutta, 1951.

7) *Tattvasandarbha*: Published by the Acyutagranthamālākāryālaya, Vārāṇasī, 1957; includes commentaries of Baladeva and Rādhāmohana.

8) *Tattvasandarbha*: Edited by Sitanath Goswami, Jadavpur University, Calcutta, 1967; includes Baladeva's commentary and notes from Rādhāmohana's commentary, as well as introduction and notes in English.

Of the above mentioned editions, that of Purīdāsa comes closest to representing a complete critical edition, although here also not all variant readings are mentioned. Seven different manuscripts and each of the five editions previous to his were consulted by the editor, and the variant readings which are given are all listed according to manuscript or edition.

The edition of Nityasvarūpa Brahmacārī and Kṛṣṇacandra Gosvāmī, while not based on as many manuscripts, also gives variant readings, as well as readings attested to by Rādhāmohana's commentary but not found in available manuscripts. The Bengali translation is extremely faithful to the text, and the notes from the editor helpful, although critical discussions regarding textual problems and the variant interpretations of the commentators are generally absent.

Sitanath Goswami's edition is the only available edition of the *Tattvasandarbha* with English notes. Although variant readings have also been noted here, the editor has unfortunately failed to consult the earlier edition of Purīdāsa, and consequently his edition is not based on some of the more reliable manuscripts. The comments of the editor are often quite helpful, although not altogether reliable throughout.[9]

Since several editions of the *Tattvasandarbha* are still available, and since most of the variant readings of the text are either trivial or obvious scribal errors, it has not been felt necessary to prepare a new critical edition. However, since no single edition has been followed exclusively, and since the most reliable edition, that of Purīdāsa, is no longer in print, we have decided to present the Sanskrit text along with the English translation and notes. The readings adopted by Purīdāsa will be generally accepted, and variant readings will be mentioned only in cases where the commentators differ as to the original text, or where the meaning is significantly affected. Some variations also exist regarding the division of the sections, or *anucchedas*, of the text, and in this regard the division and numbering adopted by Sitanath Goswami will be followed, being the system most commonly adopted by the other editors.

It will be our policy in this section to restrict ourselves mainly to the remarks found in the commentaries of Baladeva and Rādhāmohana, as well as to relevant portions of Jīva's *Sarvasaṃvādinī*, Śrīdhara's *Bhāgavata* commentary (the *Bhāvārthadīpikā*), and Kṛṣṇadāsa Kavirāja's *Caitanya Caritāmṛta*. We will offer our own comments only when necessary to clarify certain portions of the text or commentaries, or to emphasize points crucial to this study. Aside from noting instances where Jīva deviates from his own claims to follow the interpretations of Śrīdhara or the natural sense of the *Bhāgavata*, no attempt will be made in our notes to critically evaluate the relative merits of Jīva's philosophical system, such comments being reserved for the conclusion of this study.

1. Each of the remaining five *sandarbhas* opens with the following verse:
tau santoṣayatā santau śrīlarūpasanātanau |
dākṣiṇātyena bhaṭṭena punar etad vivicyate ||
"Moreover, this has been declared by the Bhaṭṭa from the South, bringing contentment to the venerable pair, Rūpa and Sanātana."

2. *vadanti tat tattvavidas tattvaṃ yaj jñānam advayam |*
brahmeti paramātmeti bhagavān iti śabdyate ||

3. The terms *abhidheya* and *prayojana* are used by Jīva in a special sense, corresponding to the notions of *sādhana* and *sādhya*, or means and ends. The same usage is also found in the *Caitanya Caritāmṛta* and seems to be peculiar to the Gauḍīya Vaiṣṇava school.

4. These verses occur in section 21 and are explained in sections 21-23. They are also found in Kṛṣṇadāsa's *Caitanya Caritāmṛta* (m. 25/137) and in the *Haribhaktivilāsa* (10/283). Though some of the most important verses for the Gauḍīya Vaiṣṇavas, they are nowhere identified by chapter and verse number, and are presumably not found in current editions of the *Garuḍa Purāṇa*. It is possible that these are some of the verses which Jīva had seen in the writings of Madhva, although some have taken a more skeptical attitude. Rāmmohan Roy writes in his essay *Gosvāmir Sahita Vicāra* ("Discussion with a Gosvāmin"):

> In our country there is practically no reliable tradition regarding the transmission of Purāṇas, and one could easily compose Purāṇic verses in simple Sanskrit. Taking advantage of this fact, the Vaiṣṇavas of this region have composed verses, attributing them to the *Garuḍa Purāṇa*, in order to have an authority for calling the *Bhāgavata* a commentary [on the *Brahmasūtra*]... (Rāmmohan: 1815: 49-50)

5. S. K. De writes in this regard:

> It is well-known that Madhva, in his voluminous writings, quotes many Śruti and Purāṇa passages which are unknown and have remained untraced; and it is often suggested that the passages are fabricated. (De: 1961: 412)

Cf. also Sharma: 1960: 112, for a defence of Madhva against such denouncers, chief of whom seems to have been the Advaitin, Appayya Dīkṣita.

6. It is curious that Jīva specifically mentions the name of Rāmanuja here, since he is not known to have written any work on the *Bhāgavata*, or even to have mentioned the Purāṇa in any of his philosophical works. The idea seems to be that Jīva will apply some of the doctrines of Rāmānuja found in his *Brahmasūtra* commentary and other writings to the verses of the *Bhāgavata*.

7. The term *samādhi* is used in Vedānta and Yoga to signify the steady and concentrated dwelling of the mind on a single object. In devotional literature, however, the term is used to indicate the absorption of the mind in a spiritual mood, wherein one communes with the object of his devotion, and enjoys visions and experiences, all of which are considered to be objectively real and to represent direct communication with the divine. Thus, the vision which Vyāsa had prior to his writing of the *Bhāgavata* is considered by Jīva to be sufficient grounds for classifying the *Bhāgavata* as revealed literature. It should also be noted that the description of Vyāsa's *samādhi* is only one of several different versions of the origin of the *Bhāgavata*. Other descriptions show Vyāsa receiv-

ing a summarized version of the *Bhāgavata* directly from the divine sage Nārada, who himself heard it either directly from Nārāyaṇa, or through his father, Brahmā. (Cf. Tagare: 1976: xxxviii for a discussion on the transmission of the *Bhāgavata* to Vyāsa.)

8. The author of *Svarṇalatā* has generally followed Baladeva's interpretations, without, however, attributing the same importance to Madhva. According to the introduction of his edition, Gaurkisor's real intention was to comment on the whole of the *Bhāgavatasandarbha*, although the remaining portions, if written at all, do not seem to have ever been published.

9. Examples of this are: the statement that there are four *anubandhas* (p. xvii), that there are only two commentaries on the *Tattvasandarbha* (p. xxi), that Caitanya declared his philosophical ideals to be "closely similar" to those of Madhva (p. 61), that the category of *viśeṣa* is logically equivalent to that of *acintyaśakti* (p. 116), etc.

CHAPTER VI

TATTVASANDARBHA :
TEXT, TRANSLATION, NOTES

śrīkṛṣṇo jayati /
Kṛṣṇa reigns supreme !

1) kṛṣṇavarṇaṃ tviṣākṛṣṇaṃ sāṅgopāṅgāstrapārṣadam /
yajñair saṅkīrtanaprāyair yajanti hi sumedhasaḥ //

1) "The wise worship Kṛṣṇa Caitanya,[1] whose complexion is fair[2] due to its brilliance, and who is accompanied by his 'limbs', 'ornaments', 'weapons', and attendants,[3] through sacrifices consisting chiefly of singing the praises of the Lord.[4]" (Bh. P. 11/5/32)

1. *kṛṣṇavarṇam* : Although the primary meaning of this compound is "dark-complected", apparently referring to Śrī Kṛṣṇa, Jīva ignores this interpretation, and offers a series of alternate explanations in S. S., all of which identify Caitanya as the object of worship in this *Bhāgavata* verse.

This verse, which incidentally occurs five times in C. C. as well, represents the conclusion of Karabhājana Muni's reply to the query of King Nimi (Bh.P. 11/5/19) regarding the different forms the various *avatāras* will assume in the different *yugas*, and how they will be worshipped in each. Karabhājana, having already described the *avatāras* of the first three *yugas* (as white, red, and dark respectively), uttered the above-quoted verse as his description of the *avatāra* of the fourth, or Kali Yuga.

According to Śrīdhara, the verse in question refers to the dark-skinned Kṛṣṇa. He writes, "With this (statement), he demonstrates the supremacy of the Kṛṣṇa *avatāra* in the Kali Yuga." (*anena kalau kṛṣṇāvatārasya prādhānyaṃ darśayati* /) And as Jīva himself points out, the belief in a Kṛṣṇa *avatāra* in the Kali Yuga is supported by the *Viṣṇudharmottara*, among other scriptures, which maintains that the Dvāpara Yuga *avatāra* will be "(green) like the wings of a parrot" (*śukapakṣavarṇa*), and the Kali Yuga *avatāra* "(dark) blue like a rain cloud" (*nīlaghanavarṇa*).

Jīva nevertheless maintains that the belief in a Kṛṣṇa *avatāra* in the Kali Yuga is untenable, based primarily on Bh.P. 10/8/13, which states: "In the previous *yugas*, (*bhagavat*) assumed bodies of three different colors, white, red, and yellow. Now (in this *yuga*), his complexion has become dark." (*āsan varṇās trayo hy asya gṛhṇato 'nuyugaṃ tanuḥ / śuklo raktas tathā pīta idānīṃ kṛṣṇatāṃ gataḥ //*) Jīva explains the word *idānīm* ("now") as referring to the Dvāpara Yuga, well-known as the appointed period for the advent of Kṛṣṇa, a fact which is also verified by Karabhājana's depiction of the Dvāpara Yuga *avatāra* as "dark in color (*śyāma*), clad in yellow garments, etc." Since the white and red *avatāras* belong to the first two *yugas*, Jīva concludes by a process of elimination that the yellow, or fair-complected, *avatāra* (namely Caitanya, famed for his golden complexion) belongs to the present Kali Yuga. The fact that the yellow-skinned *avatāra* is spoken of as belonging to an earlier *yuga* is explained by Jīva as referring to the Kali Yuga from the previous cycle which, presumably, followed the same pattern as the present one. Thus, having demonstrated, to his own satisfaction at least, the unacceptability of the primary meaning of *kṛṣṇavarṇa* as referring to the dark-skinned Kṛṣṇa, Jīva proceeds with his own explanations.

In the first of Jīva's interpretations, he explains the word *varṇa* as indicating not "color", but "syllable", and consequently analyses the compound *kṛṣṇavarṇa* as meaning "he whose name contains the two syllables *kṛ* and *ṣṇa*, namely Kṛṣṇa Caitanya." (*kṛṣṇety etau varṇau yatra yasmin śrīkṛṣṇacaitanyadevanāmni...*) Or the compound may mean "he who spreads the fame (*varṇayati*) of Kṛṣṇa" or "the preceptor of knowledge of Kṛṣṇa." As a fourth option, Jīva utilizes the more obvious meaning, "dark-complected", and explains that Caitanya appeared in that form, i.e. as the "dark-skinned Śyāmasundara", to a few rare souls (such as Rāmānanda; cf. C. C. m. 8/267-68), while all others saw him as fair. (*sarvalokadṛṣṭāv akṛṣṇaṃ gauram api bhaktaviśeṣadṛṣṭau. . .kṛṣṇavarṇaṃ tādṛśaśyāmasundaram eva santam ityarthaḥ /*)

Baladeva understands the compound *kṛṣṇavarṇa* in its primary sense, as meaning "whose complexion, or color, is dark", but adds that the implied meaning is "dark within", referring to Caitanya who, though fair in complexion, is in reality identical with the dark-complected Kṛṣṇa. (*kṛṣṇo varṇo rūpaṃ yasyāntar itiśeṣaḥ*) B.D.'s interpretation is based on the belief that the verse immediately following this one in *Tattvasandarbha* (T.S.2), represents Jīva's actual understanding of this *Bhāgavata* verse. This idea is also found in C. C. ā.3/79-80, in which T. S. 2 is quoted as part of K. K.'s explanation of Bh.P. 11/5/32.

2. *akṛṣṇam* : Jīva glosses *akṛṣṇa* (literally "non-dark") as *gaura*, a term which means "fair in complexion", and is a common epithet of Caitanya.

According to Śrīdhara, the adjective *akṛṣṇa* implies that Kṛṣṇa's complexion, though dark, shines brightly "like a sapphire, dark in color but brilliant in lustre" (*indranīlamaṇivad ujjvalam*). He also considers the variant reading, *tviṣā kṛṣṇam*, in which the two words are not joined by sandhi, giving the meaning "The wise worship Kṛṣṇa, who is dark in color..."

3. *sāṅgopāṅgāstrapārṣadam* : In its primary sense, this expression refers to the various characteristics or adornments traditionally associated with *avatāras*, such as a specific number of limbs (*aṅga*)—both the Kṛta and Tretā Yuga *avatāras* are "four-armed"—divine ornaments or embellishments (*upāṅga*)—the Kṛta Yuga *avatāra* wears a string of Rudrākṣa beads, and the Dvāpara Yuga *avatāra* bears the mark Śrīvatsa—divine weapons (*astra*) such as a discus or mace, and a retinue of companions or attendants (*pārṣada*). Thus, Śrīdhara understands *upāṅga* as referring to Kaustubha, a jewel worn on Kṛṣṇa's

chest, *astra* as referring to his discus known as Sudarśana, and *pārṣada* to his attendants such as Sunanda.

Since such outward signs of divinity were, for the most part, not seen in Caitanya, Jīva gives a figurative interpretation to this expression. He writes, "Caitanya's only weapons are his limbs, since they are so charming, and his embellishments, since they are so majestic. And since they unfailingly accompany him, they may also be considered his companions." (*tathāṅgāni paramamanoharatvād upāṅgāni bhūṣaṇādīni mahāprabhāvavattvāt tāny evāstrāṇi sarvadaikāntavāsitvāt tāny eva pārṣadāḥ*)

Jīva offers a second interpretation which identifies Advaitācārya and such other great souls as Caitanya's "limbs" and "ornaments". This latter interpretation is taken up in C. C. where Advaita and Nityānanda are identified as Caitanya's two "limbs", and Śrīvāsa and others as his attendants. (ā. 3/71, 74) B. D. likewise considers Advaita and Nityānanda to be Caitanya's two "limbs", and calls Śrīvāsa and others his "ornaments", the names of *bhagavat* his weapons, since they pierce through ignorance, and Gadādhara, Govinda and others his retinue.

4. *saṅkīrtanaprāyair* : Jīva understands this as a reference to the mode of worship made famous by Caitanya and his followers, and describes it as "the joy of gathering together in a large group and singing the praises of Kṛṣṇa." (*saṅkīrtanaṃ bahubhir militvā tadgānasukhaṃ śrīkṛṣṇagānam*)

It may also be noted that Jīva, in his opening remarks in S. S., eulogizes Caitanya as "the presiding deity for the thousands belonging to his own *sampradāya*" (*svasampradāyasahasrādhidaivam*). B. D., on the other hand, indicates his reverence for Madhva in his opening verses, as well as his animosity towards the doctrines of Advaitavāda. He writes, "Glory to Ānanda Tīrtha (Madhva), who, like the sun, has violently destroyed the doctrine of Māyāvāda, which is like a mass of darkness, with the burning rays of Vedic utterances, and who has taught the world devotion to Viṣṇu." (*māyāvādaṃ yas tamaḥstomam uccair nāśaṃ ninye vedavāgaṃśujālaiḥ / bhaktir viṣṇor darśitā yena loke jīvāt so 'yaṃ bhānur ānandatīrthaḥ //*)

2) antaḥkṛṣṇaṃ bahirgauraṃ darśitāṅgādivaibhavam /
kalau saṅkīrtanādyaiḥ smaḥ kṛṣṇacaitanyam āśritāḥ //

2) We take refuge in Kṛṣṇa Caitanya in the Kali Yuga by means of *saṅkīrtana* etc.—in him who is dark (Kṛṣṇa) within and fair (Gaura) without, and whose "limbs" etc. reveal his divine nature.

As mentioned earlier, B.D. considers the significance of this verse to be identical with that of the preceding verse. He writes, "On the pretext of commenting on the verse beginning *kṛṣṇavarṇam*, Jīva actually relies on its meaning for his own verse." (*kṛṣṇavarṇapadvavyākhyāvyājena tadartham āśrayati—antar iti*)

Rādhāmohana writes that this verse "pays reverence to Kṛṣṇa, who incarnated with a fair complexion, i.e. as Gaura, in order to initiate a *sampradāya* dedicated to his own worship." (*svabhajanasya sampradāyapravartanāyāvatīrṇaṃ gaurarūpeṇa śrīkṛṣṇam praṇamati* /)

3) jayatāṃ mathurābhūmau śrīlarūpasanātanau /
yau vilekhayatas tattvaṃ jñāpakau pustikām imām //

3) May Rūpa and Sanātana reign supreme in the land of Mathurā, the two preceptors of the highest truth, at whose behest this book is being written.

4) ko'pi tadbāndhavo bhaṭṭo dakṣiṇadvijavaṃśajaḥ /
vivicya vyalikhad granthaṃ likhitād vṛddhavaiṣṇavaiḥ//

4) A certain friend of theirs,[1] a Bhaṭṭa[2] born in the line of South Indian *brāhmaṇas*, had written a book after studying the writings of the eminent Vaiṣṇavas.[3]

1. *tadbāndhavaḥ* : According to B. D., the pronoun *tat* refers to Rūpa and Sanātana (*tayo rūpasanātanayor bandhuḥ*).

2. *bhaṭṭaḥ* : This term is used both in a general sense, as referring to a learned *brāhmaṇa*, and as a specific title or proper name. B. D. identifies this Bhaṭṭa as Gopāla Bhaṭṭa, the only one of the six Gosvāmins to have come directly from South India. According to C. C., he was born in Śrīraṅgam, and had the privilege of a four month visit by Caitanya during the latter's tour of South India.

3. *vṛddhavaiṣṇavaiḥ*: These "eminent Vaiṣṇavas" are identified by Jīva as Rāmānuja, Madhvācārya, Śrīdhara Svāmin, etc. B.D., however, simply writes "Śrī Madhva etc."

5) tasyādyaṃ granthanālekhaṃ krāntavyutkrāntakhaṇḍitam /
paryālocyātha paryāyaṃ kṛtvā likhati jīvakaḥ //

5) Now, Jīva,[1] having noticed that while some portions of this text were in proper order, others were not, and still others were missing completely, will now write it out in proper sequence.

1. *jīvakaḥ* : Out of a sense of humility, Jīva refers to himself with a term which also carries the meaning of "a simple soul".

6) yaḥ śrīkṛṣṇapadāmbhojabhajanaikābhilāṣavān /
tenaiva dṛśyatām etad anyasmai śapatho 'rpitaḥ //

6) May this be seen by him alone whose chief desire is to worship the lotus feet of Kṛṣṇa. All others are debarred.[1]

1. *śapatho 'rpitaḥ* : This expression literally means "a curse is cast upon them". However, as B. D. explains, this prohibition is meant for their own good, since the study of this text by those without devotion would not conduce to their welfare; the prohibition is not made out of fear of criticism of the text. (...*tasyāmaṅgalaṃ syād iti tanmaṅgalāyaitad na tu granthāvadyabhayāt* /)

7) atha natvā mantragurūn gurūn bhāgavatārthadān /
śrībhāgavatasandarbhaṃ sandarbhaṃ vaśmi lekhitum//

7) Now, having paid homage to the Mantra-gurus, the preceptors who elucidate the meaning of the *Bhāgavata*, I wish to write this treatise, the *Bhāgavatasandarbha*.

8) yasya brahmeti saṃjñāṃ kvacid api nigame yāti cinmātrasattāpy aṃśo yasyāṃśakaiḥ svair vibhavati vaśayann eva māyāṃ pumāṃś ca /
ekaṃ yasyaiva rūpaṃ vilasati paramavyomni nārāyaṇākhyaṃ sa śrīkṛṣṇo vidhattāṃ svayam iha bhagavān prema tatpādabhājām //

8) May Kṛṣṇa, whose being is consciousness itself and who is designated *brahman* in certain Śruti texts,[1] a portion of whom manifests[2] as his own partial incarnations[3] and rules over *māyā* as the *puruṣa*[4], and who, in his principal form, goes by the name, Nārāyaṇa,[5] and sports[6] in Paramavyoman[7]—may that Kṛṣṇa, *bhagavat* himself,[8] bestow the boon of *preman*[9] on those here who worship his feet.

1. *nigame* : The Śruti texts referred to here are identified by Jīva, B. D., and R. M. as Upaniṣadic mantras such as *satyaṃ jñānam anantaṃ brahma* / ("*Brahman* is truth, knowledge, and infinity." Tai. U. 2/1/1). B. D. also mentions the phrase from the *Kaṭha Upaniṣad, astīty evopalabdhavyaḥ* / ("It should be realized simply as existing." Ka.U. 2/3/13). It is significant that all three

commentators cite verses in which the *ānanda*, or blissful, aspect of *brahman* is not mentioned, since, according to Gauḍīya Vaiṣṇava thought, this quality is most fully manifest in *bhagavat,* and conspicuously absent in *brahman.*

2. *vibhavati*: R.M. explains this simply as "manifesting in various forms" (*vibhavati vividho bhavati* /). B. D., however, understands this verb in a technical sense as indicating the manifestation of a special type of *avatāra* known as *vibhava* (or *vaibhava*), described as being identical in essence with *bhagavat,* but possessing a lesser degree of power. (*vibhavasaṃjñakān līlāvatārān prakaṭayatītyarthaḥ*)

3. *aṃśakaiḥ svaiḥ*: Jīva explains this as meaning "in the form of *līlāvatāras* and *guṇāvatāras.*" The former category includes the twenty-two *avatāras* mentioned in the first *skandha,* third *adhyāya* of the *Bhāgavata,* the fourteen *manvantarāvatāras,* the four *yugāvatāras,* and numerous minor *avatāras,* alluded to in Bh.P. 1/3/26 (*avatārā hy asaṅkhyeyā*...). The *guṇāvatāras* are Brahmā, Viṣṇu, and Śiva, representing the *rajoguṇa, sattvaguṇa,* and *tamoguṇa* respectively, based on their respective functions of creation, preservation, and dissolution.

R. M. interprets this phrase to mean, "He manifests, through association with the *guṇas* of *prakṛti,* with the characteristics of *jīvas* in consonance with his own true nature." (*tadguṇayogena svair aṃśakaiḥ svasvarūpabhūtajīvātmadharmair vibhavati* /) The idea is that the *avatāras* bear the characteristics of living creatures, but without the attendant imperfections natural to them.

4. *pumān* : Jīva explains this term as referring to the *puruṣa,* the indweller of all, technically known as *paramātman.* (*pumān puruṣah sarvāntaryāmī paramātmākhyaḥ* /) B. D. understands this as a reference to the doctrine of the *puruṣāvatāra,* a variation on the Nārāyaṇīya *caturvyūha* theory. He writes, "Saṅkarṣaṇa, the thousand-headed *puruṣa* lying on the Ocean of Causality, is a partial aspect of Kṛṣṇa, and the master of *māyā.* He controls *prakṛti* who, being disturbed by his glance, creates the cosmic eggs. As the thousand-headed Pradyumna, he dwells within the cosmic eggs, half-filled with water, and manifests as Matsya etc." (*kāraṇārṇavaśāyī sahasraśīrṣā puruṣaḥ saṅkarṣaṇaḥ kṛṣṇāṃśaḥ prakṛter bhartā tāṃ vaśe sthāpayann eva svavikṣaṇakṣubdhayā tayāṇḍāni sṛṣṭvā teṣāṃ garbheṣv ambubhir ardhapūrṇeṣu sahasraśīrṣā pradyumnaḥ san svair aṃśakair matsyādibhir vibhavati*..)

The third *puruṣāvatāra* is Aniruddha, the indweller of all beings; though not mentioned by name, he is referred to by Jīva in S. S. as the *antaryāmin.* Thus, the third *pāda* of this verse in praise of the *puruṣa,* indirectly describes the three different manifestations of the *puruṣa*: 1) as the ruler of *prakṛti* (Saṅkarṣaṇa), 2) as the source of the various *līlāvatāras* and *guṇāvatāras* (Pradyumna), and 3) as the indweller of all beings (Aniruddha).

5. *nārāyaṇākhyam*: Nārāyaṇa, described by Jīva as the "Lord of Vaikuṇṭha" and the "Consort of Śrī", is considered to be the highest of all partial manifestations of Kṛṣṇa, fully endowed with all the lordly attributes (*aiśvarya*), but lacking in the aspect of sweetness (*mādhurya*).

6. *vilasati* : B. D. understands this verb in a technical sense (as he did earlier with regard to the verb *vibhavati*) as referring to a special kind of *avatāra* known as a *vilāsa,* described as having "nearly the same attributes as *bhagavat,* but a different form etc." (*prāyas tatsamaguṇavibhūtir ākṛtyādibhir anyadṛk tu vilāsa iti*)

7. *paramavyomni* : Jīva identifies Paramavyoman (or Paravyoman)

with Mahāvaikuṇṭha, described in the *Padma Purāṇa* as follows: "Between the Pradhāna (mortal world) and Paramavyoman flows the holy Virajā River, rushing with the waters born of the vapor of the *vedāṅgas*. On its bank lies the supreme, three-fold abode of Paravyoman, eternal, immortal, everlasting, and infinite." (*pradhānaparamavyomnor antare virajā nadī/ vedāṅgasvedajanitais toyaiḥ prasrāvitā śubhā / tasyāḥ pāre paravyoma tripādbhūtaṃ sanātanam / amṛtaṃ śāśvataṃ nityam anantaṃ paramaṃ padam //* Pa.P. 255/57, 58)

The following interpretation of these two verses is found in C. C.m.21/42-53: "The highest dwelling place, known as Goloka or Vṛndāvana, is a store-house of both lordly power and sweetness, compassion and the like. Beneath that, in Paravyoman, lies Viṣṇuloka, the abode of Nārāyaṇa etc. This is the middle abode of Kṛṣṇa and the storehouse of the six lordly attributes. Below this, on the other side of the Virajā River, is the abode of the mortals, the numerous universes known (collectively) as Devīdhāman."

B. D. describes Paramavyoman as being "situated beyond the eight sheaths" (*āvaraṇāṣṭakād bahiḥsthe*), a reference to the theory, elaborated on by Jīva in the *Kṛṣṇasandarbha*, that the fourteen mortal worlds are covered by eight sheaths corresponding to *prakṛti, mahat, ahaṅkāra*, and the five *mahābhūtas*, beyond which lie Siddhaloka (the abode of *nirguṇa brahman*), Paravyoman, and Goloka, all on the far side of the Virajā River, or Kāraṇasamudra (the Ocean of Causality).

8. *svayam...bhagavān* : Jīva cites the well-known phrase from Bh.P. 1/3/28, *kṛṣṇas tu bhagavān svayam* ("but Kṛṣṇa is *bhagavat* himself") as his authority for this claim. The intention of the *Bhāgavata* verse mentioned by Jīva is to distinguish Kṛṣṇa from the other *avatāras* spoken of in this section of the *Bhāgavata*, who are described as mere partial manifestations of the *puruṣa*, while Kṛṣṇa is identified with *bhagavat*. Despite the fact that this verse represents the single instance in the *Bhāgavata* wherein Kṛṣṇa is distinguished from the other *avatāras* on such grounds, the Gauḍīya Vaiṣṇavas consider it to have the highest authority and to take precedence over all statements in conflict with it.

9. *prema*: Jīva characterizes *preman* as "unbounded love" (*prītyatiśayam*). It is considered by the Gauḍīya Vaiṣṇavas to be the highest goal of life, and, as such, is often called the *pañcamapuruṣārtha*, superior even to final liberation.

As Jīva himself explains, T. S. 8 is not merely a *maṅgala* verse dedicated to Kṛṣṇa, but also a concise statement of the main ideas found in the entire *Bhāgavatasandarbha*. (*sarvagranthārthaṃ saṅkṣepeṇa darśayann api maṅgalam ācarati /*) R. M. writes that this section actually represents Jīva's understanding of the famous *Bhāgavata* verse 1/2/11 (cf. T. S. 51) which forms the basis for the theory of the three-fold conception of Kṛṣṇa as *bhagavat, paramātman*, and *brahman*.

According to this theory, *brahman* represents the unqualified aspect of Kṛṣṇa, metaphorically spoken of as the glow emanating from Kṛṣṇa's body (words like *tanubhā, aṅgakānta*, and *aṅgaprabhā* are used). Kṛṣṇadāsa Kavirāja compares the vision of *brahman* to looking directly into the sun with naked eyes and seeing only an undifferentiated brilliance, without being able to distinguish the sun's own color, shape, etc. (*carmmacakṣe dekhe yaiche sūryya nirvviśeṣa / jñānamārge laite nāre tāhāra viśeṣa //* C. C.ā.1/13) While the Gauḍīya

Vaiṣṇava definition of *brahman* as pure, undifferentiated consciousness is not substantially different from that of the Advaitins, the Gauḍīya Vaiṣṇavas consider the concept of *brahman* to be an incomplete description of reality, and hence assign to it a lower position in their metaphysical hierarchy.

Paramātman is considered to be a partial manifestation of Kṛṣṇa, insofar as he represents the ground for only the non-essential powers, known as the *bahiraṅgaśakti*, or external power (also called *māyāśakti*), which gives rise to the phenomenal universe, and the *taṭasthaśakti*, or peripheral power (also called *jīvaśakti*), which gives rise to living beings. In addition, the *paramātman* is also the source of the various *avatāras*, as well as the indweller and inner controller of all beings.

The concept of *bhagavat* differs from that of *paramātman* in that it describes the absolute in relation to its essential powers and attributes, the *antaraṅgaśakti* (also known as the *svarūpaśakti*) alone, without reference to the universe or its inhabitants. *Bhagavat* is distinguished from *brahman* in that he is not described as pure consciousness, but rather as a spiritual being (*saccidānandavigraha*), identified as Kṛṣṇa, who possesses infinite attributes, foremost of which is the *hlādinīśakti* (the delighting power), represented by his eternal consort, Rādhā.

The concepts *brahman*, *paramātman*, and *bhagavat* do not represent three distinct entities, but refer to one and the same reality as seen from three different aspects. As pure consciousness, this reality is termed *brahman*; as the ground for phenomenal existence, it is termed *paramātman*; and in its essential being, it is termed *bhagavat*. To continue with the metaphor of the sun, just as one can see the sun as undifferentiated brilliance, as the source of innumerable rays, or as a self-existent entity with its own essential characteristics, so can one view the one reality as *brahman*, *paramātman*, or *bhagavat*.

In the C. C., Kṛṣṇadāsa Kavirāja explains these three concepts in terms of the different types of individuals who seek to realize them. He writes, "There are three types of *sādhana* by which one attains Kṛṣṇa: *jñāna*, *bhakti*, and *yoga*, each with its own characteristics. *Bhagavat* appears with three different natures in accordance with these three *sādhanas*. *Bhagavat*, *paramātman*, and *brahman*—these are the three manifestations...On the path of *jñāna*, he appears as the unconditioned *brahman*, on the path of *yoga*, as the indweller... following the path of passionate devotion (*rāgabhakti*), one attains *bhagavat* himself." (C.C.m.24/75, 76, 79, 81)

9) athaivaṃ sūcitānāṃ śrīkṛṣṇatadvācyavācakatālakṣaṇasambandhatadbhajanalakṣaṇavidheyasaparyāyābhidheyatatpremalakṣaṇaprayojanākhyānām arthānāṃ nirṇayāya tāvat pramāṇaṃ nirṇīyate / tatra puruṣasya bhramādidoṣacatuṣṭayaduṣṭatvāt sutarām alaukikācintyasvabhāvavastusparśāyogyatvāc ca tatpratyakṣādīny api sadoṣāṇi /

9) Now, in order to determine the meaning of those topics

just alluded to[1], namely: the *sambandha*, or relationship between the topic under discussion, i.e. Kṛṣṇa, and the medium through which it is expressed; the *abhidheya*,[2] or means, which is the worship of Kṛṣṇa, taught in the form of scriptural injunction; and the *prayojana*[3], or goal, which is characterized by love of Kṛṣṇa, the standard of valid knowledge[4] will be duly decided.

Since people are subject to four kinds of defects,[5] confusion, etc., and more importantly, since they are incapable of grasping the essentially supernatural and inconceivable reality, their sense-perception etc. will prove unreliable in this realm.

1. *sūcitānām* : B. D. explains this as a reference to the preceding section. In his remarks on T. S. 8, he wrote that the *maṅgala* verse found there represented a brief statement of the *anubandhas* (cf. below for a discussion of *anubandhas*), which he considers to be four in number, adding *viṣaya* (subject matter) to the three explicitly mentioned. R. M. also finds reference to the *abhidheya* and *prayojana* in section 8 with the phrase "may he bestow *preman* (the *prayojana*) on his worshippers (the *abhidheya*)." He finds the *sambandha*, however, indicated in section 7, in which Jīva states his intention to write this treatise on the *Bhāgavata Purāṇa*.

2. *abhidheya* : The term *abhidheya* normally conveys the meaning "what is signified". Jīva, however, qualifies the term with the expression *vidheyasaparyāya*, i.e. "in the sense of something to be performed." The term *vidheya* also connotes something prescribed in scriptures, i.e. a *vidhi*. B. D. writes, "...it is the worship of him which is to be performed, characterized by listening to his glories (*śravaṇa*) , singing his praises (*kīrtana*), etc.," a reference to the famous *Bhāgavata verse* describing the nine characteristics of *bhakti*. (*śravaṇaṃ kīrtanaṃ viṣṇoḥ smaraṇaṃ pādasevanam / arcanaṃ vandanaṃ dāsyaṃ sakhyam ātmanivedanam // iti puṃsārpitā viṣṇau bhaktiś cen navalakṣaṇā /* Bh.P. 7/5/23-24)

3. *prayojana* : B. D. defines *prayojana* as *puruṣārtha*, or goal of life, a reference to the belief that *preman* constitutes the fifth and highest *puruṣārtha*, beyond *artha*, *kāma*, *dharma*, and *mokṣa*.

4. *pramāṇam* : The *pramāṇas*, or the means of acquiring valid knowledge, are generally considered to be six in number by the followers of Vedānta: *pratyakṣa* (sense-perception), *anumāna* (inference), *upamāna* (analogy), *śabda* (revelation or valid testimony), *abhāva* (proof from non-existence) or *anupalabdhi* (proof based on the non-perceptibility of an entity), and *arthāpatti* (inference from circumstance). Jīva lists ten *pramāṇas* in S. S., adding *ārṣa* (the statements of *devas* and *ṛṣis*), *sambhava* (probability), *aitihya* (traditional knowledge), and *ceṣṭā* (gesture) to the six already mentioned. B. D. lists and defines eight of these, eliminating *ārṣa* and *ceṣṭā*, although he accepts only *pratyakṣa*, *anumāna*, and *śabda* in his

Prameyaratnāvalī. R. M. mentions only *anumāna*, *upamāna*, and *anupalabdhi* in addition to *śabda* and *pratyakṣa*.

5. *bhramādidoṣacatuṣṭaya* : Jīva identifies these four defects as *bhrama* (confusion), *pramāda* (inadvertence), *vipralipsā* (deception), and *karaṇāpāṭava* (faultiness of the senses). B. D. defines these as follows: "*Bhrama* is that understanding due to which one sees something which is not actually there, such as when one thinks he sees a person while looking at a tree stump (*atasmiṃs tadbuddhir bhramaḥ, yena sthāṇau puruṣabuddhiḥ* /). *Pramāda* is inadvertence or absent-mindedness, due to which one does not notice a song sung nearby (*anavadhānatānyacittatālakṣaṇaḥ pramādaḥ, yenāntike gīyamānaṃ gānaṃ na gṛhyate* /) *Vipralipsā* is the desire to deceive, due to which a teacher might conceal something from a student which he himself knows (*vañcanecchā vipralipsā, yayā śiṣye svajñāto 'py artho na prakāśyate* /). *Karaṇāpāṭava* is dullness of the senses due to which one might fail to correctly recognize an object even though giving it his full attention (*indriyamāndyaṃ karaṇāpāṭavam, yena dattamanasāpi yathāvad vastu na paricīyate*/)."

A statement of the *anubandhas*, giving the reader a brief acquaintance with the nature and contents of the text he is about to study, is considered to be an obligatory prerequisite for this type of philosophical treatise. The *Vedāntasāra* of Sadānanda (sec. 5) mentions four *anubandhas*, namely: *adhikāra* (a statement of the necessary qualifications of the student); *viṣaya* (the subject matter of the text); *sambandha* (the connection between the subject matter and the text); and *prayojana* (the purpose of the text). The *anubandhas* mentioned by Jīva in this section are not without precedent, however, as they are also mentioned by Śaṅkara in the introduction to his *Bhagavadgītā* commentary. (...*viśiṣṭaprayojanasambandhābhidheyavadgītāśāstram*...)

The question of *pramāṇas* which is raised in the second line of this section is dealt with extensively by Jīva in S. S. In fact, as much space is devoted to the exposition of this topic as to all others taken together; a summary of the major points is given below.

After enumerating the ten *pramāṇas*, Jīva states that *śabda* alone, being free from the four defects mentioned above, can be considered a fool-proof *pramāṇa* since it is not based on any of the other *pramāṇas*, and can function in the realm of metaphysical questions.

Jīva then categorizes *pratyakṣa* (sense-perception) into six groups according to the five external sense organs and the internal sense organ, the mind. Each of these may be either *savikalpa* (mediate) or *nirvikalpa* (immediate), and either *vaiduṣa* (based on *śabda*) or *avaiduṣa* (not based on *śabda*), the *vaiduṣa pratyakṣa* alone being trustworthy.

Next comes a description of *anumāna* (inference) and the five-sided syllogism. The possibility of erroneous inference is explained as the result of the false assumption of universal concomitance. For example, if one sees smoke rising from behind a mountain, he concludes that there is a fire burning on the other side of the mountain, based on the belief that "where there is smoke there is fire". However, in the case of a fire which has been extinguished by rain, smoke will also be seen to rise, resulting in the erroneous conclusion that a fire is still burning. Since the remaining *pramāṇas* are all based either on *pratyakṣa* or *anumāna*, they are prone to the same errors.

After describing the remaining seven *pramāṇas*, Jīva returns to the question of *śabda*, and makes a distinction between mere verbal testimony and revelation, the latter alone being reliable. He writes, "That alone is accepted as *śabda* which is regularly studied by all for the attainment of wisdom, which brings wisdom to all who study it, and by virtue of which their sense-perception etc. become purified; it is that whose existence is self-established, since it is eternal. It is the basis for all time-honored knowledge, and the embodiment of the *mahāvākyas*; it is the holy scriptures, the Veda itself, established on the strength of itself. None but these eternally existent words of *bhagavat*, the universal cause, which are manifest from time to time, and again at the beginning of creation, but have no human author, can be considered free from the errors of confusion etc. They alone must be studied for knowledge regarding the creator of the universe. They alone constitute the one, infallible source of knowledge."

Jīva next offers arguments in favor of the eternal nature of the Vedas, the origin of the universe from the Vedas, and the authoritative nature of both imperative and declarative statements of the Vedas. In the course of his arguments, Jīva cites verses from both Śruti and Smṛti texts, which he borrows from the *Brahmasūtra bhāṣyas* of Śaṅkara, Rāmānuja, and Madhva. He also quotes a section of Vācaspati Miśra's *Bhāmatī* concerning the authority of the Vedas, and quotes Śaṅkara's *bhāṣya* on Br. S. 2/1/1 regarding the inability of reason to overturn the words of the Vedas.

Having established the Vedas to be the source of all knowledge, Jīva discusses different theories of language and meaning. He refutes the doctrine of Sphoṭavāda, which posits an indefinable power, or *sphoṭa*, above and beyond the linguistic elements of words, in order to explain the emergence of their meanings, and embraces the doctrine of Varṇavāda, which reduces the meaning of words to their elements which, being both universal and eternal, render the Vedas also universal and eternal. Jīva supports his arguments by quoting Śaṅkara's *bhāṣya* on Br. S. 1/3/28 which he relies on heavily for his exposition of this topic.

Jīva next classifies and discusses the different *vṛttis*, or functions, of words. The major categories *mukhyā*, *lakṣaṇā*, and *gauṇī* are explained, each with its own subdivisions, as are the terms *vākya* and *mahāvākya*. Jīva closes this section by returning to his earlier assertion regarding the infallible nature of the Vedas which he supports with a quotation from Śaṅkara's *Brahmasūtra bhāṣya* (2/2/38): "The followers of *brahman* describe the nature of the cause etc. on the strength of the Vedas; they are not constrained to accept things just as they appear."

10) tatas tāni na pramāṇānīty anādisiddhasarvapuruṣaparamparāsu sarvalaukikālaukikajñānanidānatvād aprākṛtavacanalakṣaṇo veda evāsmākaṃ sarvātītasarvāśrayasarvācintyāścaryasvabhāvaṃ vastu vividiṣatāṃ pramāṇam/

10) Therefore,[1] realizing that these (*pratyakṣa* etc.) cannot serve as *pramāṇas*, let us turn to the Vedas themselves as we seek to comprehend that reality which transcends all and yet is the

substratum of all, whose nature is incomprehensible and wondrous—to the Vedas, whose utterances have no earthly origin, being the source of all knowledge, both natural and supernatural, and having been handed down in an unbroken line of succession[2] from time immemorial.

1. *tataḥ* : B. D. explains, "Since *pratyakṣa* etc. are subject to the defects, confusion, etc., they cannot lead to the highest truth" (*tato bhramādidoṣayogāt tāni pratyakṣādīni paramārthapramākaraṇāni na bhavanti* /). B. D. follows this with examples of the kinds of errors to which sense-perception and inference are prone, closely following Jīva's own exposition of this topic in S. S.

2. *paramparāsu* : B. D. writes "originating from Brahmā" (*brahmotpanneṣu*), an apparent reference to the Mādhva Sampradāya which traces its origin directly to Brahmā.

11) tac cānumataṃ tarkāpratiṣṭhānāt ityādau
acintyāḥ khalu ye bhāvā na tāṃs tarkeṇa yojayet / ityādau
śāstrayonitvāt ityādau śrutes tu śabdamūlatvāt ityādau
pitṛdevamanuṣyāṇām vedaś cakṣus taveśvara /
śreyas tv anupalabdhe 'rthe sādhyasādhanayor api //
ityādau ca //

11) This is confirmed by the following scriptural statements: *Brahmasūtra* 2/1/11 ("If it be argued that since mere reason provides no solid ground on which to base our position, then we will find some other means of inference on which to base our position, we reply 'no, you will end up in the same difficulty'."); *Mahābhārata*, *Bhīṣmaparvan* 5/12 ("One should not apply reason to those realities which are inconceivable; for it is the essence of the inconceivable to be distinct from the things of nature."); *Brahmasūtra* 1/1/3 ("Since the scriptures are the source [of the knowledge of *brahman*]."); *Brahmasūtra* 2/1/27 ("This is verified by Śruti, since revelation is the source [of the knowledge of *brahman*]."); and *Bhāgavata Purāṇa* 11/20/4 ("O Lord, this Veda of yours is the supreme 'eye', by virtue of which the *devas*, *pitṛs*, and mortals apprehend those things beyond the range of perception, regarding even the highest goal and the means of attainment.").

12) tatra ca vedaśabdasya samprati duṣpāratvād duradhigamārthatvāc ca tadarthanirṇāyakānāṃ munīnām api paras-

paravirodhād vedarūpo vedārthanirṇāyakaś cetihāsapurāṇātmakaḥ śabda eva vicāraṇīyaḥ / tatra ca yo vā vedaśabdo nātmaviditaḥ so 'pi taddṛṣṭyānumeya eveti samprati tasyaiva pramotpādakatvaṃ sthitam / tathāhi mahābhārate mānavīye ca itihāsapurāṇābhyāṃ vedaṃ samupabṛṃhayed iti pūraṇāt purāṇam iti cānyatra / na cāvedena vedasya bṛṃhaṇaṃ sambhavati na hy aparipūrṇasya kanakavalayasya trapuṇā pūraṇam yujyate / nanu yadi vedaśabdaḥ purāṇam itihāsaṃ copādatte tarhi purāṇam anyad anveṣaṇīyam / yadi tu na na tarhītihāsapurāṇayor abhedo vedena / ucyate viśiṣṭaikārthapratipādakapadakadambasyāpauruṣeyatvād abhede 'pi svarakramabhedād bhedanirdeśo 'py upapadyate / ṛgādibhiḥ saman anayor apauruṣeyatvenābhedo mādhyandinaśrutāv eva vyajyata evaṃ vā are 'sya mahato bhūtasya niḥśvasitam etad yad ṛgvedo yajurvedaḥ sāmavedo 'tharvāṅgirasa itihāsaḥ purāṇam ityādinā //

12) And here, since the Vedas are at present[1] difficult to go through completely[2] and hard to comprehend—for even the sages[3] who sought to ascertain their meaning contradict one another—we will examine *śabda* in the form of Itihāsa and Purāṇas alone, both of which partake of the nature of Vedas, and serve to ascertain the meaning of the Vedas. Furthermore, those portions of the Vedas which are not known on their own can only be inferred by examining Itihāsa and Purāṇas. For these reasons, it is evident that in the present age, Itihāsa and Purāṇas are alone capable of generating true knowledge.

Thus we find in the *Mahābhārata* and *Manu Smṛti*,[4] "One should supplement the Vedas with Itihāsa and Purāṇas" (M.Bh., *Ādiparvan* 1/267); and elsewhere, " 'Purāṇa' is so called because it completes (*pūraṇa*)." For just as a chipped gold bracelet cannot be filled with lead, so also the Vedas cannot be supplemented by something non-Vedic.

But then, if we accept Itihāsa and Purāṇas as Vedas, won't we have to look for another Purāṇa (to supplement them)?[5] Otherwise, Itihāsa and Purāṇas cannot be considered identical with the Vedas.

To this we reply, even though this cluster of verses[6], all of which pıopound the same specific view, admits of no distinction, insofar as all the verses are of divine origin, still a distinction can be made in terms of word order and accent.[7] The identity of Itihāsa and Purāṇas with the *Ṛgveda* etc., with respect to their divine origin, is expressed in the *Mādhyandina Śruti* itself: "...in the same way, my dear, what is known as the *Ṛgveda*, *Yajurveda*, *Sāmaveda*, *Atharvaveda*, Itihāsa, Purāṇa...has been breathed forth from that great being." (Bṛ.U. 2/4/10)

1. *samprati* : Jīva explains this to be a reference to the Kali Yuga, the last of the four ages, in which beings are poorly equipped to grasp spiritual truths.

2. *duṣpāratvāt* : Jīva writes that the Vedas are difficult to go through because parts of them are no longer available and the intelligence of people is limited (*apracaradrūpatvena durmedhastvena ca duṣpāratvāt* /).

3. *munīnām* : Both B. D. and R. M. identify these sages as the authors of the six Darśanas: Vyāsa, Kaṇāda, etc.

4. According to Sitanath Goswami, this line is not found in *Manu Smṛti*. (Jīva: 1967: 15.)

5. R.M. reads *purāṇādikam anyavad anveṣaṇīyam*, giving the meaning, "Purāṇas etc. must be searched for, as is the case with the others, i.e. the Vedas." The idea, according to both readings, is that if Itihāsa and Purāṇas are identical with the Vedas in all respects, then, like the Vedas, they will also have missing portions, and will require still other Itihāsa and Purāṇas to supplement them.

6. *padakadambasya*: According to B. D., the "cluster of verses" includes all those beginning with the *Ṛgveda*, up to and including the Purāṇas (*ṛgādipurāṇāntam*).

7. *svarakramabhedāt*: B. D. analyzes the first two words of this compound, *svara* and *krama*, as forming a *tatpuruṣa*, meaning "a gradation of accent". He writes, "In the portion composed of the *Ṛgveda* etc., there is a gradation of accent; such a gradation is not found, however, in the portion composed of Itihāsa and Purāṇas. Thus, a partial difference does exist" (*ṛgādibhāge svarakramo 'sti, itihāsapurāṇabhāge tu sa nāstīty etad aṃśena bhedaḥ* /). R. M. understands *svarakrama* to form a *dvandva* compound, and explains, "The distinction regarding *svara* refers to the Vedic rules of recitation involving the accents *anudātta*, *udātta*, and *svarita*. The distinction regarding *krama* concerns the special order of the words of the Vedas. It is because of these distinctions that *śūdras* are forbidden to study or listen to a recitation of the Vedas." (*svarakramabhedāt svarakramayor bhedāt...* / *tathā cānudāttodāttādisvarabhedenādhyayanavidhiviṣayatā vedasya* / *kramabhedaḥ...ānupūrvīviśeṣaḥ* / *...śūdrasyādhyayanaśravaṇādiniṣedhaviṣayatāvacchedakaṃ ca* /)

13) ata eva skāndaprabhāsakhaṇḍe
purā tapaś cacārogram amarāṇāṃ pitāmahaḥ /
āvirbhūtās tato vedāḥ saṣaḍaṅgapadakramāḥ //
tataḥ purāṇam akhilaṃ sarvaśāstramayaṃ dhruvam /

nityaśabdamayaṃ puṇyaṃ śatakoṭipravistaram /
nirgataṃ brahmaṇo vaktrāt tasya bhedān nibodhata //
brāhmaṃ purāṇaṃ prathamam ityādi /
atra śatakoṭisaṅkhyā brahmaloke prasiddheti tathoktam /
tṛtīyaskandhe ca
ṛgyajuḥsāmātharvākhyān vedān pūrvādibhir mukhaiḥ /
ityādiprakaraṇe
itihāsapurāṇāni pañcamaṃ vedam īśvaraḥ /
sarvebhya eva vaktrebhyaḥ sasṛje sarvadarśanaḥ // iti /
api cātra sākṣād eva vedaśabdaḥ prayuktaḥ purāṇetihāsayoḥ /
anyatra ca
purāṇaṃ pañcamo vedaḥ /
itihāsaḥ purāṇaṃ ca pañcamo veda ucyate /
vedān adhyāpayāmāsa mahābhāratapañcamān // ityādau
anyathā vedān ityādāv api pañcamatvaṃ nāvakalpyeta samānajātīyaniveśitatvāt saṅkhyāyāḥ / bhaviṣyapurāṇe
kārṣṇaṃ ca pañcamaṃ vedaṃ yan mahābhārataṃ smṛtam /
iti / tathā ca sāmakauthumīyaśākhāyāṃ chāndogyopaniṣadi ca
ṛgvedaṃ bhagavo 'dhyemi yajurvedaṃ sāmavedam ātharvaṇaṃ caturtham itihāsaṃ purāṇaṃ pañcamaṃ vedānāṃ vedam ityādi / ata eva asya mahato bhūtasya ityādāv itihāsapurāṇayoś caturṇām evāntarbhūtatvakalpanayā prasiddhapratyākhyānaṃ nirastam / tad uktaṃ brāhmaṃ purāṇaṃ prathamam ityādi //

13) Therefore, it is stated in the *Prabhāsa Khaṇḍa* of the *Skanda Purāṇa*: "In ancient times, Brahmā, the grandsire of the *devas*, practiced severe austerities. As a result, the Vedas became manifest along with the six auxilliary branches and the *pada* and *krama* texts. Then the entire Purāṇa, the embodiment of all the scriptures, unchanging, composed of the eternal *śabda*, sacred, and consisting of a hundred crores (of verses) issued forth from Brahmā's mouth. Listen to the different divisions of that (Purāṇa): the *Brahma Purāṇa* is first..." (Sk.P. 2/3-5) The figure "a hundred crores" is mentioned here since that is known to be the number (of verses) which exist in Brahmaloka.[1]

And in the third *skandha* (of the *Bhāgavata*): "He breathed forth the four Vedas, known as *Ṛk*, *Yajus*, *Sāman*, and *Atharvan*, one after the other, from his four mouths, beginning with the one facing east." (Bh. P. 3/12/37) And in the same context: "Then, the all-seeing Lord breathed forth Itihāsa and Purāṇas, the fifth Veda, from all of his mouths." (Bh.P. 3/12/39) And here, the actual word "Veda" is used with reference to Itihāsa and Purāṇas. Elsewhere we find: "The Purāṇa is the fifth Veda;" "Itihāsa and Purāṇas are said to be the fifth Veda;" (Bh. P. 1/4/20) "He taught the Vedas, with the *Mahābhārata* as the fifth" (M.Bh., *Mokṣadharma* 340/11) etc.

If it were not the case (that Itihāsa and Purāṇas are Vedic in nature), then the characterization of them as the "fifth" in the preceding verses would be unwarranted, since only things of the same kind can be combined to form a single sum. It is stated in the *Bhaviṣya Purāṇa*: "That which is known as the *Mahābhārata* is Kṛṣṇa Dvaipāyana's (i.e. Vyāsa's) fifth Veda." We also find in the *Chāndogya Upaniṣad* of the Kauthumīya Śākhā: "Sir, I have learned the *Ṛgveda*, the *Yajurveda*, the *Sāmaveda*, and the fourth, or *Atharvaveda*, as well as Itihāsa and Purāṇas, the fifth Veda among the Vedas." (Ch. U.7/1/2) Thus is refuted the well-known exclusion[2] (of Itihāsa and Purāṇas from the realm of Śruti), which is based on the belief that the terms, Itihāsa and Purāṇa, occurring in Bṛ.U.2/4/10[3] refer merely to historical (Itihāsa) and mythological (Purāṇa) portions of the four Vedas themselves. Therefore it is stated, " The *Brahma Purāṇa* is first..."[4]

1. As will be explained in T. S. 14, the number of Purāṇic verses found in the mortal world, four laks, represents a condensed version of the original hundred crores which are said to still exist in Brahmaloka.

2. *prasiddhapratyākhyānam* : B. D. explains the position of the opponent, the Mīmāṃsakas, as follows : "Only those ancient stories (Itihāsa) and legends exhibiting the five characteristic signs (Purāṇas) which are found in the four Vedas are to be accepted (as breathed forth from the Lord), and not those Itihāsa and Purāṇas which are reputed to have been composed by Vyāsa, and which can be heard even by *śūdras*" (*teṣv eva yat purāvṛttaṃ yac ca pañcalakṣaṇam ākhyānaṃ te eva tadbhūte grāhye na tu ye vyāsakṛtatvena bhuvi khyātē śūdrāṇām api śravye iti karmaṭhair yat kalpitaṃ tan nirastam ityarthaḥ* /).

3. In his commentary on this verse (cf. T. S. 12), Śaṅkara upholds the Mīmāṃsaka view stated above, identifying the Itihāsa portions as "the dialogue between Purūravas and Urvaśī from the *Śatapatha Brāhmaṇa* (11/4/4/1) etc." and the Purāṇic portions as "descriptions such as 'In the beginning, all this was non-existence.' (Tai. U. 2/7), etc."

4. *tad uktam* : The fact that the *Brahma Purāṇa* is mentioned by name in Sk. P. 2/5 is offered as proof that the Purāṇas mentioned in Bṛ.U. 2/4/10 refer

to the well-known eighteen Purāṇas and not merely mythological portions of the Vedas.

14) pañcamatve kāraṇaṃ ca vāyupurāṇe sūtavākyam
itihāsapurāṇānāṃ vaktāraṃ samyag eva hi /
māṃ caiva pratijagrāha bhagavān īśvaraḥ prabhuḥ //
eka āsīd yajurvedas taṃ caturdhā vyakalpayat /
cāturhotram abhūt tasmiṃs tena yajñam akalpayat //
ādhvaryavaṃ yajurbhis tu ṛgbhir hotraṃ tathaiva ca /
audgātraṃ sāmabhiś caiva brahmatvaṃ cāpy atharva-bhiḥ //
ākhyānaiś cāpy upākhyānair gāthābhir dvijasattamāḥ /
purāṇasaṃhitāś cakre purāṇārthaviśāradaḥ //
yac chiṣṭaṃ tu yajurveda iti śāstrārthanirṇayaḥ / iti /
brahmayajñādhyayane ca viniyogo dṛśyate 'mīṣāṃ yad brāhmaṇānītihāsapurāṇāni iti / so 'pi nāvedatve sambhavati / ato yad āha bhagavān mātsye
kālenāgrahaṇaṃ matvā purāṇasya dvijottamāḥ //
vyāsarūpam ahaṃ kṛtvā saṃharāmi yuge yuge / iti /
pūrvasiddham eva purāṇaṃ sukhasaṃgrahaṇāya saṃkalayāmīti tatrārthaḥ / tadanantaraṃ hy uktam
caturlakṣapramāṇena dvāpare dvāpare sadā //
tad aṣṭādaśadhā kṛtvā bhūrloke 'smin prabhāṣyate /
adyāpy amartyaloke tu śatakoṭipravistaram //
tadartho 'tra caturlakṣaḥ saṃkṣepeṇa niveśitaḥ / iti /
atra tu yac chiṣṭaṃ tu yajurveda ityuktatvāt tasyābhidheyabhāgaś caturlakṣas tv atra martyaloke saṃkṣepeṇa sārasaṃgraheṇa niveśitaḥ na tu racanāntareṇa //

14) Sūta's statement from the *Vāyu Purāṇa* explains why Itihāsa and Purāṇas are considered the fifth Veda: "The almighty Lord, Bhagavān (Vyāsa) appointed me to be the authoritative expounder of Itihāsa and Purāṇas. (At first) the *Yajurveda* alone existed; he arranged that into four parts. The four *hotṛs* (priests) arose within; thereby did he create *yajña* (sacrifice). Along with the *Yajurveda* came the office of the Adhvaryu priest; with the *Ṛgveda*, that of the Hotṛ priest; with the *Sāmaveda*, that of the Udgātṛ priest; and with the *Atharvaveda*, that of the Brahman priest." (Vā. P. 60/16-18) "(Then) O Best of the Twice-born, (Vyāsa), skilled in the meaning of Purāṇas, assembled the Pu-

rāṇas (and Itihāsa)[1] by (gathering together) *ākhyānas*,[2] *upākhyānas*,[3] and *gāthās*.[4] This remaining portion[5] also falls within that (original) *Yajurveda*[6]: this is the contention of the sacred scriptures." (Vā.P. 60/21-22)

Moreover, in the formal study of the scriptures, known as *brahmayajña*, the use of Itihāsa and Purāṇas is indicated by the words "the Brāhmaṇas, Itihāsa and Purāṇas". This would also not be possible were Itihāsa and Purāṇas not Vedic in nature.

Therefore *bhagavat* declares in the *Matsya Purāṇa*: "O Best of the Twice-born, realizing that, in course of time, men become unable to comprehend the (original) Purāṇa, I assume the form of Vyāsa, in every age, and summarize that Purāṇa." (Ma. P. 53/8-9) That is, "To insure the happiness (of people), I take the already existent Purāṇa and arrange it in a concise form." Following this it is stated: "In every Dvāpara Yuga, the Purāṇa, consisting of four laks (of verses), is divided into eighteen parts and manifested in the world of mortals. Even today, the (verses) number a hundred crores in the world of the *devas*. The four laks found here represent a condensed version of that (original Purāṇa)." (Ma.P. 53/9-11)

And the fact that Sūta said "This remaining portion also falls within that original *Yajurveda*" shows that the four laks of verses which represent the most significant portion of that (original Purāṇa), having found their way into the world of mortals as a concise summary of the essential parts of that Purāṇa, do not represent a separate composition.

1. *purāṇasaṃhitāḥ*: B. D. analyzes this as a *dvandva* compound, the second element of which, *saṃhitā*, refers to the *Mahābhārata* (*saṃhitā bhāratarūpāḥ*). According to B. D., the Purāṇas are composed of *ākhyānas*, while the *upākhyānas* and *gāthās* combine to form Itihāsa.

R. M. accepts the reading *purāṇasaṃhitām* which, though not found in any edition of T. S., is found in some editions of the *Vāyu Purāṇa*. According to this reading, the compound would be a *tatpuruṣa*, meaning "the collection of the Purāṇas" (*purāṇasaṃgraham*). Consequently, R. M. treats all of the following three elements as belonging to Purāṇas.

2. *ākhyānaiḥ* : B. D. defines *ākhyānas* as "legends containing the five characteristics associated with Purāṇas." (*ākhyānaiḥ pañcalakṣaṇaiḥ purāṇāni* /) R. M. defines them as "portions made up of questions and answers, such as the dialogue between Sūta and Śaunaka." (*praśnottaravacananibandhaiḥ sūtaśaunakasaṃvādarūpair ityarthaḥ* /) And in his commentary on a similar passage from the *Viṣṇu Purāṇa*, Śrīdhara defines *ākhyānas* as the description of events witnessed by the narrator himself.

3. *upākhyānaiḥ* : B. D. defines *upākhyānas* as "ancient tales" (*purāvṛttaiḥ*), while according to R. M., they are "portions which make the significance of the text initially known, such as the dialogue between Śuka and King Parikṣit." (*prāthamikagranthābhidheyaprakāśakaiḥ śukaparikṣitsaṃvādādirūpaiḥ* /) Śrīdhara defines them as the description of events about which one has heard, but has not seen.

4. *gāthābhiḥ* : B. D. defines *gāthās* as "varieties of meters" (*chandoviśeṣaiḥ*). R. M. defines them as "ancient tales, legends, and dialogues" (*purāvṛttetihāsa-saṃvādākhyābhiḥ*). Śrīdhara characterizes *gāthās* as "metrical songs about the worlds of the *pitṛs*, *devas*, etc." (*gāthās tu pitṛpṛthivyādigītayaḥ* /)

5. *yac chiṣṭam*: B. D. identifies this portion as the Purāṇas and Itihāsa composed of *ākhyānas*, *upākhyānas*, and *gāthās*. Since these portions did not find their way into any of the four Vedas at the time of Vyāsa's division of the *Yajurveda*, they are referred to as the "left-over" portion (*śiṣṭa*). R. M. writes that only "certain Vedas" were used in the formation of the four Vedas (*kāṃścid vedān ādāya yajurādīnām abhedena vibhāge kṛte...*), the rest being the *ākhyānas* etc. mentioned here.

6. *yajurveda iti* : From the context of this phrase, it is not clear whether the *sandhi* is to be disjoined as *yajurvede iti* (giving *yajurveda* a locative case ending), or as *yajurvedaḥ iti* (giving it a nominative case ending). While B. D. understands it in the former sense, R. M. analyzes *yajurveda* as having a nominative case ending, and explains that "the portion which was left-over after the four Vedas were formed was also called *Yajurveda*." (*yad avaśiṣṭaṃ tad api yajurvedanāmakam ityarthaḥ* /) Thus, according to R. M., there are three distinct *Yajurvedas* : the original *Yajurveda*, from which came the four Vedas, Itihāsa, and Purāṇas; the *Yajurveda* dealing with the functions of the Adhvaryu priest; and the remaining hundred crores of verses which combine to form Itihāsa and Purāṇas, also known as *Yajurveda*.

15) tathaiva darśitaṃ vedasahabhāvena śivapurāṇasya vāyavīyasaṃhitāyām

saṃkṣipya caturo vedāṃś caturdhā vyabhajat prabhuḥ /
vyastavedatayā khyāto vedavyāsa iti smṛtaḥ //
purāṇam api saṃkṣiptaṃ caturlakṣapramāṇataḥ /
adyāpy amartyaloke tu śatakoṭipravistaram //

saṃkṣiptam iti atra teneti śeṣaḥ / skāndam āgneyam ityādi-samākhyās tu pravacananibandhanāḥ kāṭhakādivat ānupūrvī-nirmāṇanibandhanā vā / tasmāt kvacid anityatvaśravaṇaṃ tv āvirbhāvatirobhāvāpekṣayā / tad evam itihāsapurāṇayor veda-tvaṃ siddham / tathāpi sūtādīnām adhikāraḥ sakalanigamaval-līsatphalaśrīkṛṣṇanāmavat / yathoktaṃ prabhāsakhaṇḍe

madhuramadhuram etan maṅgalaṃ maṅgalānāṃ
sakalanigamavallīsatphalaṃ citsvarūpam /
sakṛd api parigītaṃ śraddhayā helayā vā

bhṛguvara naramātraṃ tārayet kṛṣṇanāma // iti /
yathā coktaṃ viṣṇudharme
ṛgvedo 'tha yajurvedaḥ sāmavedo 'py atharvaṇaḥ /
adhītās tena yenoktaṃ harir ity akṣaradvayam // iti /
atha vedārthanirṇāyakatvaṃ ca vaiṣṇave
bhāratavyapadeśena hy āmnāyārthaḥ pradarśitaḥ /
vedāḥ pratiṣṭhitāḥ sarve purāṇe nātra saṃśayaḥ // ityādau /
kiñca vedārthadīpakānāṃ śāstrāṇāṃ madhyapātitābhyupagame 'py āvirbhāvakavaiśiṣṭyāt tayor eva vaiśiṣṭyam / yathā pādme
dvaipāyanena yad buddhaṃ brahmādyais tan na budhyate /
sarvabuddhaṃ sa vai veda tad buddhaṃ nānyagocaram //

15) The same idea is demonstrated in the *Vāyavīya Saṃhitā* of the *Śiva Purāṇa* by discussing the Purāṇas alongside of the Vedas: "The Lord (Vyāsa) summarized the four Vedas and divided them into their four sections. Since he divided the Vedas (*vyastaveda*), he is remembered by posterity as 'Vedavyāsa'. The Purāṇa was also condensed into four laks (of verses). Even today, (the verses) number a hundred crores in the world of the *devas*." (Śi.P. 1/33-34) Here, the word "condensed" means "condensed by him (i.e. by Vyāsa)". And the names "Skānda", "Āgneya", etc. (by which the various Purāṇas are known) refer either to those who first declared them,[1] as is the case with the Kāṭhaka[2] etc., or to those who arranged them. Therefore, if one sometimes hears (the Purāṇas) spoken of as non-eternal, it is merely with reference to the fact that they are sometimes manifest and sometimes unmanifest. Thus, the Vedic nature of Itihāsa and Purāṇas is proved.[3]

Nevertheless, *sūtas*[4] and others are allowed access (to the Purāṇas) which, like the name of Kṛṣṇa, represent "the choicest fruits of the creeper of all the Vedas". As declared in the *Prabhāsa Khaṇḍa* (of the *Skanda Purāṇa*): "O Best of the Bhṛgus, the name of Kṛṣṇa is the sweetest of the sweet, the most auspicious of the auspicious, the choicest fruit of the creeper of all the Vedas, of the nature of pure consciousness. If sung but once, whether with devotion or with contempt, the name of Kṛṣṇa will transport a mere mortal to the other shore." As stated in the *Viṣṇu Dharma*: "He who utters the two-syllabled 'Hari' reaps the fruits of the study of the *Ṛgveda*, *Yajurveda*, *Sāmaveda*, and *Atharvaveda*." And the ability (of Itihāsa and Purāṇas) to determine the meaning of the Vedas is mentioned in the *Viṣṇu Purāṇa*: "On the pretext of describing the events of the *Mahābhārata,* he illustrates the meaning of the Vedas. The Vedas all find a firm resting place in the Purāṇas—about this there is no doubt."

Moreover, even if (Itihāsa and Purāṇas) are considered to belong to the class of *śāstras* which illumine the meaning of the Vedas,[5] still, they excel all others due to the eminence of their expounder (Vyāsa). As stated in the *Padma Purāṇa,* "Vyāsa knows what even Brahmā and the others know not. He knows all that is known, while what is known to him is beyond the reach of others."

1. *pravacananibandhanāḥ* : According to B. D., the names "Skānda" etc. indicate that they were taught by Skanda etc., but not written by them. (*skandena proktaṃ na tu kṛtam iti vaktṛhetukā skāndādisaṃjñā* /)

2. *kāṭhakādivat* : The reference here may either be to the *Kaṭha Upaniṣad* or, as B. D. maintains, to a particular recension of the Black *Yajurveda,* originally mastered by the sage Kaṭha, after whom it was named. (*kaṭhenādhītaṃ kāṭhakam ityādisaṃjñāvat / kaṭhānāṃ vedaḥ kāṭhakaḥ...* /)

3. Jīva offers further evidence for the Vedic nature of Itihāsa and Purāṇas in S. S., based on statements from the *Brahmasūtra.* He writes, "The Vedic nature of Itihāsa and Purāṇas is also confirmed by B. S. 2/1/9 ("If you object that we are not allowing room for Smṛti [i.e. Sāṅkhya], we reply 'no, [if we make room for Sāṅkhya] we will be guilty of excluding other Smṛti texts.' "), since neither Itihāsa nor Purāṇas are in conflict with other Smṛti texts, as is the case with Sāṅkhya." He continues, "One might object that Purāṇas should also be considered Smṛti, based on B. S. 1/2/9 which maintains that the notion of *pradhāna* (nature, or *prakṛti*) is a distinctive feature of Smṛti (i.e. Sāṅkhya), for Vyāsa also describes the nature of *pradhāna* in the Purāṇas." Jīva answers this objection by referring to B. S. 1/4/3 which accepts *pradhāna* as a working concept, while denying that it is an independent principle, and maintains that it is in this sense alone that the concept is used in the Purāṇas, and not in the Sāṅkhyan sense.

4. *sūtādīnām* : B D. explains this as referring to *śūdras,* women, and fallen "twice-born". R. M. defines *sūtas* as those born from a *kṣatriya* father and a *brāhmaṇa* mother. (Cf. *Manu* 10/11, *kṣatriyād viprakanyāyāṃ sūto bhavati jātitaḥ* /) *sūtas* were traditionally royal charioteers who had the additional task of relating the heroics of their king. The name "Sūta" is also used to refer to the narrator of the *Bhāgavata,* Ugraśravas, a *sūta* by caste.

5. *vedārthadīpikānāṃ śāstrāṇāṃ* : B. D. identifies these *śāstras* as Smṛti texts such as *Manu* etc. (*mānavīyādīnām*), while R. M. considers them to be different kinds of commentaries on the Vedas. (*vedavyākhyāyakabhāṣyādīnām*)

16) skānde

vyāsacittasthitākāśād avacchinnāni kānicit /

anye vyavaharanty etāny urīkṛtya gṛhād iva // iti /
tathaiva dṛṣṭaṃ śrīviṣṇupurāṇe parāśaravākyam

tato 'tra matsuto vyāsaḥ aṣṭāviṃśatime 'ntare /
vedam ekaṃ catuṣpādaṃ caturdhā vyabhajat prabhuḥ //
yathātra tena vai vyastā vedavyāsena dhīmatā /
vedās tathā samastais tair vyāsair anyais tathā mayā //
tad anenaiva vyāsānāṃ śākhābhedān dvijottama /
caturyugeṣu racitān samasteṣv avadhāraya //
kṛṣṇadvaipāyanaṃ vyāsaṃ viddhi nārāyaṇaṃ prabhum /
ko 'nyo hi bhuvi maitreya mahābhāratakṛd bhavet // iti /

skānda eva

nārāyaṇād viniṣpannaṃ jñānaṃ kṛtayuge sthitam /
kiñcit tad anyathā jātaṃ tretāyāṃ dvāpare 'khilam //
gautamasya ṛṣeḥ śāpāj jñāne tv ajñānatāṃ gate /
saṅkīrṇabuddhayo devā brahmarudrapuraḥsarāḥ //
śaraṇyaṃ śaraṇaṃ jagmur nārāyaṇam anāmayam /
tair vijñāpitakāryas tu bhagavān puruṣottamāḥ //
avatīrṇo mahāyogī satyavatyāṃ parāśarāt /
utsannān bhagavān vedān ujjahāra hariḥ svayam // iti /

vedaśabdenātra purāṇādidvayam api gṛhyate / tad evam itihāsapurāṇavicāra eva śreyān iti siddham / tatrāpi purāṇasyaiva garimā dṛśyate / uktaṃ hi nāradīye

vedārthād adhikaṃ manye purāṇārthaṃ varānane /
vedāḥ pratiṣṭhitāḥ sarve purāṇe nātra saṃśayaḥ //
purāṇam anyathā kṛtvā tiryagyonim avāpnuyāt /
sudānto 'pi suśānto 'pi na gatiṃ kvacid āpnuyāt // iti /

16) As stated in the *Skanda Purāṇa*: "Others have borrowed bits and pieces[1] from the ethereal realm of Vyāsa's mind[2] for their own use, just as one would remove objects from a house and use them."

The same idea is found in the *Viṣṇu Purāṇa*, in the words of Vyāsa's father, Parāśara: "Then, in this twenty-eighth Manvantara, my son, the Lord Vyāsa, took the one Veda, consisting of four parts, and divided it into four. All the other 'Vyāsas'[3], and myself as well, (have made use of)[4] the Vedas just as the wise Vedavyāsa had arranged them. Therefore, know for certain that the different branches of the 'Vyāsas' in the four *yugas* were created for this reason alone.[5] O Maitreya, know that Kṛṣṇadvaipāyana (Vyāsa) is the Lord Nārāyaṇa himself; for who on earth but he could have composed the *Mahābhārata*?" (Vi.P. 3/4/2-5)

And in the *Skanda Purāṇa*: "In the Kṛta Yuga, the knowledge which had issued forth from Nārāyaṇa remained intact. It became somewhat distorted in the Tretā Yuga, and completely so in the Dvāpara Yuga. When, due to the curse of the sage Gautama, knowledge turned into ignorance, the bewildered *devas*, led by Brahmā and Rudra, sought shelter with the benignant, refuge-giving Nārāyaṇa, and informed Bhagavān Puruṣottama of their purpose in coming. And the great Yogin, the Lord Hari himself, descended, taking birth as the son of Satyavatī and Parāśara, and rescued the fallen Vedas." The word "Vedas" in the preceding verse indicates both Itihāsa and Purāṇas as well. It is thus established that the study of Itihāsa and Purāṇas alone[6] leads to the highest good. And of these, it is the importance of Purāṇas alone which is seen; for it is stated in the *Nārada Purāṇa*: "O Fair One (Pārvatī), I consider the significance of the Purāṇas to outweigh that even of the Vedas. The Vedas all find a firm resting place in the Purāṇas—about this there is no doubt. He who looks down on the Purāṇas will take birth in the womb of an animal, and even if well-behaved and peaceful, will find no refuge anywhere."

1. *avacchinnāni kānicit* : R. M. explains this as a reference to the utterances of Vyāsa. (*avacchinnāni yāni vākyānītyarthaḥ* /)

2. *vyāsacittasthitākāśāt* : B. D. explains, "The knowledge of Vyāsa is like the limitless sky, while that of others is but a fragment of that." (*bādarāyaṇasya jñānaṃ mahākāśam anyeṣāṃ jñānāni tu tadaṃśabhūtāni khaṇḍākāśāni*)

3. *vyāsaiḥ* : R. M. explains the plural number as indicating Vyāsa's disciples. (*vyāsair iti śiṣyābhiprāyeṇa bahuvacanam*)

4. R. M. writes that the word *vyavahṛtā* is to be supplied. (*vyavahṛtā itiśeṣaḥ* /)

5. *anenaiva* : R. M. explains that the separate branches were created because Vyāsa understood the limited intelligence of people. (*durmedhatvādidarśanena*)

6. *itihāsapurāṇavicāra eva śreyān* : R. M. qualifies this statement by adding that it leads to the highest good "for modern man who, in the Kali Yuga, is rather dull-witted, since the Vedas are so difficult to grasp." He also adds that the Vedas should be studied by the twice-born castes, and in this sense takes the adverb *eva* as modifying *śreyān* rather than *vicāraḥ*. (*itihāsapurāṇavicāra eva śreyān iti idānīntanānām ityādi / vedānāṃ durūhatayā mandabuddhīnāṃ kaliyugīyalokānāṃ yathārthāvadhāraṇasya vedato 'śakyatvād ity evakārasaṅgatiḥ / yad vā itihāsapurāṇavicāraḥ śreyān eveti yojanā* /)

17) skāndaprabhāsakhaṇḍe

vedavan niścalaṃ manye purāṇārthaṃ dvijottamāḥ /
vedāḥ pratiṣṭhitāḥ sarve purāṇe nātra saṃśayaḥ //
bibhety alpaśrutād vedo mām ayaṃ cālayiṣyati /
itihāsapurāṇais tu niścalo 'yaṃ kṛtaḥ purā //
yan na dṛṣṭaṃ hi vedeṣu tad dṛṣṭaṃ smṛtiṣu dvijāḥ /
ubhayor yan na dṛṣṭaṃ hi tat purāṇaiḥ pragīyate //
yo veda caturo vedān sāṅgopaniṣado dvijāḥ /
purāṇaṃ naiva jānāti na ca sa syād vicakṣaṇaḥ //

atha purāṇānām evaṃ prāmāṇye sthite 'pi teṣām api sāmastyenāpracaradrūpatvān nānādevatāpratipādakaprāyatvād arvācīnaiḥ kṣudrabuddhibhir artho duradhigama iti tadavastha eva saṃśayaḥ/ yad uktaṃ mātsye

pañcāṅgaṃ ca purāṇaṃ syād ākhyānam itarat smṛtam /
sāttvikeṣu ca kalpeṣu māhātmyam adhikaṃ hareḥ //
rājaseṣu ca māhātmyam adhikaṃ brahmaṇo viduḥ /
tadvad agneś ca māhātmyaṃ tāmaseṣu śivasya ca /
saṅkīrṇeṣu sarasvatyāḥ pitṝṇāṃ ca nigadyate // iti /

atrāgnes tattadagnau pratipādyasya tattadyajñasyetyarthaḥ / śivasya ceti cakārāc chivāyāś ca / saṅkīrṇeṣu sattvarajastamomayeṣu kalpeṣu bahuṣu / sarasvatyāḥ nānāvāṇyātmakatadupalakṣitāyā nānādevatāyā ityarthaḥ / pitṝṇāṃ karmaṇā pitṛlokaḥ iti śrutes tatprāpakakarmaṇām ityarthaḥ //

17) As stated in the *Prabhāsa Khaṇḍa* of the *Skanda Purāṇa*: "O Best of the Twice-born, I consider the significance of the Purāṇas to be unchanging, like that of the Vedas. The Vedas all find a firm resting place in the Purāṇas—about this there is no doubt. The Veda is afraid of those of little knowledge, thinking 'They will twist my meaning'; and so the meaning of the Veda was fixed in ancient times by means of Itihāsa and Purāṇas. For what is not found in the Vedas, O Twice-born, is found in Smṛti; and what is not found in either, is related in the Purāṇas. He who knows the four Vedas, together with the Vedāṅgas and Upaniṣads, without knowing the Purāṇas, is not to be thought of as wise." (Sk.P. 2/90-93)

But now, even though the authoritative nature of Purāṇas has been thus established, the following doubt still remains: since the Purāṇas are also not available in their entirety, and since they are chiefly concerned with establishing the superiority of various deities, won't their meaning also be difficult to comprehend for modern man of meagre intelligence? As stated in the *Matsya Purāṇa*: "A Purāṇa should consist of five parts, as opposed to an Ākhyāna.[1] The glory of Hari is greater in *sāttvika kalpas*[2]; the glory of Brahmā is greater in *rājasika kalpas*; and that of Agni and Śiva greater in *tāmasika kalpas*.[3] In mixed *kalpas*, the glory of Sarasvatī and the *pitṛs* is said to be greater." (Ma.P. 190/13-14) The name "Agni" in the preceding verse refers to the various *yajñas* which are offered in the different fires. The conjunction *ca* in the phrase *śivasya ca* indicates that Śivā (Śiva's consort, Pārvatī) is also meant. The term "mixed *kalpas*" refers to the many *kalpas* composed of *sattva*, *rajas*, and *tamas*. "Sarasvatī" refers to various deities indicated by Sarasvatī, who is the embodiment of various words. And the *pitṛs* refers to the sacrificial acts which lead to the attainment of the world of the *pitṛs*, as declared in Śruti: "Through *karman* one attains Pitṛloka." (Br.U. 1/5/16)

1. *ākhyānam itarat* : R. M. offers two possible interpretations of this phrase. In the first, he explains "Ākhyāna" as the name of a type of *śāstra*, distinct from Purāṇas. In the second explanation, he considers Ākhyānas to be a special type of Purāṇic element distinct from the five *lakṣaṇas*. (*itarat purāṇabhinnam / ākhyānam ākhyānākhyaṃ śāstram / yad vā itarad viśvasargādipañcalakṣaṇātiriktam api prasaṅgād ākhyānam / ākhyāyakam iti purāṇaviśeṣaṇam /*) (Cf. T. S. 61 for a discussion of the five characteristics of Purāṇas.)

2. *kalpeṣu* : According to R. M., the word *kalpa* refers to scriptures such as Purāṇas etc. (*kalpeṣu purāṇādiśāstreṣu /*)

3. The classification of the eighteen major Purāṇas according to the three *guṇas* is found in several Purāṇas, although with some variation. According to the *Padma Purāṇa* (*Uttara Khaṇḍa* 263/81-84), the *Viṣṇu*, *Nārada*, *Bhāgavata*, *Garuḍa*, *Padma*, and *Varāha Purāṇas* are *sāttvika*; the *Brahmāṇḍa*, *Brahmavaivarta*, *Brahma*, *Vāmana*, and *Bhaviṣya Purāṇas* are *rājasika*: and the *Matsya*, *Kūrma*, *Liṅga*, *Śiva*, *Agni*, and *Skanda Purāṇas* are *tāmasika*.

18) tad evaṃ sati tattatkalpakathāmayatvenaiva mātsya eva prasiddhānāṃ tattatpurāṇānāṃ vyavasthā jñāpitā tāratamyaṃ tu kathaṃ syāt yenetaranirṇayaḥ kriyeta / sattvāditāratamyenaiveti cet sattvāt saṃjāyate jñānam iti sattvaṃ yad brahmadarśanam iti nyāyāt sāttvikam eva purāṇādikaṃ paramārthajñānāya prabalam ity āyātam/ tathāpi paramārthe 'pi nānābhaṅgyā vipratipadyamānānāṃ samādhānāya kiṃ syat / yadi sarvasyāpi vedasya purāṇasya cārthanirṇayāya tenaiva śrībhaga-

vatā vyāsena brahmasūtraṃ kṛtaṃ tadavalokanenaiva sarvo 'rtho nirṇeya ity ucyate tarhi nānyasūtrakāramunyanugatair manyeta / kiñcātyantagūḍhārthānām alpākṣarāṇāṃ tatsūtrāṇām anyārthatvaṃ kaścid ācakṣīta tataḥ katarad ivātra samādhānam / tad eva samādheyaṃ yady ekatamam eva purāṇalakṣaṇam apauruṣeyaṃ śāstraṃ sarvavedetihāsapurāṇānām arthasāraṃ brahmasūtropajīvyaṃ ca bhavad bhuvi sampūrṇaṃ pracaradrūpaṃ syāt/ satyam uktaṃ yata eva ca sarvapramāṇānāṃ cakravartibhūtam asmadabhimataṃ śrīmadbhāgavatam evodbhāvitaṃ bhavatā //

18) This being the case, the categories into which the various well-known Purāṇas fall are described in the *Matsya Purāṇa* itself, based solely on stories concerning the different *kalpas*; but what means can be adopted by which the relative importance of these Purāṇas can be determined? If we base our decision on the relative importance of the three *guṇas*, *sattva*, *rajas* and *tamas*, then, on the strength of such statements as "From *sattva* comes knowledge" (Bh.G. 14/17) and "*Sattva* is the basis for the realization of *brahman*", we will have to conclude that only *sāttvika* Purāṇas etc. are capable of leading us to the highest truth.

But then (it might be asked),[1] how can you reconcile the divergent views which are propounded by means of various specious arguments with regard even to the highest truth? If you propose that the entire significance can be determined merely by studying the *Brahmasūtra*, composed by the Lord Vyāsa himself in order to fix the meaning of all the Vedas and Purāṇas, the followers of the other sages who wrote *sūtra* texts will not accept your proposal. Furthermore, someone might interpret the significance of these cryptic and terse *sūtras* in a distorted manner; how then can one know which one represents the correct interpretation? This issue could be settled once and for all if only you could point to one among the many scriptures, which exhibits the characteristics of a Purāṇa, is divinely composed, represents the essence of all the Vedas, Itihāsa, and Purāṇas, is based on the *Brahmasūtra*,[2] and is available throughout the land in its complete form.

Well said! (we reply), for you have just described the very *Bhāgavata Purāṇa* which we consider to be the sovereign ruler of all *pramāṇas*.

1. *tathāpi* : This phrase introduces the remarks of a second person (indicated by the word *bhavatā* at the end of this section). B. D. writes : *pṛcchati tathāpīti* /.

2. *brahmasūtropajīvyam* : B. D. explains : "By means of which the meaning of the *Brahmasūtra* is fixed." (*yena brahmasūtraṃ sthirārthaṃ syād ityarthaḥ* /)

19) yat khalu sarvapurāṇajātam āvirbhāvya brahmasūtraṃ ca praṇīyāpy aparituṣṭena tena bhagavatā nijasūtrāṇām akṛtrimabhāṣyabhūtaṃ samādhilabdham āvirbhāvitaṃ yasminn eva sarvaśāstrasamanvayo dṛśyate sarvavedārthasūtralakṣaṇāṃ gāyatrīm adhikṛtya pravartitatvāt / tathā hi tatsvarūpaṃ mātsye

yatrādhikṛtya gāyatrīṃ varṇyate dharmavistaraḥ /
vṛtrāsuravadhopetaṃ tad bhāgavatam iṣyate //
likhitvā tac ca yo dadyād dhemasiṃhasamanvitam /
prauṣṭhapadyāṃ paurṇamāsyāṃ sa yāti paramāṃ gatim /
aṣṭādaśasahasrāṇi purāṇaṃ tat prakīrtitam // iti /

atra gāyatrīśabdena tatsūcakatadavyabhicāridhīmahipadasambalitatadartha eveṣyate / sarveṣāṃ mantrāṇāṃ ādirūpāyās tasyāḥ sākṣātkathanānarhatvāt / tadarthatā ca janmādyasya yataḥ tene brahma hṛdā iti sarvalokāśrayatvabuddhivṛttiprerakatvādisāmyāt / dharmavistara ity atra dharmaśabdaḥ paramadharmaparaḥ dharmaḥ projjhitakaitavo 'tra paramaḥ ity atraiva pratipāditatvāt / sa ca bhagavaddhyānādilakṣaṇa eveti purastād vyaktībhaviṣyati //

19) Even after manifesting the complete body of Purāṇas, and composing the *Brahmasūtra*, Bhagavān Vyāsa was still not content, and so gave form to that which serves as a natural commentary on his own *Brahmasūtra*, which was revealed to him in *samādhi* (see pp. 63, 64), and which alone illustrates the common significance of all the scriptures, as seen in the fact that it begins by referring to the *Gāyatrī*, characterized as a concise statement of the significance of all the Vedas. For its true nature has thus been described in the *Matsya Purāṇa*: "That is to be known as the *Bhāgavata*, which, basing itself on the *Gāyatrī*, describes *dharma* in all its fullness, and which narrates the slaying of the *asura* Vṛtra. Whosoever will make a copy of this *Bhāgavata* and offer it away, mounted on a throne of gold[1] during the full moon of Bhādra, will attain the supreme goal. This Purāṇa is said to contain eighteen thousand (verses)." (Ma.P. 53/20, 22)

The word *gāyatrī* in the preceding verse refers only to the meaning of the *Gāyatrī*, contained in the word *dhīmahi* ("we meditate"), which occurs unchanged[2] in the *Bhāgavata*, and thus directly indicates the *Gāyatrī*; for an outright quotation of this mantra, which is the prototype of all mantras, would not have been proper.[3] The fact that the *Bhāgavata* has the same significance as that of the *Gāyatrī* is seen in the phrases *janmādyasya yataḥ* ("from whom comes the origin etc. of the universe") and *tene brahma hṛdā* ("who revealed the Veda [to the creator Brahmā] through his heart") (Bh.P. 1/1/1), which form identical explanations regarding the substratum of the entire universe and the ability to inspire the workings of the intellect, with those of the *Gāyatrī*.[4] The word *dharma* in the phrase *dharmavistaraḥ* signifies the "supreme *dharma*", for it is declared in the *Bhāgavata* itself: "The supreme *dharma*, devoid of all ulterior motive, is found in this *Bhāgavata*." (Bh. P. 1/1/2) And it will be made clear in a subsequent section that *dharma* is characterized only by such practices as contemplation of *bhagavat* etc.

1. *hemasiṃhasamanvitam* : R. M. interprets this to mean "mounted on a throne of gold, since it is king among Purāṇas" (*hemasiṃhāsanam ārūḍhaṃ purāṇarājatvād iti* /); and this is the sense in which Śrīdhara understands the compound (cf. T. S. 22). It is more likely, however, that the intended meaning is "together with a golden lion", based on the fact that similar prescriptions are found in this section of the *Matsya Purāṇa* regarding the other Purāṇas, which are to be offered together with such objects as a golden fish, golden swan, etc.

2. *tatsūcakatadavyabhicāridhīmahipada* : The word *dhīmahi* occurs in Bh.P. 1/1/1 (*satyaṃ paraṃ dhīmahi*) as well as in the *Gāyatrī Mantra* (*bhargo devasya dhīmahi*). The form of this verb is distinctively Vedic, and the fact that it occurs in a Purāṇic text such as the *Bhāgavata* is understood by Jīva to be an unmistakable reference to the *Gāyatrī*.

3. *sākṣātkathanānarhatvāt* : R. M. reads *likhana* for *kathana*, and writes, "since it would not be proper to write the actual words of the *Gāyatrī* in a text which can be heard by women, *śūdras*, etc. (*sākṣāllikhanānarhatvād iti strīśūdrādyadhikāraśravaṇayogyagranthādau gāyatrīsvarūpalikhanasyāyogyatvād ityarthaḥ* /) Since the word *likhana* occurs in an identical compound in Jīva's *Kramasandarbha* (1/1/1), it is likely that R. M.'s reading is correct.

4. The connection between the *Bhāgavata* and the *Gāyatrī Mantra* (*Ṛgveda* 3/62/10 etc.) is mentioned in various Purāṇas, and has been noted by most commentators as well. Aside from the presence of the word *dhīmahi*, Jīva mentions the phrases from *Bhāgavata* 1/1/1, *janmādyasya yataḥ* and *tene brahma hṛdā* which, according to the commentator Vijayadhvaja of the Mādhva school,

correspond to the *Gāyatrī* phrases *tat savitur...devasya* ("of the divine Savitṛ") and *dhiyo yo naḥ pracodayāt* ("may he inspire our intellects").

Śrīdhara also discusses the relationship between the *Bhāgavata* and the *Gāyatrī* in his remarks on Bh.P. 1/1/1. He writes: "By opening the *Bhāgavata* with the word *dhīmahi* from the *Gāyatrī*, this Purāṇa is shown to be of the nature of *brahmavidyā*, known as *Gāyatrī*." (*dhīmahīti gāyatryā prārambhena ca gāyatryākhyābrahmavidyārūpam etat purāṇam iti darśitam* /) He also writes: "With the phrase *tene brahma hṛdā* the significance of the *Gāyatrī* in terms of inspiring the workings of the intellect is indicated." (*anena buddhivṛttipravartakatvena gāyatryārtho darśitaḥ* /) Śrīdhara's influence on Jīva's treatment of this theme can be further seen from the fact that all three of the Purāṇic verses cited by Śrīdhara in his comments on Bh.P. 1/1/1 are also quoted by Jīva in this and the following section.

The same theme is also found in C. C. in Caitanya's dialogue with the Advaitin Prakāśānanda. He says: "This composition begins with the meaning of the *Gāyatrī*. *Satyaṃ param* ("the supreme reality") indicates the subject matter of the text, and *dhīmahi* ("we meditate") indicates the aim of spiritual practices." (*gāyatrīr arthe ei grantha ārambhana* / *satyaṃ paraṃ sambandha dhīmahi sādhane prayojana* // C.C.m. 25/140)

20) evaṃ skānde prabhāsakhaṇḍe ca
yatrādhikṛtya gāyatrīm ityādi /
sārasvatasya kalpasya madhye ye syur narāmarāḥ /
tadvṛttāntodbhavaṃ loke tac ca bhāgavataṃ smṛtam //
likhitvā tac ca ityādi ca /
aṣṭādaśasahasrāṇi purāṇaṃ tat prakīrtitam // iti /

tad evam agnipurāṇe ca vacanāni vartante / ṭīkākṛdbhiḥ pramāṇīkṛte purāṇāntare ca

grantho 'ṣṭādaśasāhasro dvādaśaskandhasammitaḥ /
hayagrīvabrahmavidyā yatra vṛtravadhas tathā //
gāyatryā ca samārambhas tad vai bhāgavataṃ viduḥ //

atra hayagrīvabrahmavidyā iti vṛtravadhasāhacaryeṇa nārāyaṇavarmaivocyate / hayagrīvaśabdenātrāśvaśirā dadhīcir evocyate / tenaiva ca pravartitā nārāyaṇavarmākhyā brahmavidyā / tasyāśvaśirastvaṃ ca ṣaṣṭhe yad vā aśvaśiro nāma ity atra prasiddhaṃ nārāyaṇavarmaṇo brahmavidyātvaṃ ca

etac chrutvā tathovāca dadhyaṅṅ ātharvaṇas tayoḥ /
pravargyaṃ brahmavidyāṃ ca satkṛto 'satyaśaṅkitaḥ //

iti svāmiṭīkotthāpitavacanena ceti / śrīmadbhāgavatasya bhagavatpriyatvena bhāgavatābhīṣṭatvena ca paramasāttvikatvam / yathā pādme ambarīṣaṃ prati gautamapraśnaḥ

purāṇaṃ tvaṃ bhāgavataṃ paṭhase purato hareḥ /
caritaṃ daityarājasya prahlādasya ca bhūpate //

tatraiva vyañjulīmāhātmye tasya tasminn upadeśaḥ

rātrau tu jāgaraḥ kāryaḥ śrotavyā vaiṣṇavī kathā /
gītā nāmasahasraṃ ca purāṇaṃ śukabhāṣitam /
paṭhitavyaṃ prayatnena hareḥ santoṣakāraṇam //

tatraivānyatra

ambarīṣa śukaproktaṃ nityaṃ bhāgavataṃ śṛṇu /
paṭhasva svamukhenāpi yadīcchasi bhavakṣayam //

skānde prahlādasaṃhitāyāṃ dvārakāmāhātmye

śrīmadbhāgavataṃ bhaktyā paṭhate harisannidhau /
jāgare tatpadaṃ yāti kulavṛndasamanvitaḥ //

20) Thus, we also find in the *Skanda Purāṇa*, *Prabhāsa Khaṇḍa*: "That is to be known as the *Bhāgavata* which, basing itself on the *Gāyatrī*, describes *dharma* in all its fullness, and which narrates the slaying of the *asura* Vṛtra. And that is known in the world as the *Bhāgavata* which has its origin in tales concerning the gods and men who live in the Sārasvata Kalpa. Whosoever will make a copy of this *Bhāgavata* and offer it away, mounted on a throne of gold during the full moon of Bhādra, will attain the supreme goal. This Purāṇa is said to contain eighteen thousand (verses)." (Sk.P. 2/39-42)[1] And these same lines are found in the *Agni Purāṇa* as well.[2]

And in another Purāṇa cited by the commentator (Śrīdhara): "That is known as the *Bhāgavata* which contains descriptions of the Brahmavidyā of Hayagrīva and accounts of the slaying of Vṛtra, which opens with reference to the *Gāyatrī*, and which consists of twelve *skandhas* and eighteen thousand (verses)." And the fact that the term "Hayagrīvabrahmavidyā" from the preceding verse occurs alongside of the phrase "the slaying of Vṛtra" shows that the reference is to "Nārāyaṇavarman" (the armor of Nārāyaṇa).[3] The name "Hayagrīva" in this verse refers to the horse-headed Dadhīci, who inaugurated the knowledge of *brahman* known as "Nārāyaṇavarman". The fact that he bore the head of a horse is established in the sixth *skandha* (Bh.P. 6/9/52) with the phrase "having the name 'Aśvaśiras' ('Horse-headed')"; and the fact that "Nārāyaṇavarman" signifies "Brahmavidyā" is indicated in the verse cited by Śrīdhara in his commentary on Bh.P. 6/9/52: "Hearing this, Dadhīci, the son of Atharvan, having been respectfully received by the twin Aśvins, instructed them in the Pravargya ceremony[4] and the Brahmavidyā, fearful of breaking his promise to them."

Since the *Bhāgavata* is dear to *bhagavat*, and cherished by his devotees, it is the most *sāttvika* (of Purāṇas). As stated in Gautama's question to Ambarīṣa in the *Padma Purāṇa*: "O King, do you recite the *Bhāgavata* in front of Hari, containing accounts of the King of Daityas (Hiraṇyakaśipu) and (his son) Prahlāda ?" (Pa.P., *Uttara Khaṇḍa* 22/115)

In the same section, Gautama instructs Ambarīṣa in the greatness of the Vyañjulī vow: "One should remain awake throughout the night (of the 'Vyañjulī Mahādvādaśī') and listen to compositions concerning Viṣṇu: the *Bhagavadgītā*, the *Thousand Names of Viṣṇu*, and the Purāṇa taught by Śuka (the *Bhāgavata*). These bring contentment to Hari, and should be recited with great care."

Elsewhere in the same section: "O Ambarīṣa, if you wish to put an end to the cycle of birth and death, listen daily to the *Bhāgavata* taught by Śuka, and recite it also with your own lips."

And in the *Dvārakāmāhātmya* from the *Prahlāda Saṃhitā* of the *Skanda Purāṇa*: "He who remains awake (on the 'Harivāsara'), and recites the *Bhāgavata* with devotion, in the presence of Hari, attains the abode of Viṣṇu, together with his entire family."

1. The three verses cited here by Jīva are found both in the *Matsya Purāṇa*, as indicated in the previous section, and in the *Skanda Purāṇa*, as indicated here. In the earlier section, only the first and third verses were quoted, probably since only these two are quoted by Śrīdhara in his commentary on Bh.P. 1/1/1; consequently, these two verses are indicated by Jīva in this section by their opening few words alone, while the middle verse, which had not been mentioned earlier, is quoted here in full.

According to R.M., the first of these three verses is meant only to introduce the verse which follows it. He writes: "The word 'etc.' following *gāyatrīm* actually means 'after the verse beginning with the words *yatrādhikṛtya gāyatrīm*'." (*gāyatrīm ityādīti ityādyanantaram ityarthaḥ* /) Perhaps due to the confusing nature of this portion of T. S. 20, and also due to the fact that B. D. leaves this part uncommented on, these first three verses are omitted in many manuscripts and editions.

2. This line is also not found in most editions, and is not commented upon by either B. D. or R. M. The verses referred to here are *Agni Purāṇa* 272/6-7.

3. *hayagrīvaśabdena*: B. D. writes that Jīva's explanation is meant to "remove a false impression regarding the words *hayagrīva* and *brahmavidyā*". (*hayagrīvādiśabdayor bhrāntiṃ nirākurvan vyācaṣṭa atra hayagrīvetyādinā* /) Although no further explanation is offered by B. D., the idea seems to be this: In *Bhāgavata*

6/6/30, 6/10/19, 7/2/4, and 8/10/21, Hayagrīva is spoken of as a Dānava, or enemy of the gods; in Bh.P. 2/7/2, Hayagrīva is mentioned as a *līlāvatāra* of Viṣṇu; and in Bh.P. 6/9/52, there is reference to the sage Dadhīci, who is called "Aśvaśiras", another name for Hayagrīva, also meaning "horse-headed". The question naturally arises, "Which Hayagrīva is indicated in the verse under consideration, and how does his identification help explain the significance of the term 'Brahmavidyā'?"

As Jīva points out, the solution to this riddle hinges on the reference to the slaying of the *asura* Vṛtra, found in the second half of this line. According to Bh.P. 6/9/51-55, Nārāyaṇa instructs Indra regarding the slaying of Vṛtra as follows: "O Indra, good fortune to you! Go quickly to the great sage Dadhīci and request his body, made firm through knowledge, vows, and the practice of austerities. He taught the full knowledge (of *brahman*) to the twin Aśvins, by virtue of which they have become liberated while living; hence is this knowledge know as 'Aśvaśiras'. (Dadhīci had earlier been forbidden by Indra to teach this sacred knowledge to the Aśvins, who were of the low *vaidya*, or medical, caste, under penalty of having his head cut off. As a precaution, the Aśvins removed and preserved Dadhīci's head, and grafted in its place the head of a horse, through which the sage taught the Aśvins the knowledge of *brahman*. Later, when Indra severed the horse's head of Dadhīci, the Aśvins restored his own head to its rightful place.) The impenetrable 'armor' (*varman*) which you have received had been given (or taught) earlier by Dadhīci to Tvaṣṭṛ; Tvaṣṭṛ taught it to Viśvarūpa, and he taught it to you. It represents my essential being. Dadhīci is a virtuous man. If requested by the Aśvins, he will give up his own limbs. Have Tvaṣṭṛ construct a great weapon (a thunderbolt) out of his bones, with which you will sever the head of Vṛtra, fortified by my power. Having slain him, you will regain your former power, weapons, and treasures. You will prevail, for none can do harm to my devotees." (Bh.P. 6/9/51-55) (Cf. van Gulik: 1935: 11-14).

4. *pravargyam*: B. D. explains this as the "science of life" (*prāṇavidyām*). Actually, the Pravargya ceremony is part of the Agniṣṭoma sacrifice, in which offerings of hot milk are made to the Aśvins. (Cf. van Buitenen: 1968 for a full description of this ceremony.)

21) gāruḍe ca

pūrṇaḥ so 'yam atiśayaḥ /
artho 'yaṃ brahmasūtrāṇāṃ bhāratārthavinirṇayaḥ //
gāyatrībhāṣyarūpo 'sau vedārthaparibṛṃhitaḥ /
purāṇānāṃ sāmarūpaḥ sākṣādbhagavatoditaḥ //
dvādaśaskandhayukto 'yaṃ śatavicchedasaṃyutaḥ /
grantho 'ṣṭādaśasāhasraḥ śrīmadbhāgavatābhidhaḥ // iti/

brahmasūtrāṇām arthas teṣām akṛtrimabhāṣyabhūta ityarthaḥ / pūrvaṃ sūkṣmatvena manasy āvirbhūtaṃ tad eva saṃkṣipya sūtratvena punaḥ prakaṭitaṃ paścād vistīrṇatvena sākṣāc chrībhāgavatam iti / tasmāt tadbhāṣyabhūte svataḥsiddhe tasmin saty arvācīnam anyad anyeṣāṃ svasvakapolakalpitaṃ tadanugatam evādaraṇīyam iti gamyate / bhāratārthavinirṇayaḥ

nirṇayaḥ sarvaśāstrāṇāṃ bhārataṃ parikīrtitam //
bhārataṃ sarvavedāś ca tulām āropitāḥ purā /
devair brahmādibhiḥ sarvair ṛṣibhiś ca samanvitaiḥ //
vyāsasyaivājñayā tatra tv atyaricyata bhāratam /
mahattvād bhāravattvāc ca mahābhāratam ucyate //

ityādyuktalakṣaṇasya bhāratasyārthavinirṇayo yatra saḥ / śrībhagavaty eva tātparyaṃ tasyāpi / tad uktaṃ mokṣadharme nārāyaṇīye śrīvedavyāsaṃ prati janamejayena

idaṃ śatasahasrād dhi bhāratākhyānavistarāt /
āmathya matimanthena jñānodadhim anuttamam //
navanītaṃ yathā dadhno malayāc candanaṃ yathā /
āraṇyaṃ sarvavedebhya oṣadhībhyo 'mṛtaṃ yathā //
samuddhṛtam idaṃ brahman kathāmṛtam idam tathā /
taponidhe tvayoktaṃ hi nārāyaṇakathāśrayam // iti //

21) And in the *Garuḍa Purāṇa*: "This composition is exceedingly perfect. It contains the meaning of the *Brahmasūtra* and determines the meaning of the *Mahābhārata*[1]. It functions as a commentary on the *Gāyatrī* and fortifies the meaning of the Vedas. It is the *Sāmaveda* of Purāṇas, declared by *bhagavat* himself. It contains twelve *skandhas*, numerous *vicchedas*, and eighteen thousand (verses), and goes by the name *Śrīmadbhāgavata*."[2]

"It contains the meaning of the *Brahmasūtra*": That is, it represents a natural commentary on the *sūtras*. Previously, it had been revealed in the heart (of Vyāsa) in a subtle form; that was then summarized and made manifest in the form of *sūtras*. Later, that appeared in its expanded form as the *Bhāgavata* itself. Therefore, since the *Bhāgavata* represents a self-revealed commentary on the *Brahmasūtra*, it follows that only those modern, self-styled commentaries which are in consonance with the *Bhāgavata* are to be respected.[3] "It determines the meaning of the *Mahābhārata*": That is, it contains the determination of the meaning of that *Mahābhārata* which is characterized as follows: "The *Mahābhārata* is extolled as determining the significance of all the scriptures. In olden times, Brahmā and the other *devas*, along with all the *ṛṣis*, gathered together at the command of Vyāsa, and weighed the *Mahābhārata* against all the Vedas. The scales tipped in favor of the *Mahābhārata*. (Therefore) because of its greatness (*mahattva*) and its heaviness (*bhāravattva*), it is known as the *Mahābhārata*."

The import of the *Mahābhārata* (like that of the *Bhāgavata*) revolves around *bhagavat* alone. Thus, the following verses are uttered by Janamejaya to Vyāsa in the *Nārāyaṇīya* section of the *Mokṣadharma* (*Mahābhārata*): "O Brāhmaṇa, O Treasure-house of austerities, just as fresh butter is extracted from curds and sandalwood from the Malaya breeze, the Upaniṣads from all the Vedas and nectar from herbs, so too, by churning the ocean of the highest wisdom with the churning rod of knowledge, have these nectar-like words which you have uttered, based on stories concerning Nārāyaṇa, been extracted from the legends found in the *Mahābhārata*, strewn throughout these hundred thousand verses." (M.Bh., *Mokṣadharma* 170/11-14)

1. *bhāratārthavinirṇayaḥ*: There is a verse in the *Skanda Purāṇa* to the effect that the *Mahābhārata* was composed later than the eighteen Purāṇas, in which case the *Bhāgavata* could not be considered to determine the meaning of the *Mahābhārata*. In reply to this, Jīva claims that although composed earlier than the *Bhāgavata*, the *Mahābhārata* was not revealed to Janamejaya and others until a'ter the composition of the *Bhāgavata*. (*atra prabhāsakhaṇḍe yad aṣṭādaśapurāṇāvirbhāvānantaram eva bhāratam prakāśitam iti śrūyate tat śrībhāgavatavirodhāt bhāratārthavinirṇayaḥ iti...pūrvaṃ kṛtam api bhāratam tatpaścāj janamejayādiṣu pracāritam ity apekṣyaiva jñeyam* /)

2. The different elements of this verse will now be discussed serially by Jīva in this and the following two sections. For a discussion of the identity of this verse, see footnotes 4 and 5 from the preceding chapter.

3. *ādaraṇīyam* : B. D. adds the following restriction to this claim: "Only those modern commentaries which do not contradict the *Bhāgavata*, and which are written by Vaiṣṇava teachers, are to be respected. Those which contradict the *Bhāgavata*, such as the commentaries of Śaṅkara, Kumārila, and Bhāskara, are to be rejected." (*anyad vaiṣṇavācāryaracitam ādhunikaṃ bhāṣyaṃ tadanugataṃ śrībhāgavatāviruddham evādartavyaṃ tadviruddhaṃ śaṅkarabhaṭṭabhāskarādiracitaṃ tu heyam ityarthaḥ* /)

22) tathā ca tṛtīye
munir vivakṣur bhagavadguṇānāṃ
sakhāpi te bhāratam āha kṛṣṇaḥ /
yasmin nṛṇāṃ grāmyasukhānuvādair
matir gṛhītā nu hareḥ kathāyām // iti //

22) So also in the third (*skandha*): "(O Maitreya) even

your friend, the sage Kṛṣṇa Dvaipāyana (Vyāsa) felt a desire to describe the virtues of *bhagavat*, and so narrated the *Mahābhārata*, in which the hearts of men are drawn towards stories concerning Hari, through repeated accounts of lower pleasures."[1] (Bh.P. 3/5/12)

1. *grāmyasukhānuvādaiḥ* : B. D. reads *kathā* in place of *sukha*, and explains, "(through the repetition of) stories relating to everyday life, indicating the duties to be performed by householders, and supplemented by illustrations involving cats and mice, and vultures and jackals." (*grāmyā gṛhidharmakartavyatādilakṣaṇā vyāvahārakī mūṣikaviḍālagṛdhragomāyudṛṣṭāntopetā ca kathā/*).

Śrīdhara accepts the reading *grāmyasukha*, and quotes the following verses by way of explanation: "What good does it do to describe lust to a lustful person or greed to a greedy person ? Is it not like hurling a blind man into a dark well ? After describing these (lust and greed) in order to attract the minds of men, Vyāsa then denounces them here itself by means of legends which purify the mind. Otherwise, why would the wise and compassionate sage describe these two (lust and greed), which only lead to bondage to this frightful round of birth and death ?" (*kāmino varṇayan kāmaṃ lobhaṃ lubdhasya varṇayan / naraḥ kiṃ phalam āpnoti kūpe 'ndham iva pātayan // lokacittāvatārārthaṃ varṇayitvātra tena tau/itihāsaiḥ pavitrārthaiḥ punar atraiva ninditau // anyathā ghorasaṃsārabandhahetū janasya tau / varṇayet sa kathaṃ vidvān mahākāruṇiko muniḥ //*)

R. M. also reads *grāmyasukha* and offers an explanation which closely follows the verses quoted by Śrīdhara. He writes: "The repetition of accounts of lower pleasures is meant to initially engage the minds of even lustful people. Ultimately, the truth concerning *bhagavat* is made known through the denunciation of these lower pleasures, found in the very same accounts, so as to lead to the welfare (of the listener)." (*grāmyasukhānuvādas tu prathamataḥ kāminām api pravṛttyartham / tataś ca tatraiva grāmyasukhanindayā bhagavattattvam āveditaṃ śreyase /*)

The single verse which has been treated here as the whole of section 22 is actually only the beginning of a very lengthy and confused section, the latter portion of which will be treated as comprising two sub-sections, designated "22a" and "22b" respectively. The reasons for this division are as follows: The initial portion, designated "22", represents a continuation of Jīva's remarks on the phrase *bhāratārthavinirṇayaḥ* from the *Garuḍa Purāṇa* verse quoted in section 21, and is found in all editions. The portion designated "22a" represents Jīva's comments on the remaining phrases from the same verse. This portion is commented on by B.D., and occurs in some, but not all, manuscripts. The portion which follows this, designated "22b", deals with the same topics, but in much greater detail. This portion is commented on by R.M., and referred to by Jīva in his *Kramasandarbha*. It is also not found in all editions, presumably because of B.D.'s failure to comment on it.

The relationship between the two latter portions is not very clear.

Some lines from the earlier portion are repeated verbatim in the latter portion, and some of the explanations given in one differ from those of the other, leading to the conclusion that one of the two, presumably the latter and more detailed portion, was meant as a replacement for the other. On the other hand, parts of the latter portion seem to refer directly to comments made in the earlier portion, leading to the conclusion that the second portion was meant to serve as a supplement to the first. It is possible that the second portion was written as a result of Jīva's dissatisfaction with the first, either because of its brevity or the nature of some of the explanations found therein, but that the actual function that portion was to play was never fully resolved.

22a) gāyatrībhāṣyarūpo 'sau / tathaiva hi viṣṇudharmottarādau tadvyākhyāne bhagavān eva vistareṇa pratipāditaḥ / atra janmādyasya ity asya vyākhyānaṃ ca tathā darśayiṣyate / vedārthaparibṛṃhitaḥ / vedārthasya paribṛṃhaṇaṃ yasmāt / tac coktam itihāsapurāṇābhyām ityādi / purāṇānāṃ sāmarūpaḥ / vedeṣu sāmavat sa teṣu śreṣṭha ityarthaḥ / ata eva skānde

śataśo 'tha sahasraiś ca kim anyaiḥ śāstrasaṃgrahaiḥ /
na yasya tiṣṭhate gehe śāstraṃ bhāgavataṃ kalau //
kathaṃ sa vaiṣṇavo jñeyaḥ śāstraṃ bhāgavataṃ kalau /
gṛhe na tiṣṭhate yasya sa vipraḥ śvapacādhamaḥ //
yatra yatra bhaved vipra śāstraṃ bhāgavataṃ kalau /
tatra tatra harir yāti tridaśaiḥ saha nārada //
yaḥ paṭhet prayato nityaṃ ślokaṃ bhāgavataṃ mune /
aṣṭādaśapurāṇānāṃ phalaṃ prāpnoti mānavaḥ // iti /

śatavicchedasaṃyutaḥ/pañcatriṃśadadhikaśatatrayādhyāyaviśiṣṭa ityarthaḥ / spaṣṭārtham anyat / tad evaṃ paramārthavivitsubhiḥ śrībhāgavatam eva sāmprataṃ vicāraṇīyam iti sthitam /

22a) "It functions as a commentary on the *Gāyatrī*" : For it is so explained in those sections of the *Viṣṇudharmottara* etc. which contain expositions on the *Gāyatrī*,[1] that *bhagavat* alone is described in detail (in the *Gāyatrī*). A similar explanation will also be given in this regard in the commentary on Bh. P. 1/1/1.

"It fortifies the meaning of the Vedas" : That is, by virtue of the *Bhāgavata*, the meaning of the Vedas is fortified. Therefore it is said, "One should supplement the Vedas with Itihāsa and Purāṇas." (M.Bh., *Ādiparvan* 1/267)

"It is the *Sāmaveda* of Purāṇas" : That is, just as the *Sāmaveda* is the most perfect of Vedas, so is the *Bhāgavata* the most perfect of Purāṇas. Therefore, we find in the *Skanda Purāṇa*: "If the *Bhāgavata* is not kept in one's house in the Kali Yuga, of what avail are collections of other scriptures by the hundreds and thousands? How can he be considered a Vaiṣṇava who, in the Kali Yuga, does not keep the *Bhāgavata* in his house? Even if he is a *brāhmaṇa*, he is lower than an outcaste. O Nārada, O Sage, wherever the *Bhāgavata* is found in the Kali Yuga, there Hari goes together with all the *devas*. O Muni, that pious soul who daily recites a verse from the *Bhāgavata* reaps the fruits of the eighteen Purāṇas." (Sk. P., *Viṣṇu Khaṇḍa* 16/40, 42, 44, 331)

"It contains numerous *vicchedas*": That is, it is characterized as having 335 *adhyāyas*. The meaning of the rest is clear. It is therefore thus established that in the present age, those seeking to know the highest truth need only study the *Bhāgavata Purāṇa*.

1. *tadvyākhyāne* : The fact that the pronoun *tat* in this compound refers to the *Gāyatrī* is confirmed in the corresponding portion of section 22b in which verses are quoted from the *Gāyatrīnirvāṇakathana* section of the *Agni Purāṇa*.

22b) hemādrer vratakhaṇḍe

strīśūdradvijabandhūnāṃ trayī na śrutigocarā /
karmaśreyasi muḍhānāṃ śreya evaṃ bhaved iha /
iti bhāratam ākhyānaṃ kṛpayā muninā kṛtam //

iti vākyaṃ śrībhāgavatīyatvenotthāpya bhāratasya vedārthatulyatvena nirṇayaḥ kṛta iti tanmatānusāreṇa tv evaṃ vyākhyeyaṃ bhāratārthasya vinirṇayaḥ vedārthatulyatvena viśiṣya nirṇayo yatreti / yasmād evaṃ bhagavatparas tasmād eva yatrādhikṛtya gāyatrīm iti kṛtalakṣaṇaśrīmadbhāgavatanāmā granthaḥ śrībhagavatparāyā gāyatryā bhāṣyarūpo 'sau / tad uktaṃ yatrādhikṛtya gāyatrīm ityādi / tathaiva hy agnipurāṇe tasyā vyākhyāne vistareṇa pratipāditaḥ / tatra tadīyavyākhyādigdarśanaṃ yathā

taj jyotiḥ paramaṃ brahma bhargas tejo yataḥ smṛtaḥ //

ity ārabhya punar āha

taj jyotir bhagavān viṣṇur jagajjanmādikāraṇam //
śivam kecit paṭhanti sma śaktirūpam vadanti ca /
kecit sūryaṃ kecid agniṃ daivatāny agnihotriṇaḥ //
agnyādirūpo viṣṇur hi vedādau brahma gīyate / iti /

atra janmādyasya ity asya vyākhyānaṃ ca tathā darśayiṣyate / kasmai yena vibhāsito 'yam ity upasaṃhāravākye ca tac chuddham ityādi samānam evāgnipurāṇe tadvyākhyānam /

nityaṃ śuddhaṃ paraṃ brahma nityabhargam adhīśvaram //
ahaṃ jyotiḥ paraṃ brahma dhyāyema hi vimuktaye // iti //

atrāhaṃ brahmeti nādevo devam arcayet iti nyāyena yogyatvāya svasya tādṛktvabhāvanā darśitā / dhyāyemeti ahaṃ tāvat dhyāyeyaṃ sarve ca vayaṃ dhyāyemetyarthaḥ / tad etanmate tu mantre 'pi bhargaśabdo 'yam adanta eva syāt / supāṃ suluk ityādinā chāndasasūtreṇa tu dvitīyaikavacanasyāmaḥ subhāvo jñeyaḥ / yat tu dvādaśe om namas te ityādigadyeṣu tadarthatvena sūryaḥ stutaḥ tat paramātmadṛṣṭyaiva na tu svātantryeṇety adoṣaḥ / tathaivāgre śrīśaunakavākyam

brūhi naḥ śraddadhānānāṃ vyūhaṃ sūryātmano hareḥ //

iti / na cāsya bhargasya sūryamaṇḍalamātrādhiṣṭhānatvam / mantre vareṇyaśabdena atra ca granthe paraśabdena paramaiśvaryaparyantatayā darśitatvāt / tad evam agnipurāṇe 'py uktam

dhyānena puruṣo 'yaṃ ca draṣṭavyaḥ sūryamaṇḍale /
satyaṃ sadāśivaṃ brahma tad viṣṇoḥ paramaṃ padam // iti /

trilokījanānām upāsanārthaṃ pralaye vināśini sūryamaṇḍale cāntaryāmitayā prādurbhūto 'yaṃ puruṣo dhyānena draṣṭavya upāsitavyaḥ / yat tu viṣṇos tasya mahāvaikuṇṭharūpaṃ paramaṃ padaṃ tad eva satyaṃ kālatrayāvyabhicāri sadāśivam upadravaśūnyaṃ yato brahmasvarūpam ityarthaḥ / tad etadgāyatrīṃ procya purāṇalakṣaṇaprakaraṇe yatrādhikṛtya gāyatrīm ityādy apy uktaṃ agnipurāṇe / tasmāt

agneḥ purāṇaṃ gāyatrīṃ sametya bhagavatparām /
bhagavantaṃ tatra matvā jagajjanmādikāraṇam //
yatrādhikṛtya gāyatrīm iti lakṣaṇapūrvakam /
śrīmadbhāgavataṃ śaśvat pṛthvyāṃ jayati sarvataḥ //

tad evam asya śāstrasya gāyatrīm adhikṛtya pravṛttir darśitā / yat tu sārasvatakalpam adhikṛtyeti pūrvam uktaṃ tac ca gāyatryā bhagavatpratipādakavāgviśeṣarūpasarasvatītvād upayuktam eva / yad uktam agnipurāṇe

gāyaty ukthāni śāstrāṇi bhargaṃ prāṇāṃs tathaiva ca //
tataḥ smṛteyaṃ gāyatrī sāvitrī yata eva ca /
prakāśinī sā savitur vāgrūpatvāt sarasvatī // iti /

atha kramaprāptā vyākhyā vedārthaparibṛṃhita iti / vedārthānāṃ paribṛṃhaṇaṃ yasmāt tac coktam itihāsapurāṇābhyām iti / purāṇānāṃ sāmarūpa iti vedeṣu sāmavat purāṇeṣu śreṣṭha ityarthaḥ / purāṇāntarāṇāṃ keṣāṃcid āpātato rajastamasī juṣamāṇais tatparatvāpratītatve 'pi vedānām kāṇḍatrayavākyaikavākyatāyāṃ yathā sāmnā tathā teṣāṃ śrībhāgavatena pratipādye śrībhagavaty eva paryavasānam iti bhāvaḥ / tad uktam

vede rāmāyaṇe caiva purāṇe bhārate tathā /
ādāv ante ca madhye ca hariḥ sarvatra gīyate // iti /

pratipādayiṣyate ca tad idaṃ paramātmasandarbhe / sākṣādbhagavatodita iti kasmai yena vibhāsito 'yam ity upasaṃhāravākyānusāreṇa jñeyam / śatavicchedasaṃyuta iti vistarabhiyā na vivriyate / tad evaṃ śrīmadbhāgavataṃ sarvaśāstracakravartipadam āptam iti sthite hemasiṃhasamanvitam ity atra hemasiṃhāsanam āruḍham iti ṭīkākārair yad vyākhyātaṃ tad eva yuktam / ataḥ śrīmadbhāgavatasyaivābhyāsāvaśyakatvaṃ śreṣṭhatvaṃ ca skānde nirṇītam

śataśo 'tha sahasraiś ca kim anyaiḥ śāstrasaṃgrahaiḥ / tad evaṃ paramārthavivitsubhiḥ śrībhāgavatam eva sāmprataṃ vicāraṇīyam iti sthitam //

22b) The following *Bhāgavata* verse, quoted in the *Vrata Khaṇḍa* (of the *Caturvargacintāmaṇi*) of Hemādri determines the meaning of the *Mahābhārata* to be equivalent to that of the Vedas: "The sage Vyāsa compassionately composed the epic, *Mahābhārata*, with the idea in mind that it would lead to the welfare of women, *śūdras*, and fallen Twice-born who are not entitled to hear the three Vedas, and are thus deluded as to what action would lead to their ultimate good." (Bh.P. 1/4/25) Thus, according to this view, the phrase "it determines the meaning of the *Mahābhārata*" should be interpreted to mean "the meaning of the *Mahābhārata* is determined in the *Bhāgavata* as being equivalent to that of the Vedas."[1]

Since the composition known as the *Śrīmadbhāgavata* and characterized by the phrase "based on the *Gāyatrī*" is thus concerned with *bhagavat* alone, it may be said to serve as a commentary on the *Gāyatrī* which is itself concerned solely with *bhagavat*. Therefore it is stated, "That is to be known as the *Bhāgavata* which, basing itself on the *Gāyatrī*, describes *dharma* in all its fullness..." A similar detailed explanation is presented in the expository account of the *Gāyatrī* found in the *Agni Purāṇa*. A brief survey of that account is given below.

"That 'light' (mentioned in the *Gāyatri*) is the supreme *brahman*, for the word *bhargas* indicates the light of consciousness." (Ag.P. 216/3) He continues, "That 'light' is *bhagavat*, Viṣṇu, the source of the origin, preservation, and dissolution of the universe. There are some who repeat the name 'Śiva' (in place of 'Viṣṇu'), some 'Śakti', 'Sūrya', or that of other deities, while the Agnihotṛ priests repeat the name 'Agni'.[2] Verily it is Viṣṇu who has assumed the form of Agni and the rest, and is praised in the Vedas etc. as *brahman*." (Ag.P. 216/7-9)

A similar explanation will also be given in this regard[3] in the commentary on Bh.P. 1/1/1. And in the concluding section of the *Bhāgavata*, the final line of verse 12/13/19, beginning *tac chuddham*,[4] is identical in import with the explanation of the *Gāyatrī* found in the *Agni Purāṇa*:[5] "Let us meditate on the eternal, pure, supreme *brahman*, the everlasting light, and the highest Lord, (thinking) 'I am the light, the supreme *brahman*', in order to attain liberation."[6] (Ag.P. 216/6, 7) Here, the phrase "I am *brahman*" indicates a kind of meditation in which one assumes an attitude of identity between oneself and *brahman* in order to be fit for worship according to the principle "One who is not himself divine may not worship the divine." The verb *dhyāyema* ("Let us meditate") means "May I, and all of us as well, meditate."[7]

But then, on the strength of this verse, one would expect to find the *adanta* stem, *bharga*, in the *Gāyatrī* as well.[8] This can be explained, however, with the help of *Pāṇini Sūtra* 7/1/39 as an instance of a Vedic irregularity in which the singular accusative ending *am* is replaced by the ending *su*.[9]

And in the prose passages which praise the sun as the object of worship in the *Gāyatrī* (Bh.P. 12/6/67-69), the sun should not be viewed as an independent entity, but rather as indicating *paramātman*, rendering those passages free from blemish. The words of Śaunaka at the end of the *Bhāgavata* are similarly to be understood: "Tell us, who are full of faith, of the manifestations of Hari, in the form of the sun." (Bh.P. 12/11/28)

And the "light" (mentioned in the *Gāyatri*) does not refer to that which dwells in the physical sun alone, for, as indicated by the word *vareṇya* ("most excellent") from the *Gāyatrī* and the word *para* ("supreme") from the *Bhāgavata* (1/1/1 and 12/13/19), its application extends as far as the majesty of *īśvara*. Therefore it is stated in the *Agni Purāṇa* "Through meditation, the *puruṣa* can be seen dwelling in the disc of the sun. (But) the supreme abode of Viṣṇu, *brahman*, is alone real and ever-blessed."[10] (Ag.P. 216/16, 17) That is, through meditation, the *puruṣa*, who manifests as the indweller within the disc of the sun, which will itself perish at the time of dissolution, so that the inhabitants of the three worlds may worship him, can be seen, i.e. worshipped. But the supreme abode of Viṣṇu, in the form of Vaikuṇṭha, is alone real, unchanging in the past, present, and future, since it partakes of the nature of *brahman*.

After thus explaining the *Gāyatrī*, the *Agni Purāṇa* also makes use of the verse beginning *yatrādhikṛtya gāyatrīm* (Ag.P. 272/6) in the section which deals with the characteristics of Purāṇas.[11] Thus we find the following verses: "The *Agni Purāṇa* considers the *Gāyatrī* to be concerned with *bhagavat* alone, who is held therein to be the source of the origin, preservation, and dissolution of the universe. The *Bhāgavata*, characterized by the phrase, 'based on the *Gāyatrī*', ever flourishes throughout the land."[12] Thus is the origin of the *Bhāgavata* demonstrated to be based on the *Gāyatrī*.

And the earlier statement regarding the Sārasvata Kalpa[13] is also appropriate since Sarasvatī, whose distinguishing characteristic is speech illustrative of *bhagavat*, represents the essence of the *Gāyatrī*. As stated in the *Agni Purāṇa*, "It is called *Gāyatrī* since it sings (*gāyati*), or reveals,[14] Vedic texts, scriptures, the divine light, and the vital forces. It is called Sāvitrī (the daughter of the sun) since it has the power of enlightening. And since speech represents the essence of the sun, it is also called Sarasvatī." (Ag.P. 216/1,2)[15]

Now the next phrase will be explained. "It fortifies the meaning of the Vedas" : That is, by virtue of the *Bhāgavata*, the meaning of the Vedas is fortified. Therefore it is said, "One should supplement the Vedas with Itihāsa and Purāṇas." (M.Bh., *Ādiparvan* 1/267)

"It is the *Sāmaveda* of Purāṇas": That is, just as the *Sāmaveda* is the most perfect of Vedas, so is the *Bhāgavata* the most perfect of Purāṇas. For just as the *Sāmaveda* brings out the one common theme running through the three *kāṇḍas* of the Vedas (*karmakāṇḍa*, *upāsanākāṇḍa*, and *jñānakāṇḍa*), so does the *Bhāgavata* demonstrate the fact that some of the other Purāṇas which occasionally seem to partake of the nature of *rajas* and *tamas*, and do not appear to be concerned with *bhagavat*, ultimately find their resolution in *bhagavat* alone, as presented in the *Bhāgavata*. Therefore it is said, "In the Vedas, *Rāmāyaṇa*, *Purāṇas*, and *Mahābhārata*, Hari is everywhere praised, in the beginning, the middle, and the end." The truth of this statement will be demonstrated in the *Paramātmasandarbha*.

"Declared by *bhagavat* himself": This is to be understood in accordance with the concluding words of the *Bhāgavata*: "Let us meditate on *bhagavat*, who revealed the *Bhāgavata* to Brahmā..." (Bh.P. 12/13/19)

"It contains numerous *vicchedas*": This phrase will not be discussed, out of fear of unduly lengthening this text.[16] Thus, Śrīdhara's interpretation of the phrase *hemasiṃhasamanvitam*[17] as meaning "mounted on a throne of gold" is fitting indeed, for as has just been demonstrated, the *Bhāgavata* occupies the position of sovereign ruler of all scriptures. Consequently, both the superiority of the *Bhāgavata*, and the need for its repeated study are established in the *Skanda Purāṇa*: "Of what avail are collections of other scriptures by the hundreds and thousands...?" (Sk.P. 16/40) It is therefore thus established that in the present age those seeking to know the highest truth need only study the *Bhāgavata Purāṇa*.

1. *tanmatānusāreṇa tu* : As indicated by the particle *tu*, the verses quoted here represent an alternate explanation of the phrase *bhāratārthavinirṇayaḥ*. In the previous section, T. S. 21, Jīva had quoted verses from the *Mahābhārata* to the effect that it was "heavier" than the Vedas. That position is somewhat modified here, as Jīva now considers the Vedas and the *Mahābhārata* to be of "equal weight" (*tulyatvena*).

2. *agniṃ daivatāny agnihotriṇaḥ* : Jīva's reading of this portion of the verse gives the impression that the Agnihotṛ priests repeat the names of other deities, and not that of Agni. The reading found in the Ānandāśrama edition of the *Agni Purāṇa*, *agniṃ vedagā agnihotriṇaḥ*, is clearly a better reading, and clarifies the fact that the Agnihotṛ priests, "being followers of the Vedas", repeat the name of Agni.

3. *atra* : R. M. explains this as meaning "concerning the interpretation of the *Gāyatrī*." (*atra gāyatrīvyākhyāne*)

4. The full *pāda* reads: *tac chuddhaṃ vimalaṃ viśokam amṛtaṃ satyaṃ paraṃ dhīmahi* /. This line is cited by Jīva for several reasons. First, it clearly refers to the *Gāyatrī* by its use of the word *dhīmahi*. It also echoes Bh.P. 1/1/1 with

the phrase *satyaṃ paraṃ dhīmahi*, the verse which the *Agni Purāṇa* specifically points to as being based on the *Gāyatrī*. And it shares the words *śuddham* and *param* with the *Agni Purāṇa* verse quoted here with respect to the *Gāyatrī*.

5. The Ānandāśrama edition of the *Agni Purāṇa* gives the following reading of this verse: *nityaṃ śuddhaṃ buddham ekam satyaṃ tad dhīmahīśvaram* // (216/6) *ahaṃ brahma paraṃ jyotir dhyāyema hi vimuktaye* / (216-7).

6. *vimuktaye* : R. M. explains that "the attitude of identity with *brahman* is for those seeking to attain liberation, while those who cherish pure *bhakti* think in terms of the attitude 'I am the servant of *bhagavat*', for this is the sense in which they understand the *mahāvākyas*, such as *tat tvam asi*." (*idaṃ tu brahmābhedena svātmacintanaṃ mumukṣupakṣe ata eva vimuktaye iti vacane darśitam /... śuddhabhaktānāṃ tu bhagavaddāso 'smītyādicintanaṃ tat tvam asyādiśrutīnāṃ tathaiva tātparyakalpanād iti* /)

7. *dhyāyema* : Jīva's explanation of this phrase stems from the fact that a first person plural verb form (*dhyāyema*) is found in the same line as the first person singular pronoun *aham*. According to R. M., the use of the plural verb form does not indicate a plural meaning, but is rather Vedic license for an irregular singular verb ending. (*dhyāyemeti atra bahutvam avivakṣitam / bahuvacanaprayogo 'pi chāndasa iti dyotayann āha ahaṃ dhyāyeyam iti* /)

8. The regular accusative singular ending of the *adanta* (i.e. "ending in *a*") stem, *bharga*, is *bhargam*, and this is the form which occurs in the *Agni Purāṇa* verse cited by Jīva. The problem is that the form *bhargas* occurs as the accusative singular form in the *Gāyatrī*. Hence, the necessity for Jīva's explanation here.

9. Rather than admit that the form *bhargas*, found in the *Gāyatrī*, is the regular accusative singular of the neuter stem *bhargas*, Jīva interprets it as an irregular Vedic form of the masculine stem *bharga*. Jīva offers no justification for this interpretation beyond the fact that the *adanta* stem *bharga* occurs in the *Agni Purāṇa* verse describing the *Gāyatrī*, implying, in his mind, that this is the stem which must have also been employed in the *Gāyatrī*.

10. Once again, Jīva has quoted the final line of one verse, and the initial line of the following verse. His reading of the second line also seems defective to some extent. The Ānandāśrama edition reads as follows: *janmamṛtyuvināśāya duḥkhasya trividhasya ca / dhyānena puruṣo 'yaṃ ca draṣṭavyaḥ sūryamaṇḍale // tattvaṃ sad asi cid brahma viṣṇor yat paramaṃ padam / devasya savitur bhargo vareṇyaṃ hi turīyakam* // (Ag. P. 216/16, 17). ("One should behold the *puruṣa* dwelling in the disc of the sun, in order to put to an end the round of birth and death, and the three kinds of misery, meditating as follows: 'You are the real, the true, pure consciousness, *brahman*, the supreme abode of Viṣṇu, and the supreme, absolute light of the Lord Savitṛ.' ") Although Jīva does not interpret the second of these two verses as representing the words of the meditation, R.M. understands it as such, and writes, "They describe the meditation with the words *satyam* etc." (*dhyānam āha satyam iti*)

11. The two sections of the *Agni Purāṇa* alluded to here are the 216th *adhyāya* entitled *Gāyatrīnirvāṇakathana*, and the 272nd *adhyāya* entitled *Purāṇadānādimāhātmyakathana*.

12. R. M. reads *sammatya* for *sametya* in the first of these two verses, and explains that the *Agni Purāṇa* demonstrates the significance of the *Gāyatrī* by

means of etymological interpretations. (*niruktavyākhyānena pradarśya...*) The reference is again to the 216th *adhyāya* in which the name *Gāyatrī*, as well as the key words of the mantra, are explained in terms of their verbal roots, or similar-sounding roots. Thus, the word *gāyatrī* is explained by means of the roots *gai* and *trai*, *vareṇya* by the root *vṛ*, *dhīmahi* by *dhā*, etc.

13. *sārasvatakalpam adhikṛtyeti*: The use of the particle *iti* normally indicates that the words preceding it represent a direct quotation. However, since the words *sārasvatakalpam adhikṛtya* are not found prior to this in the text of T.S., it may be assumed that either a portion of the text is missing, or that the particle *iti* is not to be understood in its usual sense. It is possible that the *iti* was interpolated by a scribe who, on the strength of the frequently quoted phrase *yatrādhikṛtya gāyatrīm*, took this also for a quotation, and indicated it as such. If the implication of the *iti* is ignored, the phrase in question may then be interpreted as a reference to the *Skanda Purāṇa*, verse 2/40, cited in T.S. 20, which associates the *Bhāgavata* with the Sārasvata Kalpa.

14. *gāyati*: R. M. glosses this as *prakāśayati* and explains: "It reveals *ukthas*, i.e. scriptures made up of Vedic mantras, since, as the primordial mantra, all other mantras depend on the *Gāyatrī* for their existence." (*gāyaty ukthānīti ukthāni vaidikamantrātmakaśāstrāṇi gāyati prakāśayati sarvamantrāṇām ādibhūtāṃ gāyatrīm upajīvyaiva mantrāntarāṇām āvirbhāvāt* /)

15. As earlier, Jīva has here failed to cite the initial line of this *Agni Purāṇa* verse, and has given a reading of the second line which differs substantially from available editions of the text. The difficulty of the reading presented by Jīva is vouched for by the numerous alternate explanations offered by R. M. The Ānandāśrama version of these two verses runs as follows: *evaṃ sandhyāvidhiṃ kṛtvā gāyatrīṃ ca japet smaret / gāyañ śiṣyāṇy atas trayet bhāryāṃ* (*kāyaṃ*) *prāṇāṃs tathaiva ca // tataḥ smṛteyaṃ gāyatrī sāvitrīyaṃ tato yataḥ / prakāśanāt sā savitur vāgrūpatvāt sarasvatī //* (Ag.P. 216/1,2). ("After thus performing his Sandhyā rites, one should repeat and meditate on the *Gāyatrī*. By singing the *Gāyatrī*, one protects his disciples, his wife (or his body), and his vital forces as well; therefore is it called the *Gāyatrī* (from the roots *gai*, to sing, and *trai*, to protect). Since it enlightens, it is called *Sāvitrī*; and since Savitṛ has speech as its essence, the *Gāyatrī*, or *Sāvitrī*, is also called *Sarasvatī*.") R.M., obviously familiar with a similar reading of these two verses, also derives the meaning of the name *Gāyatrī* from the roots *gai* and *trai*. He writes, "It sings and it protects; hence is it called *Gāyatrī*." (*gāyati trāyati ceti gāyatrīti paryavasitam*/)

16. *vistarabhiyā*: In the previous section (22a), Jīva interpreted the phrase *śatavicchedasaṃyutaḥ* to mean "having 335 *adhyāyas*". His hesitation in defending that interpretation here is probably, as Sitanath Goswami suggests, based on the fact that Śrīdhara, in his *Bhāgavata* commentary, characterizes the *Bhāgavata* as having only 332 *adhyāyas*. Thus, rather than contradict Śrīdhara and get involved in a lengthy discussion, Jīva chooses to leave the phrase uncommented on here. (Jīva: 1967: 44.)

17. *hemasiṃhasamanvitam* : This expression, quoted earlier in section 19 as belonging to Ma.P. 53/22, is also found in Bh.P. 12/13/13 in an identical verse. Although the verses are the same, the contexts are different, and whereas Śrīdhara's interpretation of this expression as meaning "mounted on a throne of gold" is appropriate for the *Bhāgavata* verse, it is not necessarily so in the verse cited by Jīva. (Cf. T. S. 19, footnote 1)

23) ata eva satsv api nānāśāstreṣv etad evoktam kalau naṣṭadṛśām eṣa purāṇārko 'dhunoditaḥ / iti / arkatārūpakeṇa tadvinā nānyeṣāṃ samyagvastuprakāśakatvam iti pratipadyate / yasyaiva śrīmadbhāgavatasya bhāṣyabhūtam śrihayaśīrṣapañcarātre śāstraprastāve gaṇitaṃ tantrabhāgavatābhidhaṃ tantram / yasya sākṣācchrīhanumadbhāṣyavāsanābhāṣyasambandhoktividvatkāmadhenutattvadīpikābhāvārthadīpikāparamahaṃsapriyāśukahṛdayādayo vyākhyāgranthāḥ tathā muktāphalaharilīlābhaktiratnāvalyādayonib andhāś ca vividhā eva tattanmataprasiddhamahānubhāvakṛtā virājante / yad eva ca hemādrigranthasya dānakhaṇḍe purāṇadānaprastāve matsyapurāṇīyatallakṣaṇadhṛtyā praśastam / hemādripariśeṣakhaṇḍasya kālanirṇaye ca kaliyugadharmanirṇaye kaliṃ sabhājayanty āryāḥ ityādikaṃ yadvākyatvenotthāpya yatpratipāditadharma eva kalāv aṅgīkṛtaḥ/ atha yad eva kaivalyam apy atikramya bhaktisukhavyāhārādiliṅgena nijamatasyāpy upari virājamānārthaṃ matvā yad apauruṣeyaṃ vedāntavyākhyānaṃ bhayād acālayataiva śaṅkarāvatāratayā prasiddhen avakṣyamānasvagopanādihetukabhagavadājñāpravartitādvayavādenāpi tanmātravaıṇitaviśvarūpadarśanakṛtavrajeśvarīvismayaśrīvrajakumārīvasanacauryādikaṃ govindāṣṭakādau varṇayatā taṭasthībhūya nijavacaḥsāphalyāya spṛṣṭam iti //

23) Thus, even though there exists a variety of scriptures, it is the *Bhāgavata* alone which is described as follows: "This Purāṇa has risen like the sun for those bereft of sight in the Kali Yuga." (Bh.P. 1/3/44) It is thus demonstrated that, aside from the sun-like *Bhāgavata*, no other scripture is capable of properly illuminating reality.

The Tantra known as *Tantrabhāgavata* is considered, in the section of the *Hayaśīrṣapañcarātra* which classifies scriptures, to represent a virtual commentary on the *Bhāgavata*. Actual commentaries on the *Bhāgavata* include the *Hanumadbhāṣya*, *Vāsanābhāṣya*, *Sambandhokti*, *Vidvatkāmadhenu*, *Tattvadīpikā*, *Bhāvārthadīpikā*, *Paramahaṃsapriyā*, *Śukahṛdaya*, etc. There also exists[1] a variety of Nibandhas,[2] composed by distinguished authors, well-known for their particular interpretations, such as the *Muktāphala*, *Harilīlā*, *Bhaktiratnāvalī*, etc. The *Bhāgavata* is also praised in the *Dānakhaṇḍa* of Hemādri's *Caturvargacintāmaṇi*, in the section dealing with the gift of Purāṇas, as embodying the characteristics mentioned in the *Matsya Purāṇa* (53/20-23). And in the *Pariśeṣakhaṇḍa* of the same work by Hemādri, in determining the *dharma* appropriate to the Kali Yuga, in the *Kālanirṇaya* section, the *dharma* which the *Bhāgavata* propounds for the Kali Yuga is accepted, and the *Bhāgavata* verse, 11/5/36 quoted: "The noble ones praise the Kali Yuga..."[3]

Śaṅkara, however, commonly accepted to be an *avatāra* of Śiva, realized the significance of the *Bhāgavata*, characterized by utterances concerning the joys of *bhakti* which surpass even the joy of liberation, to be superior to his own doctrines, and was afraid to upset the views found in this divinely composed exposition on Vedānta. As will be explained later, he propagated the doctrine of Advaita at the command of *bhagavat*, in order that the latter's true nature might remain hidden. Still, Śaṅkara desired his own words to be fruitful, and so touched on the *Bhāgavata* indirectly, by describing in such works as his *Govindāṣṭaka* etc. certain events found only in the *Bhāgavata*, such as Yaśodā's amazement at the vision of the universal form (of Kṛṣṇa), Kṛṣṇa's theft of the Gopī's clothes, etc.[4]

1. *virājante*: B. D. interprets this to mean "currently available" (*samprati pracarantītyarthaḥ* /), implying that there are others which are no longer available.

2. *nibandhāḥ* : R. M. defines these Nibandhas, or digests, as "works which gather together those portions of a text which embody its significance." (*nibandhas tattātparyavarṇātmakatadekadeśasaṃgrahaḥ*/)

3. *yatpratipāditadharmaḥ*: B. D. writes that the *dharma* for the Kali Yuga is characterized by Kṛṣṇa *saṃkīrtana*. (*tatpratipādito dharmaḥ kṛṣṇasaṃkīrtanalakṣaṇaḥ*/) This interpretation is based on the second line of the *Bhāgavata* verse cited by Jīva (Bh.P. 11/5/36): *yatra saṃkīrtanenaiva sarvaḥ svārtho 'bhilabhyate.* ("...wherein one attains his desired end through the practice of *saṃkīrtana* alone.")

4. B. D. explains the import of this paragraph as follows: "Śaṅkara reflected, 'I am in charge of the dissolution of the universe, and am the devotee of Hari. I have honored his command by commenting on the Upaniṣads etc. in such a way as to distort their real meaning. If I were to disturb the meaning of his beloved *Bhāgavata* as well, the Lord would be angry with me. So, better that it not be disturbed. But then, I will be depriving myself of both wisdom and joy, so I must somehow make contact with it.' Thinking thus, he incorporated in his own poetry certain events described only in the *Bhāgavata*, such as the vision of the universal form etc. This shows that Śaṅkara also respected the *Bhāgavata*, thereby demonstrating the fact that it is universally

honored." (*pralayādhikārī khalu harer bhakto 'ham upaniṣadādi vyākhyāya tatsiddhāntaṃ vilāpya tasyājñāṃ pālitavān evāsmi / atha tadatipriye śrībhāgavate 'pi cālite sa prabhur mayi kupyed ato na tac cālyam evaṃ sati me sārajñatā sukhasampac ca na syād ataḥ kathaṃcit tat sparśanīyam iti tanmātroktaṃ viśvarūpadarśanādi svakāvye nibabandheti tena cādṛtaṃ tad iti sarvamānyaṃ śrībhāgavatam iti/*)

R. M. explains the import of this paragraph by citing the following two verses from the *Padma Purāṇa*: (Hari to Śiva) "You may publicize yourself, but not me. Turn people away from me by composing your own scriptures. Keep me hidden, for in that way creation will go on uninterruptedly." (*prakāśaṃ kuru cātmānam aprakāśaṃ ca māṃ kuru / svāgamaiḥ kalpitais tvaṃ ca janān madvimukhān kuru / māṃ ca gopaya yena syāt sṛṣṭir eṣottarottarā // Uttara Khaṇḍa* 62/31); and (Śiva to Pārvatī) "The false doctrine of Māyāvāda is said to be Buddhism in disguise. O Devī, it was I alone who spread that doctrine in the Kali Yuga, assuming the form of a *brāhmaṇa*." (*māyāvādam asacchāstraṃ pracchannaṃ bauddham ucyate / mayaiva vihitaṃ devi kalau brāhmaṇamūrtinā // Uttara Khaṇḍa* 25/7)

(24) yad eva kila dṛṣṭvā sākṣāt tatśiṣyatāṃ prāptair api śrī madhvācāryacaraṇair vaiṣṇavamate praviśya vaiṣṇavāntarāṇāṃ tacchiṣyāntarapuṇyāraṇyādirītikavyākhyāpraveśaśaṅkayā tatra tātparyāntaraṃ likhadbhir vartmopadeśaḥ kṛta iti ca sātvatā varṇayanti / tasmād yuktam uktaṃ tatraiva prathamaskandhe

tad idam grāhayām āsa sutam ātmavatāṃ varam //
sarvavedetihāsānāṃ sāraṃ sāraṃ samuddhṛtam /

dvādaśe

sarvavedāntasāraṃ hi śrībhāgavatam iṣyate /
tadrasāmṛtatṛptasya nānyatra syād ratiḥ kvacit //

tathā prathame

nigamakalpataror galitaṃ phalaṃ
śukamukhād amṛtadravasaṃyutam /
pibata bhāgavataṃ rasam ālayaṃ
muhur aho rasikā bhuvi bhāvukāḥ //

ata eva tatraiva

yaḥ svānubhāvam akhilaśrutisāram ekam
adhyātmadīpam atititīrṣatāṃ tamo 'ndham /
saṃsāriṇāṃ karuṇayāha purāṇaguhyaṃ
taṃ vyāsasūnum upayāmi guruṃ munīnām // iti /

śrībhāgavatamataṃ tu sarvamatānām adhīśarūpam iti sūcakam/ sarvamunīnāṃ sabhāmadhyam adhyāsyopadeṣṭṛtvena teṣāṃ gurutvam api tasya tatra suvyaktam //

24) Tradition has it[1] that after seeing this same *Bhāgavata*,[2] the revered[3] Madhvācārya embraced the views of the Vaiṣṇavas,

even though himself a direct disciple of Śaṅkara;[4] and fearing that other Vaiṣṇavas might fall under the influence of commentaries written by Śaṅkara's other disciples,[5] such as Puṇyāraṇya etc.,[6] wrote a different *tātparya*[7] pointing out the true path: thus is it described by the Sātvatas.[8]

The following statements, found in the *Bhāgavata* itself, are therefore appropriate.[9] From the first *skandha*: " (Vyāsa) imparted this *Bhāgavata* to his son (Śuka), the best of the self-controlled, representing the essential extracts from all the Vedas and Itihāsa." (Bh.P. 1/3/41, 42)

And in the twelfth *skandha*: "The *Bhāgavata* is considered to represent the essence of all Vedānta. He who is satiated by its nectar-like juice, has no taste for anything else." (Bh.P. 12/13/15)

And in the first *skandha*: "O Connoisseurs of taste here on earth, drink again and again, for all your days, the juice of the *Bhāgavata*, the ripe fruit fallen from the wish-fulfilling tree of the Vedas, whose nectar-like juice flows from the lips of Śuka (like the juice of a ripe fruit from the mouth of a parrot)."[10] (Bh.P. 1/1/3)

Thus, in the same *skandha*: "I seek refuge with (Śuka), the son of Vyāsa and most venerable of sages,[11] who, out of compassion for worldly beings desirous of going beyond the blinding darkness (of ignorance), recited the 'secret one' among Purāṇas, of uncommon majesty,[12] the essence of all Śruti, unparalleled, and the illuminator of Self-knowledge." (Bh.P. 1/2/3) It is thus indicated that the doctrines found in the *Bhāgavata* are the overlord, as it were, of all other doctrines.

Śuka took his seat in the midst of the assembly of all the sages, and fully exhibited his superiority over them by assuming the role of preceptor.[13]

1. *kila* : The particle *kila*, though virtually untranslatable, carries the implication that this statement is based either on an older tradition, or second-hand information. The closing words of this line, *iti ca sātvatā varṇayanti*, are further evidence that Jīva is referring here to older beliefs, the truth of which he apparently accepts, but is unable to verify.

2. *yad eva* : The use of a relative pronoun followed by the adverb *eva* is evidence that the reference is to the *Bhāgavata*, since relative pronouns were similarly used in the previous section to indicate the *Bhāgavata* (e.g. *yasyaiva*, *yasya*, *yad eva*); and some manuscripts actually read *śrībhāgavatam* for *yad*. B.D.,

however, interprets the pronoun to refer to the previous section in general. He writes, "The meaning is, 'having realized that Śaṅkara did not simply avoid the *Bhāgavata*, but actually respected it.' " (*śaṅkareṇa naitad vicālitaṃ kintu ādṛtam eveti vibhāvyetyarthaḥ* /)

3. *śrīmadhvācāryacaraṇaiḥ* : B. D. writes that the use of the plural number indicates Jīva's extreme respect for Madhva, based on the fact that Madhva was the original propounder of the doctrines accepted by Jīva. (*atyādarasūcakabahutvanirdeśaḥ svapūrvācāryatvād iti bodhyam* /)

4. *sākṣāt tacchiṣyatāṃ prāptair api* : Although this phrase is not found in all editions, it is accepted here on the strength of R.M.'s commentary. He writes, "discipleship with him, i.e. with Śaṅkara". (*tacchiṣyatāṃ śaṅkarācāryaśiṣyatām*) Moreover, the use of the adjective *antara* in the compound beginning *tacchiṣyāntra* ("his, i.e. Śaṅkara's, *other* disciples") would be meaningless in the absence of this phrase. We also find a similar phrase in section 28, although also not found in all editions, *śrīmacchaṅkarācāryaśiṣyatāṃ labdhvāpi*, providing further evidence for the correctness of this reading.

5. *tacchiṣyāntara* : Not only does B.D. not comment on the above phrase, he also ignores the implication of the word *antara* ("other") in this compound, commenting only on *tacchiṣya* and *puṇyāraṇyādi* etc. He writes, "The *Bhāgavata* was falsely explained by his disciples, Puṇyāraṇya etc." (*tacchiṣyaiḥ puṇyāraṇyādibhir etad anyathā vyākhyātam*)

6. *puṇyāraṇyādi* : Although there is no *Bhāgavata* commentary associated with the name of Puṇyāraṇya currently available, Jīva does refer to it in other volumes of the *Bhāgavatasandarbha*, often in conjunction with the *Bhāgavata* commentary of the Advaitin, Citsukha. B. N. K. Sharma accepts both of these commentaries as authentic and earlier than Madhva's *Bhāgavatatātparya*. He further states, "The evidence furnished by Madhva in his B. T. shows that he was contending with powerfully established Advaitic commentaries on the Purāṇa. His comments, being as usual, too brief, it is not possible to fix the identity of those assailed by him." (Sharma: 1960: 96, 169)

7. *tātparyāntaram*: B. D. takes this to mean "an interpretation different from that of the others, showing the import of the *Bhāgavata* to rest on *bhagavat*, and not on the attributeless *brahman*." (*nirguṇacinmātraparam...tātparyāntaraṃ bhagavatparatārūpaṃ tato 'nyat tātparyam*) It is also possible that Jīva is referring to Madhva's other famous commentary containing the word *tātparya* in its title, the *Bhāratatātparya*.

8. *sātvatāḥ* : Neither B. D. nor R. M. comments on Jīva's reference to the Sātvatas in this section. In its technical sense, the term may refer to a particular group of Bhāgavatas mentioned in the *Nārāyaṇīya* section of the *Mahābhārata*. However, since the word *sātvata* occurs twice in T. S. (sections 26 and 30), both times as part of *Bhāgavata* verses, and both times in a general sense, as meaning "related to Kṛṣṇa", it seems safe to assume that Jīva is using the term here as a simple synonym for "Vaiṣṇava".

In any event, the tradition that Madhva was a direct disciple of Śaṅkara is one which both Jīva and R. M. apparently respect, despite the fact that a gap of a few hundred years must have existed between the two great teachers, and that the tradition mentioned here is not acknowledged by the followers of either Madhva or Śaṅkara. B. D., on the other hand, is not even willing to recognize the reference to this tradition in this section of T. S., as seen in his failure to comment on the phrase *tacchiṣyatāṃ prāptair api* (which, as the earlier of the two commentators, he must have been aware of) or on the adjective *antara*. (Cf. footnotes 4 and 5 above.)

B. D. probably had good reasons for remaining silent on this question. For one thing, because of his early association with the Mādhva school, he must have been familiar with their own biographical literature on Madhva, according to which accounts, Madhva was formally initiated into *sannyāsa* by an Advaitin named Acyutaprekṣa. Later, while on pilgrimage to Badarī, Madhva is said to have had the direct vision of Vyāsa, by virtue of which he was empowered to establish the Brahma Sampradāya. Thus, Jīva's account of Madhva's initiation is in direct contradiction to the accounts of the Mādhvas. Furthermore, B. D.'s own claims regarding Caitanya's affiliation with the Mādhva Sampradāya would lose all their force were Madhva's own spiritual descent to be traced back only as far as Śaṅkara, since the legitimacy of the Mādhva Sampradāya stems from its ability to trace its roots back to Nārāyaṇa, by way of Brahmā, Nārada, Vyāsa, and Madhva. Thus, B. D.'s silence here also represents a desire to protect his own claims regarding Caitanya's affiliation with the Mādhva Sampradāya, claims which played such an important role in his teachings and sectarian activities. It may also be speculated that B.D.'s unhappiness with the phrases in this section concerning Madhva's relationship to Śaṅkara played an instrumental role in their subsequent deletion in many manuscripts, and that, were it not for R. M.'s mention of such phrases in his commentary, there might be no record that they ever existed today.

Even accepting the phrases commented on by R. M., which greatly improve the reading of this line, it seems clear that the reading is defective in other respects. For one thing, there is the problematic use of the conjunction *ca* following *iti*, implying a second statement also followed by *iti*. Also, R. M. comments on a phrase beginning *yasyaiva* which is not, however, found in the text. From his commentary, it seems that the missing phrase was in connection with Madhva's *tātparya* on the *Bhāgavata* (*yasyaiva*), explaining it as an interpretation of complete statements, as opposed to a word-by-word commentary, or *bhāṣya*. (*yasyaivetyādau yadpadānām uttaravākyasthatayā na tatpadāpekṣeti*/)

9. *tasmāt* : Despite the controversial nature of the opening line of this section, it is clear from Jīva's use of the word *tasmāt* ("therefore") that he was primarily interested in showing the great appeal of the *Bhāgavata*, and was not trying to make any statement of importance regarding sectarian questions.

10. *śukamukhāt* : There is a pun here on the word *śuka*, indicating both a parrot and the son of Vyāsa, Śuka. The metaphor employed in this verse is based on the reputation parrots have for eating only the ripest and sweetest fruits.

11. *guruṃ munīnām* : R. M. writes that Śuka is referred to as "guru" here due to his superior wisdom, and not because he gave instructions to the sages. (*gurutvaṃ jñānātiśayanaṃ na tūpadeṣṭṛtvam*)

12. *svānubhāvam* : B. D. glosses *asādhāraṇaprabhāvam*.

13. *upadeṣṭṛtvena* : R. M. interprets this to mean "as the preceptor of Parikṣit." (*parikṣitaṃ praty upadeṣṭṛtvenetyarthaḥ* /) The reason for R. M.'s insistence on this point is the fact that both Vyāsa and Nārada, Śuka's guru and grand-guru, were both present there. (Cf. section 26)

25) yataḥ

tatropajagmur bhuvanaṃ punānā
mahānubhāvā munayaḥ saśiṣyāḥ /
prāyeṇa tīrthābhigamāpadeśaiḥ
svayaṃ hi tīrthāni punanti santaḥ //
atrir vasiṣṭhaś cyavana śaradvān
ariṣṭanemir bhṛgur aṅgirāś ca /
parāśaro gādhisuto 'tha rāma
utathya indrapramadedhmavāhau //
medhātithir devala ārṣṭiṣeṇo
bharadvājo gautamaḥ pippalādaḥ /
maitreya aurvaḥ kavaṣaḥ kumbhayonir
dvaipāyano bhagavān nāradaś ca//
anye ca devarṣibrahmarṣivaryā
rājarṣivaryā aruṇādayaś ca /
nānārṣeyapravarāṃs tān sametān
abhyarcya rājā śirasā vavande //
sukhopaviṣṭeṣv atha teṣu bhūyaḥ
kṛtapraṇāmaḥ svacikīrṣitaṃ yat /
vijñāpayām āsa viviktacetā
upasthito 'gre nigṛhītapāṇiḥ //

ityādyanantaram

tataś ca vaḥ pṛcchyam idam vipṛcche
viśrabhya viprā itikṛtyatāyām /
sarvātmanā mriyamāṇaiś ca kṛtyaṃ
śuddhaṃ ca tatrāmṛśatābhiyuktaḥ //

iti pṛcchati rājñi

tatrābhavad bhagavān vyāsaputro
yadṛcchayā gām aṭamāno 'napekṣaḥ /
alakṣyaliṅgo nijalābhatuṣṭo
vṛtaś ca bālair avadhūtaveṣaḥ //

tataś ca pratyutthitās te munayaḥ svāsanebhyaḥ ityādyante

sa saṃvṛtas tatra mahān mahīyasāṃ
brahmarṣirājarṣisurarṣivaryaiḥ /
vyarocatālaṃ bhagavān yathendur
graharkṣatārānikaraiḥ parītaḥ //

ity uktam //

25) For it is said:[1] "The world-purifying, high-souled sages went there with their disciples: Atri, Vasiṣṭha, Cyavana, Śaradvat, Ariṣṭanemi, Bhṛgu, Aṅgiras, Parāśara, Viśvāmitra (the son of Gādhi), Rāma, Utathya, Indrapramada, Idhmavāha, Medhātithi, Devala, Āṛṣṭiṣeṇa, Bharadvāja, Gautama, Pippalāda, Maitreya, Aurva, Kavaṣa, Kumbhayoni, Dvaipāyana (Vyāsa), the venerable Nārada, as well as other *devarṣis*, *brahmarṣis*, and *rājarṣis*, including Aruṇa and others—for often holy men, on the pretext of making pilgrimage to a holy place, actually purify those places by their own presence. King Parikṣit welcomed the assembled chiefs of the various holy clans, worshipping them with bowed head. And the wise king again saluted the sages who were filled with joy, and, standing before them with joined palms, informed them of his intention." (Bh.P. 1/9/12)

Then (the king said): "Thus, O wise ones, having confided in you fully, let me ask a pressing question concerning duty. What pure action should be performed with all one's soul by those who are about to die? Please consider this jointly among yourselves." (Bh.P. 11/9/24)

As the king was asking this question: "(Śuka), the son of Vyāsa, appeared, wandering about the earth at will, free from care, bearing no distinguishing marks, content within himself,[2] in the garb of an *avadhūta*, and surrounded by children." (Bh.P. 11/12/25)

And then: "The sages all rose from their seats..." and "that most noble Bhagavān Śuka, surrounded there by these most eminent *brahmarṣis*, *rājarṣis*, and *surarṣis*, shone brilliantly, like the moon surrounded by clusters of planets, constellations, and stars." (Bh.P. 1/9/28, 30)

1. *yataḥ..ity uktam* : As B. D. explains, the words *ity uktam* occuring at the end of this section are to be construed with the word *yataḥ* from the beginning of the section. (*yata ity asya ityuktam iti pareṇa sambandhaḥ*) Actually, this entire section is a continuation of section 24, and explains, as B. D. points out, the sense in which Śuka is considered the "guru" of the sages. (*munīnāṃ gurum ity uktaṃ tat katham ity atrāha yata iti* /)

2. *nijalābhatuṣṭaḥ* : B. D. interprets this to mean "content through the gain of his Lord, Kṛṣṇa, the granter of purity." (*nijasya śuddhipūrtikartuḥ svasvāminaḥ kṛṣṇasya lābhena tuṣṭaḥ* /)

26) atra yady api tatra śrīvyāsanāradau tasyāpi guruparamagurū tathāpi punas tanmukhaniḥsṛtaṃ śrībhāgavataṃ tayor apy aśrutacaram iva jātam ity evaṃ śrīśukas tāv apy upadideśa deśyam ity abhiprāyaḥ / yad uktaṃ śukamukhād amṛtadravasaṃyutam iti / tasmād evam api śrībhāgavatasyaiva sarvādhikyam / matsyādīnāṃ yat purāṇādhikyaṃ śrūyate tat tv āpekṣikam iti / aho kiṃ bahunā śrīkṛṣṇapratinidhirūpam evedam / yata uktaṃ prathamaskandhe

kṛṣṇe svadhāmopagate dharmajñānādibhiḥ saha //
kalau naṣṭadṛśām eṣa purāṇārko 'dhunoditaḥ / iti /

ata eva sarvaguṇayuktatvam asyaiva dṛṣṭaṃ dharmaḥ projjhitakaitavo 'tra ityādinā

vedāḥ purāṇaṃ kāvyaṃ ca prabhur mitraṃ priyeva ca /
bodhayantīti hi prāhus trivṛd bhāgavataṃ punaḥ //

iti muktāphale hemādrikāravacanena ca / tasmān manyantāṃ vā kecit purāṇāntareṣu vedasāpekṣatvaṃ śrībhāgavate tu tathā sambhāvanā svayam eva nirastety api svayam eva labdhaṃ bhavati / ata eva paramaśrutirūpatvaṃ tasya / yathoktam

kathaṃ vā pāṇḍaveyasya rājarṣer muninā saha /
saṃvādaḥ samabhūt tāta yatraiṣā sātvatī srutiḥ // iti /

atha yat khalu sarvaṃ purāṇajātam āvirbhāvyetyādikaṃ pūrvam uktaṃ tat tu prathamaskandhagataśrīvyāsanāradasaṃvādenaiva prameyam //

26) Even though Vyāsa, Śūka's guru, and Nārada, his grandguru, were both present there, still, the *Bhāgavata* flowed forth from Śuka's lips in such a manner that it seemed to them as if they had never heard it before. This is the sense in which it is said that Śuka instructed[1] the two of them as well. As it was said, "...whose nectar-like juice flows from the lips of Śuka." (Bh.P. 1/1/3) Thus, the superiority of the *Bhāgavata* is seen in this sense also.[2]

Those statements, then, which one hears regarding the superiority of other Purāṇas, such as the *Matsya* etc., are only relatively true. But what is the need for so much argument ? The *Bhāgavata* is Kṛṣṇa's very own stand-in (on earth). As stated in the first *skandha*: "Now that Kṛṣṇa has returned to his own abode, along with *dharma* and knowledge, etc., this Purāṇa has risen like the sun for those bereft of sight in the Kali Yuga." (Bh.P. 1/3/43, 44)

The *Bhāgavata* is thus seen to be endowed with all virtues, as demonstrated in the verse, "The supreme *dharma*, devoid of all ulterior motive, is found in this *Bhāgavata*..." (Bh.P. 1/1/2) This fact is further demonstrated by the words of Vopadeva in the *Muktāphala*: "The Vedas, Purāṇas, and Kāvya give council like a ruler, a friend, and a beloved, but the *Bhāgavata* is said to give council like all three combined." Thus, even if some consider other Purāṇas to be dependent on the Vedas, the same supposition with regard to the *Bhāgavata* is dispelled by the *Bhāgavata* itself; this is also self-evident. Therefore the *Bhāgavata* represents the highest form of Śruti. As it is said, "How then, my child, did the dialogue between the royal sage Parikṣit and the sage Śuka come about, as a result of which this Sātvatī Śruti became manifest?" (Bh.P. 1/4/7)

And the fact that Vyāsa composed the *Bhāgavata* only after completing all of the other Purāṇas, as stated earlier,[3] can be verified by examining the dialogue between Vyāsa and Nārada, recorded in the first *skandha*.[4]

1. *upadideśa* : R. M. writes that Śuka only "reminded" them (*smārayām āsa*), since they are the ones who taught the *Bhāgavata* to him. As an alternate explanation, R. M. writes that it was Śuka's expertise in delivering his charming exposition which he taught to Vyāsa and Nārada. (*deśyaṃ madhuravyākhyānakauśalyam upadideśaivetyarthaḥ* /)

2. *evam api*: B. D. explains, "insofar as its narrator, Śuka, is superior to all". (*tadvaktuḥ śukasya sarvagurutvenāpītyarthaḥ* /)

3. Cf. section 19.

4. The reference is to the 5th and 6th *adhyāyas* of the first *skandha* of the *Bhāgavata*.

27) tad evaṃ paramaniḥśreyasaniścayāya śrībhāgavatam eva paurvāparyāvirodhena vicāryate / tatrāsmin sandarbhaṣaṭkātmake granthe sūtrasthānīyam avatārikāvākyaṃ viṣayavākyaṃ śrībhāgavatavākyam / bhāṣyarūpā tadvyākhyā tu samprati madhyadeśādau vyāptān advaitavādino nūnaṃ bhagavanmahimānam avagāhayituṃ tadvādena karvuritalipīnāṃ paramavaiṣṇavānāṃ śrīdharasvāmicaraṇānāṃ śuddhavaiṣṇavasiddhāntānugatā cet tarhi yathāvad eva vilikhyate / kvacit teṣām evānyatradṛṣṭavyākhyānusāreṇa draviḍādideśavikhyātaparamabhāgavatānāṃ teṣām eva bāhulyena tatra vaiṣṇavatvena prasiddhatvāt śrībhāgavata eva

kvacit kvacin mahārāja draviḍeṣu ca bhūriśaḥ /
ity anena prathitamahimnāṃ sākṣācchrīprabhṛtitaḥ pravṛtta-sampradāyānāṃ śrīvaiṣṇavābhidhānāṃ śrīrāmānujabhagavat-pādaviracitaśrībhāṣyādidṛṣṭamataprāmāṇyena mūlagrantha-svārasyena cānyathā ca / advaitavyākhyānaṃ tu prasiddhatvān nātivitāyate //

27) Therefore, we will examine the *Bhāgavata* alone, observing consistency between the earlier and later portions, in order to determine what is the supreme good. Here, in this composition of six volumes, the introductory remarks will occupy the position of *sūtras*, and the words of the *Bhāgavata*, the subject matter. Our interpretation of the words of the *Bhāgavata*, representing a kind of *bhāṣya*,[1] will be written in accordance with the views of the great Vaiṣṇava, the revered Śrīdhara Svāmin, only when they conform to the strict Vaiṣṇava standpoint, since his writings are interspersed with the doctrines of Advaita so that an appreciation for the greatness of *bhagavat* may be awakened in the Advaitins who nowadays pervade the central regions etc.[2] In some places we will follow Śrīdhara's interpretations found elsewhere.[3] In other instances, our interpretation will be based on the doctrines found in the writings of the venerable Rāmānuja, such as his *Śrībhāṣya* etc., (adhered to) by the Śrī Vaiṣṇavas, whose renowned *sampradāya* has originated from the goddess Śrī herself, and who are celebrated as great Bhāgavatas of the Draviḍa region etc.; for as the *Bhāgavata* itself states, there are many in this area well known as Vaiṣṇavas: "O Great King, some (devotees of Nārāyaṇa) can be found here and there, but their numbers are great in the Draviḍa regions."[4] (Bh.P. 11/5/39) And in some instances, our interpretations will differ from both (Śrīdhara and Rāmānuja),[5] and will follow the natural sense of the *Bhāgavata*. As the Advaita doctrines are well-known, they need not be delineated here.

1. *bhāṣyarūpa* : Since the *Bhāgavatasandarbha* deals with only selected verses from the *Bhāgavata*, it cannot be considered a full-fledged *bhāṣya*. Jīva's *Kramasandarbha*, which comments on the whole of the *Bhāgavata*, represents his actual *bhāṣya* on that Purāṇa.

2. B. D. considers Śrīdhara a Vaiṣṇava because his commentaries contain remarks to the effect that the form, attributes, manifestations, and abodes of *bhagavat* are eternal, as are the bodies of his attendants,

and that the devotees of *bhagavat* belong to the highest class and are headed towards liberation. (*taṭṭīkāsu bhagavadvigrahaguṇavibhūtidhāmnāṃ tatparṣadatanūnāṃ ca nityokteḥ bhagavadbhakteḥ sarvotkṛṣṭamokṣānuvṛttyor ukteś ca* /) B. D. then likens the Advaita doctrines of Śrīdhara to the meat on the end of a hook, meant to lure fish. (*baḍiśāmiṣārpaṇanyāyenaiva*) R. M. adds that Śrīdhara's attempt to enlighten the Advaitins stems from the fact that he belongs to the same *sampradāya* as they do. (*avagāhayituṃ bodhayituṃ tatsampradāyāntargatatvād iti* /)

3. *teṣām evānyatrādṛṣṭavyākhyā* : Both commentators understand *teṣām* as referring to Śrīdhara, but are not specific regarding the meaning of the word *anyatra* ("elsewhere"). The reference may either be to Śrīdhara's commentaries on the *Viṣṇu Purāṇa* and *Bhagavadgītā*, or to remarks from his *Bhāgavata* commentary on verses other than those cited by Jīva. This latter interpretation may be the correct one since, at least in the *Tattvasandarbha*, no reference is made to either of Śrīdhara's other two commentaries

4. *draviḍādideśa*: R. M. understands the *ādi* in this compound, and the plural ending in the word *draviḍeṣu* to indicate the regions of Karṇāṭa and Teliṅga as well. (*ādinā kārṇāṭatailaṅgādiparigrahaḥ* / *draviḍesv iti bahuvacanena kārṇāṭādiparigrahaḥ* /)

5. *anyathā ca* : The presence of the conjunction *ca* seems to indicate that Jīva's interpretations will also differ from the natural sense of the *Bhāgavata* at times. Since such a statement would not be possible in a work specifically meant to explain the meaning of the *Bhāgavata*, the implications of the conjunction *ca* must be ignored. R. M. accordingly interprets the phrase *anyathā ca* as indicating that Jīva will at times abandon the interpretations of the other commentators in explaining the various *Bhāgavata* verses. (*etena kvacit tattanmataparityāgenāpi vyākhyeyam iti sūcitam* /) B. D. understands this portion in a similar light and writes that it indicates Jīva's promise not to base his comments merely on his own personal opinions, but on accepted authority. (*matkapolakalpanaṃ kiñcid api nāstīti pramāṇopetātra ṭīketyarthaḥ* /)

28) atra ca svadarśitārthaviśeṣaprāmāṇyāyaiva na tu śrīmadbhāgavatavākyaprāmāṇyāya pramāṇāni śrutipurāṇādivacanāni yathādṛṣṭam evodāharaṇīyāni kvacit svayam adṛṣṭākarāṇi ca tattvavādagurūṇām anādhunikānāṃ śrīmacchaṅkarācāryaśiṣyatāṃ labdhvāpi śrībhagavatpakṣapātena tato vicchidya pracurapracāritavaiṣṇavamataviśeṣāṇāṃ dakṣiṇādideśavikhyātaśiṣyopasiṣyībhūtaśrīvijayadhvajabrahmatīrthav – yāsatīrthādivedavedārthavidvadvarāṇāṃ śrīmadhvācāryacaraṇānāṃ śrībhāgavatatātparyabhāratatātparyabrahmasūtrabhāṣyādibhyaḥ saṃgṛhītāni / taiś caivam uktaṃ bhāratatātparye

śāstrāntarāṇi saṃjānan vedāntasya prasādataḥ /
deśe deśe tathā granthān dṛṣṭvā caiva pṛthagvidhān //
yathā sa bhagavān vyāsaḥ sākṣānnārāyaṇaḥ prabhuḥ /
jagāda bhāratādyeṣu tathā vakṣye tadīkṣayā // iti /

tatra taduddhṛtā śrutiś caturvedaśikhādyā purāṇaṃ ca gāruḍādīnāṃ samprati sarvatrāpracaradrūpam aṃśādikaṃ saṃhitā ca mahāsaṃhitādikā tantraṃ ca tantrabhāgavatādikaṃ brahmatarkādikam iti jñeyam //

28) And here, the authoritative words of Śruti, the Purāṇas, etc. will be quoted just as I have seen them; they are meant to establish the validity of the various interpretations presented by me, and not the validity of the words of the *Bhāgavata.* In some cases, I have been unable to personally see certain verses, and so have taken them from the *Bhāgavatatātparya*, *Bhāratatātparya*, and *Brahmasūtrabhāṣya*, etc. of the venerable Madhvācārya,[1] the ancient[2] preceptor of the doctrine of Tattvavāda,[3] who, even after accepting discipleship with the revered Śaṅkarācārya[4], separated himself from him, and siding with the worshippers of *bhagavat,* advanced many distinctively "Vaiṣṇava" doctrines,[5] who was chief among knowers of the Vedas and their meaning, and whose disciples and grand-disciples include Vijayadhvaja, Brahma Tīrtha, Vyāsa Tīrtha, etc.,[6] of great renown in the South and elsewhere.[7] As stated by Madhva in his *Bhāratatātparya*: "Having mastered the other scriptures by the light of Vedānta, and having seen different versions of the text (the *Mahābhārata*) in various parts of the country, I will examine these, and will speak just as Bhagavān Vyāsa, the Lord Nārāyaṇa himself, spoke in the *Mahābhārata* etc."[8] (2/7, 8)

The Śruti texts which will be quoted from Madhva will be the *Caturvedaśikhā* etc.; the Purāṇic texts will include those portions of Purāṇas, such as the *Garuḍa* etc., which are no longer available; the Saṃhitās will include the *Mahāsaṃhitā* etc.; and the Tantras will include the *Tantrabhāgavata* and *Brahmatarka*[9] etc.

1. *śrīmadhvācāryacaraṇānām* : B.D. characterizes Madhva as "our *ācārya*" (*asmadācārya*). In sharp contrast to this, R. M. argues here for the independence of the Caitanya Sampradāya, and the unique nature of its doctrines, which, though not reducible to those of any other *sampradāya,* represent the best features of all of them. (Cf. the chapter on Rādhāmohana for details of this discussion.)

2. *anādhunikānām* : B. D. explains this as meaning "very ancient, a contemporary of Śaṅkara". (*atiprācīnānāṃ śaṅkarasamasamayānām*) His interpretation is somewhat surprising in light of the fact that the *guru-paramparā* found in his *Govindabhāṣya* separates Madhva from Caitanya by only seventeen gurus. On the other hand, B. D. considers Madhva to be an *avatāra* of Vāyu and disciple of Vyāsa, so it is not exactly clear in what sense he considers Madhva to be "ancient". B. D. does mention the tradition of a debate between Madhva and Śaṅkara, at the end of which Vyāsa rejected the views of Śaṅkara in favor of those of Madhva. (*śaṅkareṇa saha vivāde madhvasya mataṃ vyāsaḥ svīcakre śaṅkarasya tu tatyājety aitihyam asti* /) It should be noted that some editions of B. D.'s commentary drop the word *śaṅkarasamasamayānām* ("a contemporary of Śaṅkara"), and read *kenacic chāṅkareṇa* for *śaṅkareṇa*, explaining the debate as having taken place between Madhva and "a certain follower of Śaṅkaıa". However, as the former tradition is noted in other sources as well (cf. Wilson: 1976: 141; and Vasu: 1912: app. II, p. 4), it is likely that the reading accepted here is the correct one, and that the other reading is an alteration, made either for sectarian reasons, or simply because of the unlikely chronology of the original statement.

3. *tattvavādagurūṇām* : B. D. defines Tattvavāda as "the doctrine that everything is real". (*sarvaṃ vastu satyam iti vādas tattvavādaḥ*) R. M., on the other hand, explains the doctrine as being simply an examination of ontological categories (*tattvavicāra*). Jīva's use of this particular term to indicate the Mādhva school is of some interest, in view of the fact that this is the term employed in the *Caitanya Caritāmṛta* (m. 9/249-77), in a portion which is highly unflattering to the Mādhva school, wherein Caitanya severely criticizes the doctrines of Madhva and the Tattvavādins.

4. *śrīmacchaṅkarācāryaśiṣyatāṃ labdhvāpi śrībhagavatapakṣapātena tato vicchidya*: Like the similar phrase in section 24, this is also not found in most editions, and is not commented on by B. D. R. M., however, places great emphasis on this phrase, and takes it as a precedent for the founding of the Caitanya Sampradāya. He writes, "Just as Madhva, though a disciple of Śaṅkara, initiated his own independent *sampradāya* by writing commentaries on the *Brahmasūtra* etc., after joining the Brahma Sampradāya, so also Kṛṣṇa Caitanya, though himself an *avatāra* of *bhagavat,* accepted the indispensibility of having a guru and belonging to his *sampradāya,* and initiated his own school through Advaitācārya and other intimate associates..." (*evaṃ śrīmanmadhvācāryo yathā śrīmacchaṅkarācāryaśiṣyo 'pi brahmasampradāyam āśritya brahmasūtrabhāṣyādikaṃ kṛtvā svātantryeṇa sampradāyapravartakaḥ tathā svayaṃ bhagavadavatāro 'pi śrīkṛṣṇacaitanyaḥ svamatam eva tatsampradāyāntargatatvaṃ gurvāśrayaṇasyāvaśyakatvam aṅgīkṛtya pravartitavān svasvarūpaśrīmadadvaitācāryādidvāreti...*/)

Although both Sitanath Goswami (Jīva: 1967: 62) and A. K. Majumdar (1969: 266-67.) take this as reference to Caitanya's initiation with Īśvara Purī, and his consequent entrance into the Mādhva Sampradāya of his *paramaguru,* Mādhavendra, the reference is almost certainly to Caitanya's initiation into *sannyāsa* by the Advaitin, Keśava Bhāratī. For one thing, it is clear that R. M., like Jīva, did not consider either Īśvara Purī or his guru Mādhavendra Purī to be a member of the Mādhva Sampradāya; and there is no sense in which Caitanya may be said to have broken away from the traditions initiated by Mādhavendra and passed on through Īśvara. Caitanya's initiation into *sannyāsa*, on the other hand, was to a large extent a calculated move, carried out to insure the success of his future mission. It is also clear that although Caitanya officially belonged to the Advaitic Bhāratī order, he did not adhere to the doctrines of the Advaitins, nor did he continue their traditions by initiating others into *sannyāsa* and conferring on them the Bhāratī title.

5. *vaiṣṇavamataviśeṣāṇām* : B. D. characterizes these doctrines as follows: "Only *brāhmaṇa* devotees will attain liberation; the *devas* are chief among devotees; Brahmā alone attains union (with *brahman*); and Lakṣmī is a *jīvakoṭi*, or mortal." (*bhaktānāṃ viprāṇām eva mokṣaḥ devā bhakteṣu mukhyāḥ viriñcasyaiva sāyujyaṃ lakṣmyā jīvakoṭitvam ity evaṃ mataviśeṣaḥ* /) It is interesting to note that although B. D. consistently presses for Mādhva affiliation, none of the doctrines mentioned here represents the views of the Gauḍīya Vaiṣṇavas, and it is questionable whether they may be said to accurately represent the views of the Mādhvas either.

6. *vijayadhvajabrahmatīrthavyāsatīrtha* : Most editions mention only the first and last of these three, probably because the name Brahma Tīrtha is not found in any of the lists of Mādhva gurus. However, if we take Brahma Tīrtha as referring to Brahmaṇya (Tīrtha), and Vijayadhvaja as referring to Jayadhvaja, then the three Mādhva gurus mentioned by Jīva are all found to belong to the *guruparamparā* of the Vyāsarāja (Mūla) Maṭha, which seems to have been the source for the *guruparamparās* of B.D. and Karṇapūra (although they both read Jayadharma for Jayadhvaja). This is not surprising when we consider that this was by far the best known of the various Mādhva *guruparamparās*, due to the fact that two of the school's most important authors, Jaya Tīrtha and Vyāsa Tīrtha, belonged to this line. The fact that Jīva mentions the three names found here, without mentioning that of Mādhavendra, seems to indicate that he was either not familiar with Kavi Karṇapūra's *guruparamparā* when he wrote this work, or did not accept it as genuine.

7. *dakṣiṇādideśa* : B. D. interprets this expression to mean that disciples of the Mādhva school, such as Mādhavendra etc., are often found in Bengal also. (*tena gauḍe 'pi mādhavendrādayas tadupaśiṣyāḥ katicid babhūvur ityarthaḥ* /)

8. The *Sarvamūlagranthāḥ* gives the following reading for the first line of these verses: *śāstrāntarāṇi saṃjānan vedāṃś cāsya prasādataḥ* / ("Having mastered the Vedas and other scriptures by his, i.e. Hari's, grace..."). (Madhva: 1971: 23)

9. *brahmatarka* : According to B. N. K. Sharma, the *Brahmatarka* is "quoted only by Madhva, and is not known to us through any other source, or recognized by any other system." (Sharma: 1961a: 331)

29) atha namaskurvann eva tathābhūtasya śrīmadbhāgavatasya tātparyaṃ tadvaktur hṛdayaniṣṭhāparyālocanayā saṃkṣepatas tāvan nirdhārayati

svasukhanibhṛtacetās tadvyudastānyabhāvo
'py ajitaruciralīlākṛṣṭasāras tadīyam /
vyatanuta kṛpayā yas tattvadīpaṃ purāṇaṃ
tam akhilavṛjinaghnaṃ vyāsasūnuṃ nato 'smi//

ṭīkā ca śrīdharasvāmiviracitā śrīguruṃ namaskaroti / svasukhenaiva nibhṛtaṃ pūrṇaṃ ceto yasya saḥ / tenaiva vyudasto 'nyasmin bhāvo bhāvanā yasya tathābhūto 'py ajitasya rucirābhir līlābhir akṛṣṭaḥ sāraḥ svasukhagataṃ dhairyaṃ yasya saḥ / tattvadīpaṃ paramārthaprakāśakaṃ śrībhāgavataṃ yo vyatanuta taṃ nato 'smi ity eṣā / evam eva dvitīye tadvākyam eva prāyeṇa munayo rājan ityādipadyatrayam anusandheyam / atrākhilavṛjinaṃ tādṛśabhāvasya pratikūlam udāsīnaṃ ca jñeyam / tad evam iha sambandhitattvaṃ brahmānandād api prakṛṣṭo ruciralīlāviśiṣṭaḥ śrīmān ajita eva / sa ca pūrṇatvena mukhyatayā śrīkṛṣṇasaṃjña eveti śrībādarāyaṇasamādhau vyaktībhaviṣyati / tathā prayojanākhyaḥ puruṣārthaś ca tādṛśatadāsaktijanakaṃ tatpremasukham eva / tato 'bhidheyam api tādṛśatatpremajanakaṃ tallīlāśravaṇādilakṣaṇaṃ tadbhajanam evety āyātam / atra vyāsasūnum iti brahmavaivartānusāreṇa śrīkṛṣṇavarāj janmata eva māyayā tasyāspṛṣṭatvaṃ sūcitam/ śrīsūtaḥ śrīśaunakam 12/12 //

29) Now,[1] Sūta gives a brief description of the import of this just described *Bhāgavata* to Śaunaka,[2] while offering salutations (to Śuka), by reflecting on the ideal lodged in the heart of its narrator (Śuka): "I bow down to the son of Vyāsa, the destroyer of all sins, whose mind is filled with its own bliss, who, even having cast aside all thoughts, has had his heart drawn toward the enchanting *līlās* of Ajita (i.e. Kṛṣṇa), and who has compassionately unfolded this Purāṇa, revolving around him (Kṛṣṇa), which illumines reality like a lamp." (Bh.P. 12/12/68) According to Śrīdhara's commentary: "He offers salutations to his venerable guru—to him whose mind is filled with its own bliss alone, who has cast aside all thought, i.e. worry, and who, despite being of such a disposition, has had his heart, which steadfastly dwelled in its own bliss, attracted by the enchanting *līlās* of Ajita. 'I bow down to him who unfolded the *Bhāgavata*,

the lamp of truth, the illuminator of the highest reality.'" The three verses from the second *skandha* (Bh.P. 2/1/7-9), uttered by Śuka himself, should also be examined in this connection.[3]

The expression "all sins" in this verse should be understood to signify aversion or indifference to such a feeling (of attraction to Kṛṣṇa).[4] Thus, a related principle is found here, namely that the holy Ajita, distinguished by his enchanting *līlās*, is himself superior to the bliss of *brahman*. And it will become clear (by examining) the *samādhi* of Vyāsa that Ajita, in his fullest aspect, is primarily known as "Śrī Kṛṣṇa".

It thus follows that the goal of life, technically known as *prayojana*, is nothing less than the joy which springs from love of him, engendering attachment of such a kind (as Śuka's) to him, and that the *abhidheya* also is nothing less than the worship of him, characterized by listening to accounts of his divine sport etc., engendering love of such a kind for him. According to the *Brahmavaivarta Purāṇa*, the appellation "Vyāsasūnu" ("the son of Vyāsa") is indicative of the fact that Śuka, due to a boon from Kṛṣṇa, was untouched by *māyā* from his very birth.[5]

1. *atha* : The word *atha* indicates that the preliminary portion of this text, dealing with the standards of knowledge to be applied within, has been concluded, and that the text proper is about to begin. B. D. writes, "The author, having commenced this work with the verse from section 8 describing the subject matter, i.e. the principle of reality known as 'Kṛṣṇa', the means, characterized by devotion for him, and the goal of life, characterized by love for him, introduces this portion with the word *atha*, for the sake of auspiciousness." (*atha yasya brahmeti padyoktaṃ sambandhikṛṣṇatattvaṃ tadbhaktilakṣaṇam abhidheyaṃ tatpremalakṣaṇaṃ pumarthaṃ ca nirūpayatā padyena tāvad granthaṃ pravartayan granthakṛd avatārayati atheti maṅgalārtham*/)

2. *nirdhārayati...śrīsūtaḥ śrīśaunakam* : As both B. D. and R. M. explain, the two names found at the end of this section are to be taken with the verb *nirdhārayati*. This system is used throughout the *Bhāgavatasandarbha* by Jīva to indicate the conclusion of his discussion of a particular *Bhāgavata* verse, or series of verses. In each case, the name of the speaker of the verse is accompanied by two figures, indicating the *skandha* and *adhyāya* in which the verses occur. Jiva writes: *tatra vyākhyāsamāptāv aṅkavinyāsaviśeṣasyāyam arthaḥ dvādaśaskandhe dvādaśādhyāye śrīsūtaḥ* /.

3. The verses in question read as follows:
prāyeṇa munayo rājan nivṛttā vidhiṣedhataḥ /
nairguṇyasthā ramante sma guṇānukathane hareḥ //
idaṃ bhāgavataṃ nāma purāṇaṃ brahmasammitam /
adhītavān dvāparādau pitur dvaipāyanād aham //

pariniṣṭhito 'pi nairguṇya uttamaślokalīlayā /
gṛhītacetā rājarṣe ākhyānaṃ yad adhītavān //

"O King, often sages who have gone beyond scriptural injunctions and prohibitions, and who dwell in the realm of the attributeless (*brahman*), delight in relating the virtues of Hari. At the end of the Dvāpara Yuga, I was taught this Purāṇa, the equal of the Vedas and known as the *Bhāgavata*, from my father, Vyāsa. O Parikṣit, though established in the attributeless (*brahman*), my heart was snatched away by the divine sport of the illustrious (Kṛṣṇa), and so I studied (this *Bhāgavata*)." (Bh.P. 2/1/7-9)

4. *tādṛśabhāvasya* : R. M. explains this as indicating aversion or indifference to "the nature of *bhagavat* which attracts the hearts even of those freed from bondage." (*muktānām apy ākarṣakasya bhagavadbhāvasyetyarthaḥ /*)

5. Cf. T. S. 49 for the details of this account of Śuka's birth.

30) tādṛśam eva tātparyaṃ kariṣyamāṇatadgranthapratipādyatattvanirṇayakṛte tatpravaktṛśrībādarāyaṇakṛte samādhāv api saṃkṣepata eva nirdhārayati

bhaktiyogena manasi samyak praṇihite 'male /
apaśyad puruṣaṃ pūrṇaṃ māyāṃ ca tadapāśrayam //
yayā sammohito jīva ātmānaṃ triguṇātmakam /
paro 'pi manute 'narthaṃ tatkṛtaṃ cābhipadyate //
anarthopaśamaṃ sākṣād bhaktiyogam adhokṣaje /
lokasyājānato vyāsaś cakre sātvatasaṃhitām //
yasyāṃ vai śrūyamāṇāyāṃ kṛṣṇe paramapūruṣe /
bhaktir utpadyate puṃsaḥ śokamohabhayāpahā //
sa saṃhitāṃ bhāgavatīṃ kṛtvānukramya cātmajam /
śukam adhyāpayām āsa nivṛttiniratam munim //

tatra

sa vai nivṛttiniratah sarvatropekṣako muniḥ /
kasya vā bṛhatīm etām ātmārāmaḥ samabhyasat //

iti śaunakapraśnānantaraṃ ca

ātmārāmāś ca munayo nirgranthā apy urukrame /
kurvanty ahaitukīṃ bhaktim itthambhūtaguṇo harih //
harer guṇākṣiptamatir bhagavān bādarāyaṇiḥ /
adhyagān mahadākhyānaṃ nityaṃ viṣṇujanapriyaḥ //

bhaktiyogena premṇā

astv evam aṅga bhajatāṃ bhagavān mukundo
muktiṃ dadāti karhicit sma na bhaktiyogam //

ity atra prasiddheḥ / praṇihite samāhite samādhinānusmara tadviceṣṭitam iti taṃ prati śrīnāradopadeśāt / pūrṇapadasya muktapragrahayā vṛttyā

bhagavān iti śabdo 'yaṃ tathā puruṣa ity api /
vartate nirupādhiś ca vāsudeve 'khilātmani //
iti pādmottarakhaṇḍavacanāvaṣṭambhena tathā
kāmakāmo yajet somam akāmaḥ puruṣaṃ param //
akāmaḥ sarvakāmo vā mokṣakāma udāradhīḥ /
tīvreṇa bhaktiyogena yajeta puruṣaṃ param /
ity asya vākyadvayasya pūrvavākye puruṣaṃ paramātmānaṃ prakṛtyekopādhim uttaravākye puruṣaṃ pūrṇaṃ nirupādhim iti ṭīkānusāreṇa ca pūrṇaḥ puruṣo 'tra svayambhagavān evocyate //

30) Sūta similarly[1] gives a concise explanation of the import of the *Bhāgavata*, (this time) in terms of the *samādhi* experienced by its author, wherein the principle which was to be set forth in that work was ascertained: "With his heart purified and perfectly poised through *bhaktiyoga*, he saw the *pūrṇapuruṣa*, with *māyā* resting outside of him.[2] The *jīva*, deluded by that *māyā*, considers himself to be composed of the three *guṇas*, though really beyond them, and consequently comes to grief. Vyāsa composed this *Sātvatasaṃhitā* for those people ignorant of the fact that *bhaktiyoga* directed toward Adhokṣaja (i.e. Kṛṣṇa) directly puts an end to grief. If one but hears this (*Sātvatasaṃhitā*, i.e. *Bhāgavata*), devotion for Kṛṣṇa, the supreme *puruṣa*, will grow in him, putting an end to grief, delusion, and fear. After composing and arranging this *Bhāgavatī Saṃhitā*, Vyāsa taught it to his son (Śuka), then leading a life of renunciation." (Bh.P. 1/7/4-8)

At this point Śaunaka asked, "But why did the sage (Śuka), then leading a life of renunciation, being unconcerned in all situations, and rejoicing in the Self alone, study this vast composition?" (Bh.P. 1/7/9)

In reply to Śaunaka's query, Sūta said, "Although such sages rejoice in the Self alone, and are free from all bonds, still they cherish motiveless devotion for Urukrama (i.e. Kṛṣṇa); such are the virtues of Hari. The venerable son of Vyāsa had his heart captivated by the virtues of Hari and studied this great narrative daily, holding the devotees of Viṣṇu dear to his heart." (Bh.P. 1/7/10-12)[3]

The expression *bhaktiyogena* ("through *bhaktiyoga*") means "through *preman*, or love of God", based on the use of the same term in the following verse: "Bhagavān Mukunda (i.e. Kṛṣṇa) no doubt grants liberation to those who offer him (mere) worship; but he never grants them *bhaktiyoga*." (Bh.P. 5/6/18) *Praṇihite* ("perfectly poised") means "absorbed in *samādhi*", since he had been instructed earlier by Nārada to "recall the events of Kṛṣṇa's *līlā* by means of *samādhi*". (Bh.P. 1/5/13) The word *pūrṇa* ("full" or "perfect") should be understood in its unrestricted sense, based on the statement from the *Uttara Khaṇḍa* of the *Padma Purāṇa*: "The words *bhagavat* and *puruṣa* are both free from limiting adjuncts, and refer to Vāsudeva, the Self of all." And the fact that the *pūrṇapuruṣa* mentioned here refers to *bhagavat* himself is also verified by Śrīdhara's commentary on the following verses: "The desirer of desires should worship Soma; the desireless one, the supreme *puruṣa*. The high-minded ones, whether free from desires, desiring all, or desiring liberation, should worship the supreme *puruṣa* with intense *bhaktiyoga*." (Bh.P. 2/3/9-10) According to Śrīdhara's commentary, the term *puruṣa* from the first of the two preceding verses signifies "the *paramātman*, whose sole limiting adjunct is prakṛti", while the same term from the second verse refers to the "*pūrṇapuruṣa*, free from all limiting adjuncts."[4]

1. *tādṛśam eva* : B. D. explains, "Just as earlier the ideal lodged in the heart of Śuka, the narrator of the *Bhāgavata*, was pointed out, here the ideal lodged in the heart of Vyāsa, the author of the *Bhāgavata*, is pointed out." (*granthavaktuḥ śukasya yatra niṣṭhāvadhāritā tatraiva granthakartur vyāsasyāpi niṣṭhām avadhārayitum avatārayati tādṛśam eveti*)

2. *tadapāśrayām* : R.M. characterizes *māyā* as being "external to *bhagavat*" (*tadbahirbhūtām*), a reference to the Gauḍīya Vaiṣṇava designation of *māyā* as the *bahiraṅgaśakti*. Śrīdhara, however, reads *tadupaśrayām* for *tadapāśrayām*, and interprets it to mean that Vyāsa had the vision of *īśvara* as well as of *māyā*, which is dependent on, and grounded in *īśvara*. (*īśvarāśrayāṃ tadadhīnāṃ māyām*) It is interesting to note that Jīva supports his own interpretation of this verse by citing Śrīdhara's commentary on other verses, but is silent regarding Śrīdhara's interpretation of the verse itself.

3. Jīva now begins a verse by verse explanation of the eight *Bhāgavata ślokas* just quoted, devoting the remaining portion of this section to the first of these. His remarks on this portion of the *Bhāgavata* extend through section 49, and form the basis for all of the major points found in the *Tattvasandarbha*.

4. A comparison of Śrīdhara's commentary on these two verses with his commentary on Bh.P. 1/7/4 shows that it is the first of these two *puruṣas*, the *paramātman*, or *īśvara*, with which Śrīdhara identifies the *pūrṇapuruṣa* of Bh.P. 1/7/4, and not the *puruṣa* "free from all limiting adjuncts", as Jīva maintains.

31) pūrvam iti pāṭhe pūrvam evāham ihāsam iti tatpuruṣasya puruṣatvam iti śrautanirvacanaviśeṣapuraskāreṇa ca sa evocyate / tam apaśyat śrīvedavyāsa iti svarūpaśaktimantam evety etat svayam eva labdhaṃ pūrṇaṃ candram apaśyad ity ukte kāntimantam apaśyad iti labhyate / ata eva

tvam ādyaḥ puruṣaḥ sākṣād īśvaraḥ prakṛteḥ paraḥ /
māyāṃ vyudasya cicchaktyā kaivalye sthita ātmani //

ity uktam / ata eva māyāṃ ca tadapāśrayām ity anena tasmin apa apakṛṣṭa āśrayo yasyāḥ nilīya sthitatvād iti māyāyā na tatsvarūpabhūtatvam ity api labhyate / vakṣyate ca māyā paraity abhimukhe ca vilajjamānā iti / svarūpaśaktir iyam atraiva vyaktībhaviṣyati anarthopaśamaṃ sākṣād bhaktiyogam adhokṣaje ity anena ātmārāmāś ca ity anena ca / pūrvatra hi bhaktiyogaprabhāvaḥ khalv asau māyābhibhāvakatayā svarūpaśaktivṛttitvenaiva gamyate paratra ca te guṇā brahmānandasyāpy uparicaratayā svarūpaśakteḥ paramavṛttitām evārhantīti / māyādhiṣṭhātṛpuruṣas tu tadaṃśatvena brahma ca tadīyanirviśeṣāvirbhāvatvena tadantarbhāvavivakṣayā pṛthaṅ nokte iti jñeyam/ ato 'tra pūrvavad eva sambandhitattvaṃ nirdhāritam //

31) Even if the reading *pūrvam* is accepted (for *pūrṇam*),[1] still *bhagavat* alone is indicated, based on the etymological interpretation of Śruti which derives the essential nature of the *puruṣa* from his statement, "I existed here even prior (*pūrvam*) (to the universe)."

It is self-evident that the phrase "he, i.e. Vyāsa, saw the *puruṣa*" means that he saw him endowed with his *svarūpaśakti* alone, just as when someone says, "he saw the full moon", it is understood that he saw the moon endowed with all its loveliness. Therefore Arjuna said to Kṛṣṇa, "You are the primordial *puruṣa*, the visible Lord, beyond *prakṛti*. Having cast aside *māyā* by means of your *cicchakti* (power of consciousness), you dwell in a state of supreme independence within yourself." (Bh.P. 1/7/23)

Therefore, the phrase *māyāṃ ca tadapāśrayām* indicates that *māyā* does not constitute an essential *śakti* of *bhagavat*, since, having had her ground removed from her (indicated by the preverb *apa*), she remains concealed from *bhagavat*.[2] As stated later, "*Māyā*, embarrassed to remain in his presence, flees..." (Bh.P. 2/7/47)

The nature of this *svarūpaśakti* will now be explained by means of *Bhāgavata* verses 1/7/9 and 1/7/10. In the first of these, the power of *bhaktiyoga* is understood to be a function of the *svarūpa*-

śakti, based on its ability to overpower *māyā*; and in the latter, the virtues (of Hari) deserve to be considered the highest[3] functioning of the *svarūpaśakti*, since they surpass even the bliss of *brahman*.

It should be understood that no separate mention is made of the *puruṣa* which presides over *māyā* (i.e. the *paramātman*), or of *brahman*, since both are considered to fall within the domain of the *pūrṇapuruṣa*, the former as a partial aspect of him, and the latter as his unqualified manifestation. Thus, just as before, a related principle is here set forth.

1. *pūrvam iti pāṭhe* : This is the reading preferred by Śrīdhara, who explains its implications as follows: "He saw the *puruṣa*, i.e. *īśvara*, prior (to seeing *māyā*), i.e. first." (*pūrvaṃ prathamaṃ puruṣaṃ īśvaram apaśyat* /)

2. B. D. characterizes the difference between the *svarūpaśakti* and the *māyāśakti* as that between the king's favorite wife and an attendant who remains outside his door. (*paṭṭamahiṣīva svarūpaśaktiḥ bahirdvārasevikeva māyāśaktir iti ubhayor mahadantaram bodhyam* /)

3. *paramavṛttitām* : The employment of the adjective *parama* ("highest") would seem to indicate a hierarchy within the *svarūpaśakti* itself. However, both B. D. and R. M. treat the two functions as being of equal importance, both representing an essential aspect of the *svarūpaśakti*. (B. D.: *bhagavadbhakter bhagavadguṇāṇāṃ ca svarūpaśaktisārāṃśatvam*; R. M.: *bhakteḥ svarūpabhūtacicchaktisārāṃśatvenaiva...paramavṛttitāṃ sārāṃśavṛttitām*...)

32) atha prākpratipāditasyaivābhidheyasya prayojanasya ca sthāpakaṃ jīvasya svarūpata eva parameśvarād vailakṣaṇyam apaśyad ity āha yayeti / yayā māyayā sammohito jīvaḥ svayaṃ cidrūpatvena triguṇātmakāj jaḍāt paro 'py ātmānaṃ triguṇātmakaṃ jaḍaṃ dehādisaṃghātaṃ manute tanmananakṛtam anarthaṃ saṃsāravyasanaṃ cābhipadyate / tad evaṃ jīvasya cidrūpatve 'pi yayā sammohitaḥ iti manute iti ca svarūpabhūtajñānaśālitvaṃ vyanakti prakāśaikarūpasya tejasaḥ svaparaprakāśanaśaktivat /

ajñānenāvṛtaṃ jñānaṃ tena muhyanti jantavaḥ /

iti śrīgītābhyaḥ / tad evam upādher eva jīvatvaṃ tannāśasyaiva mokṣatvam iti matāntaraṃ parihṛtavān / atra yayā sammohitaḥ ity anena tasyā eva tatra kartṛtvaṃ bhagavatas tatrodāsīnatvam / vakṣyate ca

vilajjamānayā yasya sthātum īkṣāpathe 'muyā /
vimohitā vikatthante mamāham iti durdhiyaḥ // iti /

atra vilajjamānayā ity anenedam āyāti tasyā jīvasammohanaṃ

karma śrībhagavate na rocata iti yady api sā svayaṃ jānāti tathāpi bhayaṃ dvitīyābhiniveśataḥ syād īśād apetasya iti diśā jīvānām anādibhagavadajñānamayavaimukhyam asahamānā svarūpāvaraṇam asvarūpāveśaṃ ca karoti //

32) Then, Vyāsa saw the essential distinction[1] between the *jīva* and *parameśvara* which forms the basis for the *abhidheya* and *prayojana*[2] of this work, as stated earlier.[3] Thus was it described by Sūta in Bh.P. 1/7/5.

"The *jīva*, deluded 'by that', i.e. by *māyā*, considers himself to be 'composed of the three *guṇas*', i.e. to be the insentient aggregate of the body etc., even though as a conscious entity, he is 'beyond', i.e. beyond the insentient combination of the three *guṇas*, and 'consequently', i.e. as a result of that misconception, 'comes to grief', i.e. experiences the misery of repeated birth and death."

Thus, even though the *jīva* is a conscious entity, the phrases "deluded by *māyā*" and "he considers himself (to be composed of the three *guṇas*)" reveal the fact that consciousness, which constitutes his essential nature, is an attribute of the *jīva*, just as the power of illumination, which represents the essential nature of light, is also capable of illuminating both itself and other entities. This view is verified by the words from the *Bhagavadgītā*: "Knowledge is covered by ignorance; hence are beings deluded." (5/15)

Thus, Vyāsa rejected that other doctrine[4] which maintains that it is the limiting adjuncts, or *upādhis*, which constitute the nature of the *jīva*, and it is their destruction which constitutes his liberation.

The phrase "deluded by *māyā*" indicates that she alone is responsible (for deluding *jīvas*), while *bhagavat* remains uninvolved. As stated later, "Foolish people are deluded by *māyā*, who is ashamed to stand in the presence of *bhagavat*, and speak boastingly of 'I' and 'mine'." (Bh.P. 2/5/13) Here, the word "ashamed" indicates that *māyā*, though realizing that her practice of deluding *jīvas* is not pleasing to *bhagavat*, is nevertheless unable to bear the fact that *jīvas* have been ignorantly turning their backs on *bhagavat* from time without beginning—as indicated by the line, "Those who turn away from the Lord experience fear because of their devotion to a second" (Bh.P. 11/2/37)—and so conceals their real nature, and covers it with its opposite.[5]

1. *vailakṣaṇyam* : B. D. explains that the distinction between the *jīva* and *īśvara* is based on their respective eternal attributes, the former being the worshipper and atomic in nature, and the latter being the object of worship and all-pervading. (*jīvasyeti vailakṣaṇyam iti sevakatvasevyatvāṇutvavibhu tvarūpanitya-dharmahetukam* /)

2. *sthāpakam* : R. M. explains that, were the *jīva* and *parameśvara* non-different, then the *abhidheya*, devotional practices, and the *prayojana*, the attainment of love of God, would not be possible. (*abhidheyasya sādhanabhakteḥ* / *prayojanasya premasevāyāḥ sthāpakam iti jīvaparameśvarayor abhede tayor anupapatter iti bhāvaḥ* /)

3. Cf. section 9.

4. *matāntaram* : B. D. attributes the doctrine under attack to Śaṅkara, and characterizes it as follows: "The mind is the *jīva*; the destruction of the mind results in the liberation of the *jīva*." (*antaḥkaraṇaṃ jīvaḥ antaḥkaraṇa-nāśo jīvasya mokṣa iti śaṅkaramataṃ dūṣitam* /) B. D.'s description of this doctrine represents such a distortion of Śaṅkara's actual position that Sitanath Goswami suspects the reading of B. D.'s commentary here to be faulty. (Jīva: 1967: 78) Other instances can be pointed to, however, where B. D. gives similar inaccurate accounts of Śaṅkara's position. (Cf. sections 35-43 in particular.)

5. The two powers of *māyā* referred to here are generally termed *āvaraṇa-śakti* and *vikṣepaśakti*. (Cf. *Vedāntasāra* 51)

33) śrībhagavāṃś cānādita eva bhaktāyāṃ prapañcādhikāriṇyāṃ tasyāṃ dākṣiṇyaṃ laṅghituṃ na śaknoti / tathā tadbhayenāpi jīvānāṃ svasāmmukhyaṃ vāñchann upadiśati

daivī hy eṣā guṇamayī mama māyā duratyayā /
mām eva ye prapadyante māyām etāṃ taranti te //
satāṃ prasaṅgān mama vīryasaṃvido
bhavanti hṛtkarṇarasāyanāḥ kathāḥ /
tajjoṣaṇād āśv apavargavartmani
śraddhā ratir bhaktir anukramiṣyati // iti /

līlayā śrīmadvyāsarūpeṇa tu viśiṣṭatayā tad upadiṣṭavān ity anantaram evāyāsyati anarthopaśamaṃ sākṣād iti / tasmād dvayor api tattatsamañjasaṃ jñeyam / nanu māyā khalu śaktiḥ śaktiś ca kāryakṣamatvaṃ tac ca dharmaviśeṣaḥ tasyā kathaṃ lajjādikam / ucyate evaṃ saty api bhagavati tāsāṃ śaktīnām adhiṣṭhātṛdevyaḥ śrūyante yathā kenopaniṣadi mahendramāyayoḥ saṃvādaḥ / tad āstām prastutaṃ prastūyate //

33) And *bhagavat* is unable to withhold his favor from *māyā*

who, being in charge of creation, has been his devotee from time immemorial. So, desiring that *jīvas* turn within, even if out of fear of *māyā*,[1] he instructs them as follows: "This divine *māyā* of mine, composed of the three *guṇas*, is indeed difficult to transcend. They cross over this *māyā* who take refuge in me alone." (Bh.G. 7/14) "As a result of holy company, conversations concerning my prowess take place, pleasing the heart and ear. By taking part in these, one quickly attains faith in the path of salvation, followed in turn by joy and devotion." (Bh.P. 3/25/25) And as seen in the verse immediately following this,[2] (Bh.P. 1/7/6), *bhagavat* taught this in a special way, by assuming the form of Vyāsa, through his divine sport.[3] Therefore, the respective activities of both (*bhagavat* and *māyā*)[4] should be deemed proper.

But if *māyā* is nothing but a *śakti*, and *śakti* is nothing but the capacity to perform a function, which is itself a kind of attribute, how can you speak of it as possessing such characteristics as embarrassment etc. ?

To this we reply: What you say is true. However, we do find mention in Śruti of the presiding deities of the *śaktis* which reside in *bhagavat*, such as in the dialogue between Indra and Māyā in the *Kena Upaniṣad*. But enough for now. Let us return to the topics already introduced.

1. *tadbhayenāpi* : The construction of this phrase gives the impression that it is *bhagavat* who is afraid of *māyā*. This interpretation, however, makes little sense in this context, and goes against the commentaries of both B.D. and R.M. B.D. explains this phrase as follows: *māyāto yaj jīvānāṃ bhayaṃ tenāpi hetunetyarthaḥ* /.

2. *anantaram*: The reference is to Bh.P. 1/7/5, which has been the topic under discussion in this and the previous section, and which is further analyzed in sections 34-45. Bh.P. 1/7/6, which is briefly referred to in this sentence is not fully discussed until section 46.

3. *līlayā* : B. D. takes this as indicating that Vyāsa is a *līlāvatāra* of *bhagavat* (*līlayeti līlāvatāreṇa*), who took that form specifically to put an end to the misery of *jīvas* by composing the *Bhāgavata*.

4. *tattat* : B. D. identifies these as the deluding activity of *māyā*, and the desire of *bhagavat* to turn the gaze of *jīvas* inward. (*tattad iti mohanaṃ sāmmukhyavāñchā cetyarthaḥ* /)

34) tatra jīvasya tādṛśacidrūpatve 'pi parameśvarato vailakṣaṇyaṃ tadapāśrayām iti yayā sammohita iti ca darśayati//

34) Here, the phrases "*māyā* resting outside of him" (Bh.P. 2/7/4) and "deluded by *māyā*" (Bh.P. 2/7/5)[1] indicate that the *jīva*, even though, like *parameśvara*, being essentially pure consciousness, is nevertheless distinct from *parameśvara*.

1. B. D. explains that the first of these phrases indicates *īśvara* to be the controller of *māyā*, while the second indicates the *jīva* to be controlled by *māyā*. (*īśvarasya māyāniyantṛtvam...jīvasya māyāniyamyatvaṃ ca*/)

B. D. further maintains that the word *apaśyat* ("he saw") from Bh.P. 2/7/4 indictes that Vyāsa also had the realization of the principle of time (*kāla*). He writes: "Due to the occurrence of the word *apaśyat*, *kāla* is also to be understood. Thus, the four *tattvas* (principles), *īśvara*, *jīva*, *māyā*, and *kāla* were realized by Vyāsa in *samādhi*. All of these are eternal....Of these, *īśvara*, being the ground for these *śaktis*, is independent, while the others, the *jīva* etc., are all dependent, being *śaktis* of *īśvara*.... *Īśvara* is all-pervading consciousness; the *jīva* is atomic consciousness; *māyā* is insentient substance composed of the three *guṇas*, *sattva*, *rajas*, and *tamas*; *kāla* is also insentient, but devoid of the three *guṇas*, and represents the basis for all dealings in the past, present, and future. *Karman* (the fifth *tattva*) is also beginningless, but unlike the others is destructible." (*apaśyad ity anena kālo 'py ānītaḥ / tad evam īśvarajīvamāyākālākhyāni catvāri tattvāni samādhau śrīvyāsena dṛṣṭāni / tāni nityāny eva /...īśvaraḥ śaktimān svatantraḥ jīvādayas tu tacchaktayo 'svatantrāḥ/...vibhujñānam īśvaraḥ aṇuvijñānaṃ jīvaḥ/ . sattvādiguṇatrayaviśiṣṭaṃ jaḍaṃ dravyaṃ māyā/ guṇatrayaśūnyaṃ bhūtavartamānādivyavahārakāraṇaṃ jaḍaṃ dravyaṃ tu kālaḥ/ karmāpy anādi vināśi cāsti.. /*)

These five *tattvas* are discussed in even greater detail by B. D. in his *Govinda Bhāṣya* (1/1/1). They also form the subject matter for the *Vedānta-syamantaka*, attributed variously to B. D. and his guru, Rādhādāmodara. The doctrine of five *tattvas* cannot be traced to the writings of the Gosvāmins, and, in fact, goes against the explicit statement of this text, based on the words of the *Bhāgavata*, that the *tattva*, described in section 51 as "non-dual consciousness", admits of no second reality, either similar or dissimilar.

35) yarhy eva yad ekaṃ cidrūpaṃ brahma māyāśrayatābalitaṃ vidyāmayaṃ tarhy eva tanmāyāviṣayatāpannam avidyāparibhūtaṃ cety ayuktam iti jīveśvaravibhāgo 'vagataḥ / tataś ca svarūpasāmarthyavailakṣaṇyena tad dvitayaṃ mitho vilakṣaṇasvarūpam evety āgatam //

35) It is thus erroneous to contend that one and the same *brahman*, pure consciousness itself, is simultaneously the embodiment of knowledge, as it functions as the substratum of *māyā*, as well as overpowered by ignorance, falling under the sway of

that *māyā*.[1] In fact, this is the very sense in which the distinction between *īśvara* and *jīva* is to be understood. It thus follows that, due to the respective differences in their natural capacities,[2] the two (ie. *īśvara* and *jīva*) are essentially distinct.

1. B. D. identifies this as the doctrine of Śaṅkara, and elaborates as follows: "Based on such pronouncements of Śruti as 'One without a second', '*Brahman* is consciousness and bliss', 'It admits of no diversity', etc., the absolute reality is considered to be non-dual, pure consciousness alone, the unqualified *brahman*. But through contact with *ajñāna*, having the two functions of *vidyā* and *avidyā*, and being indefinable, in that it lacks the characteristics of both existence and non-existence, the consciousness of *īśvara*, associated with *vidyā*, and that of the *jīva*, associated with *avidyā*, come into being. When, however, *ajñāna* is removed through the knowledge of one's true nature, then *īśvara* and *jīva* cease to exist, and attributeless, non-dual pure consciousness alone remains. Thus is it explained by the clever Śaṅkara." (*yat tu ekam evādvitīyam vijñānam ānandaṃ brahma nehi nānāsti kiñcana ityādiśrutibhyo nirviśeṣacinmātrādvaitaṃ brahma vāstavam / atha sadasadvilakṣaṇatvād anirvacanīyena vidyāvidyāvṛttikenājñānena sambandhāt tasmād vidyopahitam īśvaracaitanyam avidyopahitaṃ jīvacaitanyaṃ cābhūt / svarūpajñānena nivṛtte tv ajñāne na tatreśvarajīvabhāvaḥ kintu nirviśeṣādvitīyacinmātrarūpāvasthitir bhaved ity āha māyī śaṅkaraḥ /*

B. D. concludes with the apostrophe: "What sin did *brahman* commit that he had to suffer all kinds of confusion and anguish ?" (*kim aparādhaṃ tena brahmaṇā yena vividhavikṣepakleśānubhavabhājanatābhūt /*)

2. *svarūpasāmarthyavailakṣaṇyena* : R. M. interprets this to mean "due to the difference between their respective natural capacities, the one (*īśvara*) having the capacity to effectively control *māyā*, and the other (the *jīva*), the inability to remove the veil of ignorance placed on it by *māyā*." (*svarūpayoḥ svābhāvikayor māyāniyantṛtvaprayojakasāmarthyamāyākṛtāvaraṇanivartanākṣamasāmarthyayor vailakṣaṇyena.../*)

36) na copādhitāratamyamayaparicchedapratibimbatvādivyavasthayā tayor vibhāgaḥ syāt //

36) Nor can the distinction between the two (i.e. *īśvara* and *jīva*) be explained on the basis of limitation by, or reflection in, different grades of adjuncts,[1] etc.

1. *paricchedapratibimba* : B. D. describes these two doctrines as follows: "The large portion, limited by *vidyā*, is *īśvara*, and the small portion, limited by *avidyā*, is the *jīva*, just as the space limited by a pot is designated 'large', and the space limited by a cup, 'small'.... *Īśvara* is the reflection within *vidyā*, and the *jīva*, the reflection within *avidyā*. The one is considered large and the other small, like the reflection of the sun in a lake, and in a pot. Thus

is it described by Śaṅkara." (*tatra vidyayā paricchinno mahān khaṇḍa īśvaraḥ avidyayā paricchinnaḥ kanīyān khaṇḍas tu jīvaḥ / yathā ghaṭenāvacchinnaḥ śarāveṇāvacchinnas cākāśakhaṇḍo mahadalpatāvyapadeśaṃ bhajati / ...vidyāyāṃ pratibimba īśvaraḥ avidyāyāṃ pratibimbas tu jīvaḥ / yathā sarasi raveḥ pratibimbaḥ yathā ca ghaṭe pratibimbo mahadalpatvavyapadeśaṃ bhajate tadvad ity āha śaṅkaraḥ/*)

R. M., more accurately, describes the two doctrines as follows : "Just as, due to the apparent separation of space by the adjuncts of a jar, a space within the jar is created, so also, due to the apparent separation of the *ātman* by the body, the *jīva* comes into being, a separate individual, as it were. According to the second doctrine, the reflection of the sun is due to its association with the various modifications of water; the real sun remains in the sky. No real distinction can be made between the sun and its reflections ; it is the sun itself, situated in the sky, which assumes the variation of the water. Furthermore, the position of other suns (to explain the variety of reflections) is not based on any valid means of knowledge, and only complicates the issue." (*yathā ghaṭādyupādhinā mahākāśavibhāgeneva ghaṭākāśaḥ kriyate evaṃ dehenātmano vibhāgeneva jīvaḥ pṛthag iva kriyate ity evaṃ matam / matāntaraṃ ca sūryasya jalavṛttitvarūpavilakṣaṇasambandhena pratibimbatvaṃ gaganavṛttitvena bimbatvam / na ca tatra bimbapratibimbayor bhedaḥ pāramārthikaḥ gaganasthasūryasyaiva jalavṛttitvasvīkārād jale sūryāntarakalpane gauravān mānābhāvāc ca/*)

37) tatra yady upādher anāvidyakatvena vāstavatvaṃ tarhy aviṣayasya tasya paricchedaviṣayatvāsambhavaḥ / nirdharmakasya vyāpakasya niravayavasya ca pratibimbatvāyogo 'pi upādhisambandhābhāvāt bimbapratibimbabhedābhāvāt dṛśyatvābhāvāc ca / upādhiparicchinnākāśasthajyotiraṃśasyaiva pratibimbo dṛśyate na tu ākāśasya dṛśyatvābhāvād eva //

37) Here,[1] if the limiting adjuncts are objectively real, and not the result of ignorance,[2] then *brahman*, who is beyond the objective realm, cannot be subject to division by them.[3] Furthermore, that which is attributeless, all-pervading, and without "limbs" cannot be reflected, since (what is attributeless) can have no connection with adjuncts, (what is all-pervading) admits of no distinction between the object and its reflection, and (what is without "limbs") cannot be perceived. The reflection of luminous bodies resting in the sky, separated by their own adjuncts, alone can be seen, but never the reflection of the sky itself, for the simple reason that the sky possesses no visible attributes.

1. *tatra* : Both commentators take this as indicating the doctrine of *paricchedavāda*. While the first sentence of this section represents Jīva's criticisms of *paricchedavāda*, the remaining two sentences concern the doctrine of *pratibimbavāda*.

2. *anāvidyakatvena* : B. D. explains, "as a real entity and not the product of ignorance, like the imagined snake superimposed on a rope". (*anāvidyakatvena rajjubhujaṅgavadajñānaracitatvābhāvena vastubhūtatve satītyarthaḥ* /)

3. B. D. writes, "It cannot be the case that *īśvara* and *jīva* are separate portions of *brahman* divided by real adjuncts, like pieces of stone cut by a chisel, since *brahman* is indivisible and without parts." (*na ca ṭaṅkacchinnapāṣāṇakhaṇḍavad vāstavopādhicchinno brahmakhaṇḍaviśeṣa īśvaro jīvaś ca brahmaṇo 'cchedyatvād akhaṇḍatvābhyupagamāc ca...*/)

38) tathā vāstavaparicchedādau sati sāmānādhikaraṇyajñānamātreṇa na tattyāgaś ca bhavet / tatpadārthaprabhāvas tatra kāraṇam iti ced asmākam eva matasammatam //

38) Similarly, if division and reflection are real, then they cannot be negated merely by thinking that the terms *tat* and *tvam* (indicating *īśvara* and *jīva* respectively) refer to one and the same reality (namely, *brahman*).[1] If it is maintained, however, that the extraordinary power of the being denoted by the term *tat*[2] is responsible (for the removal of the limiting adjuncts), then their view concurs with our own.[3]

1. *sāmānādhikaraṇyajñānamātreṇa*: B. D. writes, "The idea that one takes on the nature of *brahman* merely by thinking 'I am *brahman*' is not possible, given the real existence of limiting adjuncts....No wretch, bound in chains, is ever seen to become a king merely by thinking 'I am king'." (*brahmaivāham iti jñānamātreṇa tadrūpāvasthitiḥ syād iti yad abhimataṃ tat khalūpādher vāstavatvapakṣe na sambhavati...na khalu nigaḍitaḥ kaścid dīno rājaivāham iti jñānamātrād rājā bhavan dṛṣṭa itibhāvaḥ*/)

R. M. interprets the compound to mean "merely by accepting the identity between *parameśvara*, indicated by the word *tat*, and the *jīva*, indicated by the word *tvam*, on the strength of the Śruti text, *tat tvam asi* ('You are That')." (*tat tvam asīti śrutyā tatpadārthaparameśvaratvampadārthajīvayor aikyagrahamātreṇetyarthaḥ* /) He adds, "Only if the *upādhis* were considered to be false superimpositions on *brahman* could their destruction be effected through the direct vision of *brahman*; this is the idea." (*brahmaṇy upādher āropitatva eva tatsākṣātkāreṇa tannāśo bhaved itibhāvaḥ*/)

2. *tatpadārthaprabhāvaḥ* : R. M. identifies this as the "power of *parameśvara*, indicated in Śruti by the term *tat*."

3. *asmākam eva matasammatam* : B. D. adds that such an admission would not only amount to an acceptance of Jīva's position, it would also represent a refutation of the Advaitin's own position. (*tathā ca tvanmatakṣatir iti* /) R.M. defines Jīva's position by citing the following words from Śruti: "Liberation is the result of the elimination of any connection with gross or subtle bodies." (*sthūlasūkṣmadehasambandhanāśe jīvānāṃ muktihetuḥ iti śrutisiddham asmākaṃ matam eva...*/)

39) upādher āvidyakatve tu tatra tatparicchinnatvāder apy aghaṭamānatvād āvidyakatvam eveti ghaṭākāśādiṣu vāstavopādhimayataddarśanayā na teṣām avāstavasvapnadṛṣṭāntopajīvināṃ siddhāntaḥ sidhyati ghaṭamānāghaṭamānayoḥ saṅgateḥ kartum aśakyatvāt / tataś ca teṣāṃ tat tat sarvam avidyāvilasitam eveti svarūpam aprāptena tena tena tat tad avasthāpayitum aśakyam //

39) If, on the other hand, the limiting adjuncts are considered to be unreal, then the division etc.[1] which they allegedly effect must also be unreal, since it simply could not take place. Thus, the doctrine of those who base their position on the analogy of the unreal dream state[2] cannot be substantiated with the help of analogies involving real limiting adjuncts, such as jars and space,[3] etc., since no logical connection can be shown to exist between that which obtains and that which does not. And so, these notions of theirs are nothing but a foolish diversion, as it is not possible to establish the existence of various phenomena[4] on the strength of these two theories, which are themselves baseless.[5]

1. *tatparicchinnatvādeḥ* : B. D. takes this to signify both the doctrines of Paricchedavāda (limitation) and Pratibimbavāda (reflection). (*paricchedādivādadvayam*) R. M., on the other hand, understands this section to represent Jīva's refutation of Paricchedavāda alone.

2. *teṣām* : B. D. identifies these individuals as "those who believe in non-dual pure consciousness alone, being intent on establishing the doctrine that one *jīva* alone exists." (*teṣāṃ cinmātrādvaitinām ekajīvavādapariniṣṭhatvāt...*)

3. *ghaṭākāśādiṣu*: B. D. explains this as referring to the Paricchedavāda analogy of space divided by a jar, as well as to the Pratibimbavāda analogy of the sky reflected in a jar of water. (*ghaṭākāśādiṣu ghaṭaparicchinnākāśe ghaṭāmbupratibimbākāśe ca*)

4. *tat tad avasthāpayitum* : R. M. writes, "to account for the variety within phenomenal existence". (*saṃsāravaicitryam*) It may be, however, that the terms *tat* and *tat* refer to *īśvara* and *jīva*, although B. D. also does not interpret them as such.

5. *svarūpam aprāptena tena tena*: B. D. interprets this phrase to mean "by the unproven Paricchedavāda and Pratibimbavāda". (*svarūpam aprāptena asiddhena / tena paricchedavādena / tena pratibimbavādena ca/*) R. M. however, not recognizing this section as dealing with the doctrine of Pratibimbavāda, takes this as meaning "(by *upādhis*) which have no empirical value". (*vyāvahārikasattvam aprāptena*)

As R. M. explains, the Advaitin seeks to refute the objection of inappropriate analogy by maintaining that objects like pots etc., which form the illustrations for their analogies, are also unreal from the ultimate point of view. To this R. M. replies that, though ultimately unreal, such objects nevertheless have an empirical value (*vyāvahārika*), as opposed to the snake in the rope, which has an illusory value (*prātibhāsika*). Since *brahman* is non-empirical, the Advaitin cannot help but admit that division results from illusory adjuncts alone. Thus, analogies involving jars and space cannot be employed; consequently, the Advaitin cannot demonstrate the empirical division of *brahman*. This is the idea. (*yady api tanmate ghaṭāder ākāśasya tatparicchedasya cāvāstavatvāt taddṛṣṭāntatāsambhavaḥ tathāpi mithyābhūtānām api brahmātiriktānāṃ dvividhaṃ sattvaṃ keṣāñcid vyāvahārikaṃ ghaṭādidehādīnāṃ keṣāñcic ca prātibhāsikaṃ yathā rajjusarpāder iti / brahmaṇaś ca niravayatvena nirvikāratvena tadupādher āvidyakatvena ca tatparicchedakasya vyāvahārikasyāghaṭamānatvam iti prātibhāsikapariccheda evāṅgīkāryaḥ iti na ghaṭākāśasya dṛṣṭāntatāsambhavaḥ...vyāvahārikabrahmaparicchedo na sidhyatītyarthaḥ /*)

40) iti brahmāvidyayoḥ paryavasāne sati yad eva brahma cinmātratvenāvidyāyogasyātyantābhāvāspadatvāc chuddhaṃ tad eva tadyogād aśuddhyā jīvaḥ punas tad eva jīvāvidyākalpitamāyāśrayatvād īśvaras tad eva ca tanmāyāviṣayatvāj jīva iti virodhas tadavastha eva syāt / tatra ca śuddhāyāṃ city avidyā tadavidyākalpitopādhau tasyām īśvarākhyāyāṃ vidyeti tathā vidyāvattve 'pi māyikatvam ity asamañjasā ca kalpanā syād ityādy anusandheyam //

40) If one, then, tries to reduce everything to *brahman* and *avidyā* alone, the end result is also a contradictory state of affairs,[2] namely that the one *brahman* which, as pure consciousness, is untainted due to a perfect absence of contact with *avidyā* (ignorance), is none other than the *jīva*, who has become tainted through contact with *avidyā*. Furthermore, this same *brahman* is considered to be *īśvara* when seen as the substratum for *māyā*, which is itself superimposed by *avidyā* belonging to the *jīva*, and is called *jīva*, when seen to fall within the domain of *māyā*, which belongs to *īśvara*. Thus, *avidyā* is said to exist within pure consciousness, and *vidyā* (knowledge) within that consciousness which is known as *īśvara*, and which possesses *upādhis* superimposed by the aforementioned *avidyā*. The unhappy result of all this is that he who is the embodiment of *vidyā* is, nevertheless, held to be the source of illusion. This and other questions merit close scrutiny.

1. B. D. writes that, finding the doctrines of Paricchedavāda and Prati-

bimbavāda unconvincing, the Advaitin will claim that these two doctrines do not represent his actual position, which according to B. D. is Ekajīvavāda, the belief that one self alone exists, and that they were only meant to awaken those of poor understanding. B. D. then characterizes this latter doctrine as follows: "Only one, non-dual, pure-conscious Self exists. Due to *avidyā*, this Self imagines two classes of entities, termed *asmat* and *yuṣmat* respectively ("ours" and "yours"). The former represents one's own true nature as the *puruṣa*; the latter indicates the insentient constituents of *prakṛti*, other *puruṣas* like oneself, and the supreme *puruṣa*, or *īśvara*. This Self considers himself to be the agent and enjoyer, and behaves like one in a dream who imagines a kingdom, king, and subjects, and considers himself to be under their jurisdiction. And just as one awakens from a dream and sees that none but he exists, so does the Self experience an awakening of knowledge to find that it alone exists as pure consciousness. (*nanu paricchedādivādadvaye nāsmākaṃ tātparyaṃ tasyājñabodhanāya kalpitatvāt kintv ekajīvavāda eva tad asti* /... *advitīyacinmātro hy ātmā* / *sa...avidyayā...asmadartham ekaṃ yuṣmadarthāṃś ca bahūn kalpayati* / *tatrāsmadarthaḥ svasvarūpaḥ puruṣaḥ* / *yuṣmadarthaś ca mahadādīni bhūmyantāni jaḍāni svatulyāni puruṣāntarāṇi sarveśvarākhyaḥ puruṣaviśeṣaś cetyevaṃ trividhaḥ* /...*kartṛtvabhoktṛtve tatrātmany adhyaste yathā svapne kaścid rājadhānīṃ rājānaṃ tatprajāś ca kalpayati tanniyamyam ātmānaṃ manyate tadvat* / *jāte ca jñāne jāgare ca sati tato 'nyan na kiñcid astīti cinmātram ekam ātmavastv iti* /

2. *virodhaḥ* : R. M. explains the fallacy to be one of mutual dependence, and explains that in the absence of the *jīva*, *īśvara* would not represent the substratum for *māyā*, and in the absence of the delusion created by *māyā*, which resides in *īśvara*, the *jīva* would not exist. (*tathā ca jīvabhāvaṃ vinā na māyāśrayatvam īśvarasya tathā īśvarāśritamāyākṛtamohaṃ vinā na jīvabhāvaḥ ity anyonyāśraya iti bhāvaḥ* /)

41) kiñca yady atrābhedavāda eva tātparyam abhaviṣyat tarhy ekam eva brahmājñānena bhinnaṃ jñānena tu tasya bhedamayaṃ duḥkhaṃ vilīyata ity apaśyad ity evāvakṣyat/ tathā śrībhagavallīlādīnāṃ vāstavatvābhāve sati śrīśukahṛdayavirodhaś ca jāyate /

41) Moreover, if the doctrine of Abhedavāda ("non-difference") represented the actual significance here,[1] then Vyāsa would have seen that it is *brahman* alone which (appears) divided due to ignorance, and that the suffering which results from this (apparent) division within *brahman* can be removed by means of knowledge; and Sūta would have described it as such.[2] Also, if the *līlā* etc. of *bhagavat* were to be considered unreal, a contradiction would result with regard to the experience of Śuka.[3]

1. *atra* : Both commentators take this as reference to the *Bhāgavata*. B. D. writes: *atra śrībhāgavate śāstre* / .

2. As B. D. explains, "If this were the case, Sūta would not have described Vyāsa as seeing the *pūrṇapuruṣa*, and realizing that the *jīva*, deluded by *māyā* resting on the *puruṣa*, experiences suffering, and that *bhakti* represents the means of removing that suffeiing." (*pūrṇaḥ puruṣaḥ kaścid asti tadāśritatayā māyayā jīvo vimohito 'nartham bhajati tadanarthopaśamanī ca pūrṇasya tasya bhaktiḥ ity apaśyad ity evaṃ nāvakṣyad ityarthaḥ* /) The reference here is to Bh.P. 1/7/4-6 quoted by Jīva in section 30.

3. *śrīśukahṛdayavirodhaḥ* : R. M. takes this as reference to the *Bhāgavata* commentary entitled *Śukahṛdaya*, mentioned by Jīva in section 23. He writes, "...since the *līlā* of *bhagavat* is described as real in the text *Śukahṛdaya*." (*...śukahṛdayagranthe śrībhagavallīlāyā vāstavikatvena kathanād iti bhāvaḥ* /) Jīva, however, explains this expression in S. S., in terms of Śuka's attraction to the *līlā* of *bhagavat*, which could not have come about were the majesty of *bhagavat* also illusory. (*atra śrīśukahṛdayavirodhaś caivaṃ yadi bhagavato 'py avidyāmayam eva vaibhavaṃ syāt tadā śrīśukasya tallīlākṛṣṭatvaṃ na syād iti...*/)

42) tasmāt paricchedapratibimbatvādipratipādakaśāstrāṇy api kathañcit tatsādṛśyena gauṇyaiva vṛttyā pravarteran / ambuvadagrahaṇāt tu na tathātvaṃ vṛddhihrāsabhāktvam antarbhavād ubhayasāmañjasyād evam iti pūrvottarapakṣamayanyāyābhyām //

42) Therefore, one should also make use of scriptures which teach such doctrines as Pratibimbavāda and Paricchedavāda, accepting these doctrines in a secondary sense, as indicating partial similarity (between the metaphor and the reality). This is corroborated by *Brahmasūtra* 3/2/19 ("But the cases are not similar, since we don't apprehend anything like water") and 3/2/20,[1] ("By entering within [its adjuncts], it participates in their increase and decrease; since both cases agree in this respect, the analogy is appropriate"), the former representing the opponent's objection, and the latter the author's reply.

1. B. D. interprets the first of these *sūtras* in two different senses. According to his first interpretation, the objection is to the view that *brahman* can be divided by *upādhis* in the same way that a section of earth is divided by water (*ambuvat*). The grounds for this objection are the fact that *brahman* lacks any apprehendable characteristics (*agrahaṇāt*). Thus, the analogy is not appropriate (*na tathātvam*). According to the second interpretation, the objection is to the view that *brahman* can be reflected in *upādhis*, like the sun in water. This objection is based on the fact that unlike the sun, which is limited, *brahman* is all-pervading.

However, since these metaphors are met with in Śruti, they must be applicable in some sense. Thus, the second of these *sūtras* explains, *vṛddhihrāsabhāktvam*, i.e. just as one portion of earth is large and another small, or as the sun partakes of increase and its reflection decrease, so is *īśvara* (vast) and the *jīva* (limited). Why? *antarbhāvāt*, i.e. since the *jīva* represents a portion of *brahman*. B. D. concludes with the statement that the author of the *sūtras* considers the *jīva* alone to be a portion or reflection of *brahman*, while the clever, godless (Advaitins) consider *īśvara* to be a portion or reflection of *brahman* as well. (*yathāmbunā bhūkhaṇḍasya paricchedaḥ evam upādhinā brahmapradeśasya sa syāt / na ambunā bhūkhaṇḍasyevopādhinā brahmapradeśasya grahaṇābhāvāt / ...ato na tathātvaṃ brahmaṇa upādhiparicchinnatvaṃ netyarthaḥ / yad vā ambuni yathā raveḥ pratibimbaḥ paricchinnasya gṛhyate evam upādhau brahmaṇaḥ pratibimbo vyāpakasya na gṛhyate /...yathā mahadalpau bhūkhaṇḍau yathā ca ravitatpratibimbau vṛddhihrāsabhājau tathā pareśajīvau syātām / kutaḥ / antarbhāvāt etasminn aṃśe śāstratātparyapūrteḥ /...brahmaṇaḥ khaṇḍaḥ pratibimbo vā jīva eveti sūtrakṛtāṃ matam / īśo 'pi brahmaṇaḥ khaṇḍaḥ pratibimbo veti māyināṃ īśavimukhānāṃ matam iti boddhavyam /*)

R. M.'s interpretation of these two *sūtras* differs from those of all the major commentators. He understands the first of these to represent the view that the *jīva* appears to be distinct from *brahman*, like water removed from a pitcher, but reassumes its identity with *brahman* on the disappearance of his *upādhis*, like water poured back into its original pitcher. The second *sūtra*, R. M. contends, refutes this idea with the expression *vṛddhihrāsabhāktvam* ("there is participation in increase and decrease"). That is, just as water which has been removed from a pitcher cannot be considered identical with the water still remaining in the pitcher, since its removal represents a decrease in the total amount of water, and its addition an increase, so also a real difference must be admitted to exist between the *jīva* and *paramātman*. Still, they may be considered non-different secondarily, insofar as the former falls within the latter (*antarbhāvāt*), like water returned to its original vessel. (*tathā caikam eva brahma tattadupādhibhedena bhinnam eva tattadupādhivigame punar aikyam ambuvat ekasmād ghaṭād uddhṛtaṃ jalaṃ punas tatraiva jale nihitam ekībhavatīti tadvad iti /...jalād uddhṛtaṃ jalam avayavavibhāgena pūrvajalanāśena jalāntaram utpannaṃ na tu tayor aikyaṃ tadādhārabhūtajalasya hrāsāt / punas tatra nikṣiptaṃ taj jalaṃ militam ubhābhyāṃ jalāntaram utpannaṃ vṛddhidarśanāt /...ekasmin jale 'parajalasyāntarbhāvāt...evaṃ jīvātmaparamātmanor api bhedaḥ pāramārthikaḥ...abhedapratītas tu antarbhāvāt upādhivigame vilakṣaṇasambandhāpāyāt /*)

It will be helpful to note Śaṅkara's own interpretation of these two *sūtras*, especially in view of the different attempts by Jīva and the two commentators to characterize his position. According to Śaṅkara, the first of these *sūtras* represents the opponent's objection to the use of the illustration of the sun and its reflection in explaining the relationship between *brahman* and *jīvas*. The objection centers on the fact that *brahman*, unlike the sun, is formless and all-pervading, and thus can have no *upādhis* into which it could be reflected. The second *sūtra* states, according to Śaṅkara, that the illustration of the sun and its reflection was never intended to be appropriate in all respects (in which case it would cease to be an illustration), and describes the intended points of similarity as follows: As the reflection of the sun increases with the increase of the water and decreases with its decrease, as it moves when the water moves, takes on the color of the water, etc., without effecting the slightest change in the sun itself, so does *brahman*, though seeming to take on the characteristics of the *jīva*, remain perfectly unchanged and unaffected. Thus, since the illustration conforms to the reality in this sense, the charge of imperfect analogy cannot stand.

43) tata evābhedaśāstrāṇy ubhayoś cidrūpatvena jīvasamūhasya tadekatve 'pi durghaṭaghaṭanāpaṭīyasyā svābhāvikatadacintyaśaktyā svabhāvata eva tadraśmiparamāṇugaṇasthānīyatvāt tadvyatirekeṇāvyatirekeṇa ca virodhaṃ parihṛtyāgre muhur api tadetadvyāsasamādhilabdhasiddhāntayojanāya yojanīyāni //

43) Therefore, those scriptures which propound non-difference can be employed to arrive at the conclusion reached by Vyāsa in *samādhi*, by both initially and repeatedly avoiding the contradiction between the views that the *jīva* is either identical with or distinct from *īśvara*;[1] for, despite the two of them being one with respect to their pure conscious nature, due to the unthinkable power natural to *īśvara*, making even the impossible possible, *jīvas* and *īśvara* (are both identical and distinct), like innumerable atomic rays and the sun.[2]

1. *virodhaṃ parihṛtya* : R. M. interprets this to mean, "avoiding the contradictions found in Śruti, Smṛti, Nyāya, etc., indicating either difference or non-difference." (*bhedābhedabodhakaśrutismṛtinyāyādivirodhaṃ parihṛtya* /)

2. B. D. explains the concept of simultaneous identity and difference, by pointing to the instance of two *brāhmaṇa* boys, one dark and one fair, who share a generic identity as *brāhmaṇas*, but are nevertheless separate individuals. (*yathā gauraśyāmayos taruṇakumārayor vā viprayor vipratvenaikyam / tataś ca jātyaivābhedo na tu vyaktyor ityarthaḥ* /)

44) tad evaṃ māyāśrayatvamāyāmohitatvābhyāṃ sthite dvayor bhede tadbhajanasyaivābhidheyatvam āyātam //

44) Therefore, since *īśvara* and *jīva* are thus shown to be distinct, the former as the substratum of *māyā* and the latter as deluded by *māyā*, it follows that the worship of *īśvara* alone constitutes the *abhidheya*.[1]

1. R. M. adds "in the *Bhāgavata*".

45) ataḥ śrībhagavata eva sarvahitopadeṣṭṛtvāt sarvaduḥkhaharatvāt raśmīnāṃ sūryavat sarveṣāṃ paramasvarūpatvāt sarvādhikaguṇaśālitvāt paramapremayogatvam iti prayojanaṃ ca sthāpitam //

45) And since *bhagavat* alone teaches what is beneficial for all, destroys all sorrow, represents the ultimate nature of all beings,[1] like the sun with respect to its rays, and is endowed with a superabundance of virtues, he alone is deserving of the highest love; thus is the *prayojana* (of the *Bhāgavata*) also established.

1. *paramasvarūpatvāt* : B.D. writes that the qualifier *parama* ("ultimate") indicates that *jīvas* are not actually one with *bhagavat*, just as the rays of the sun are not actually one with the sun (since they are limited, discrete, many, etc.), but only ultimately one with the sun (insofar as they possess luminosity as their nature). (*sūryo yathā raśmīnāṃ svarūpaṃ na kintu paramasvarūpam eva bhavaty evaṃ jīvānāṃ bhagavān iti svarūpaikyaṃ nirastam /*) R. M. analyzes the compound as a *dvandva*, meaning "since *bhagavat* is superior to all, i.e. is the embodiment of bliss par excellence, and represents the nature of all". (*paramatvāt svarūpatvāc cetyarthaḥ / paramatvaṃ ca niratiśayasukhamayatvam...*)

46) tatrābhidheyaṃ ca tādṛśatvena dṛṣṭavān api yatas tatpravṛttyarthaṃ śrībhāgavatākhyām imāṃ sātvatasaṃhitāṃ pravartitavān ity āha anartheti / bhaktiyogaḥ śravaṇakīrtanādilakṣaṇaḥ sādhanabhaktiyogaḥ na tu premalakṣaṇaḥ // anuṣṭhāṇaṃ hy upadeśāpekṣaṃ prema tu tatprasādāpekṣam iti / tathāpi tasya tatprasādahetos tatpremaphalagarbhatvāt sākṣād evānarthopaśamanatvaṃ na tv anyasāpekṣatvena yat karmabhir yat tapasā jñānavairāgyataś ca yat ityādau sarvaṃ madbhaktiyogena madbhakto labhate 'ñjasā / svargāpavargam ityādeḥ / jñānādes tu bhaktisāpekṣatvam eva śreyaḥsṛtiṃ bhaktim ityādeḥ / athavā anarthasya saṃsāravyasanasya tāvat sākṣād avyavadhānenopaśamanaṃ sammohādidvayasya tu premākhyasvīyaphaladvāretyarthaḥ / ataḥ pūrvavad evātrābhidheyaṃ darśitam //

46) And Vyāsa also realized the *abhidheya* in this sense[1] while in *samādhi*[2] for, as explained by Sūta in Bh.P. 1/7/6, he undertook the writing of this *Sātvatasaṃhitā*, known as the *Bhāgavata*, in order to initiate that (i.e. the worship of *bhagavat* which forms the *abhidheya* of the *Bhāgavata*). The term *bhaktiyoga* in

this verse[3] indicates the preliminary stages of *bhakti* (*sādhana-bhakti*), characterized by such practices as listening to the scriptures, singing the praises of the Lord, etc.; it is not characterized by the highest love of God, for devotional practices alone require instruction, while love of God depends solely on the grace of *bhagavat*.[4] Still, *bhaktiyoga* may be said to directly[5] remove misery since, as the means of acquiring the grace of *bhagavat*, it ultimately ripens into love for him; it does not require the aid of anything else (to remove misery). This is verified in the following lines: "Whatever benefits come from the performance of rituals or austerity, from knowledge or renunciation, through the practice of *yoga*, charity or virtue, or any other righteous means, my devotee attains them all without effort, through *bhaktiyoga* aimed at realizing me, whether it be heaven, liberation, my own abode, or whatever else he might desire." (Bh.P. 11/20/32-33) Knowledge etc., on the other hand, are themselves dependent on *bhakti*, as indicated in the following verse: "Those, O Lord, who take pains solely to acquire wisdom, rejecting the higher path of devotion, will receive as their gain wasted effort alone, like those who engage in the husking of chaff." (Bh.P. 10/14/4)

Or it may be[6] that *bhaktiyoga* removes only worldly suffering directly, i.e. without intermediary, but removes the double misery of delusion etc.[7] by means of its effect, love of God. Thus, the *abhidheya* is presented here (Bh.P. 1/7/6) just as it was earlier (Bh.P. 1/7/4-5).

1. *tādṛśatvena* : B. D. explains, "as capable of removing the veil of *māyā*" (*māyānivārakatvena*). R. M. writes, "as representing the means of attaining *bhagavat*, the supreme abode of love" (*paramapremāspadabhagavatprāptihetutva-puraskāreṇa*).

2. *tatra* : R. M. glosses: *samādhau*.

3. Jīva resumes, in this section, his interpretation of the *Bhāgavata* verses cited in section 30. The remaining portion of this section represents Jīva's remarks on the key words and phrases of the third of these verses, Bh.P. 1/7/6.

4. The idea is that, since Vyāsa wrote the *Bhāgavata* in order to teach *bhaktiyoga* to the ignorant, the term *bhaktiyoga* cannot refer to *preman* (love of God), since no one can teach that to anyone else, it being solely due to the grace of *bhagavat*. The reason why Jīva takes such pains here to identify the term *bhaktiyoga* with *sādhanabhakti* (practices leading to love of God), as opposed to *preman* (love of God) is that in section 30, while commenting on Bh.P. 1/7/4, he identified the same term (*bhaktiyoga*) with *preman* itself.

The devotional practices referred to here (*śravaṇa*, *kīrtana*, etc.) are enumerated in Bh.P. 7/5/23-24. (Cf. section 9, f. n. 2 for the complete verse.)

5. *sākṣāt* : Bh.P. 1/7/6 states that *bhaktiyoga* directly (*sākṣāt*) removes misery. As this claim goes against Jīva's description of *bhaktiyoga* as a mere means to the attainment of *preman*, which is the real source of freedom from misery, Jīva devotes the remainder of this section to explaining the sense in which *bhaktiyoga* may be said to directly remove misery.

6. *athavā* : The introduction of Jīva's second explanation of the word *sākṣāt* with the word *athavā* indicates his apparent dissatisfaction with the earlier explanation.

7. *sammohādidvayasya* : Both B. D. and R. M. identify the second of these two sources of misery as the false identification of oneself with the body and mind. (B. D.: *jaḍadehādirūpatāmanana*; R. M.: *dehābhimāna*)

47) atha pūrvavad eva prayojanaṃ ca spaṣṭayituṃ pūrvoktasya pūrṇapuruṣasya ca śrīkṛṣṇasvarūpatvaṃ vyañjayituṃ granthaphalanirdeśadvārā tatra tadanubhavāntaraṃ pratipādayann āha yasyām iti / bhaktiḥ premā śravaṇarūpayā sādhanabhaktyā sādhyatvāt / utpadyate āvirbhavati / tasyānuṣaṅgikaṃ guṇam āha śoketi atraiṣāṃ saṃskāro 'pi naśyatīti bhāvaḥ /

prītir na yāvan mayi vāsudeve na mucyate dehayogena tāvat iti śrīṛṣabhadevavākyāt / paramapuruṣe pūrvoktapūrṇapuruṣe / kimākāra ity apekṣāyām āha kṛṣṇe / kṛṣṇas tu bhagavān svayam ityādi śāstrasahasrabhāvitāntaḥkaraṇānāṃ paramparayā tatprasiddhimadhyapātināṃ cāsaṃkhyalokānāṃ tannāmaśravaṇamātreṇa yaḥ prathamapratītiviṣayaḥ syāt tathā tannāmnaḥ prathamākṣaramātraṃ mantrāya kalpyamānaṃ yasyābhimukhyāya syāt tadākāra ityarthaḥ / āhuś ca nāmakaumudīkārāḥ kṛṣṇaśabdasya tamālaśyāmalatviṣi yaśodāyāḥ stanandhaye parabrahmaṇi rūḍhiḥ iti //

47) Then, in order to clarify the nature of the *prayojana*, as was done earlier,[1] and to reveal the fact that the *pūrṇapuruṣa* mentioned in Bh.P. 1/7/4 is none other than Kṛṣṇa, Sūta utters the verse, Bh.P. 1/7/7, explaining another experience of Vyāsa's by indicating the effects of listening to the *Bhāgavata*.

The word *bhakti* in this verse means *preman*, since it is the goal of *sādhanabhakti* in the form of listening (to the *Bhāgavata*);[2] the verb *utpadyate* means "becomes manifest". Sūta mentions a concomitant virtue of *preman* with the phrase "destroying grief, delusion, and fear", namely, that with the manifestation of *preman*, even the subtle impressions of grief, delusion, and fear are destroyed. For in the words of the *avatāra* Ṛṣabha: "As long as one has no love for me, Vāsudeva, he will not be freed from association with a body." (Bh.P. 5/5/6)

The *paramapuruṣa* mentioned in this verse is identical with the *pūrṇapuruṣa* of Bh.P. 1/7/4. In answer to the question "What form does he take?", Sūta replies, *kṛṣṇe*. The idea is that his is the form which first comes to the mind, at the mere hearing of his name, of all those whose hearts have been nourished by thousands of scriptural statements, such as "But Kṛṣṇa is *bhagavat* himself" (Bh.P. 1/3/28), as well as to those countless individuals who have fallen under the influence of his fame through an unbroken tradition; it is that which is visualized after uttering merely the first syllable of his name, in order to see him face to face. As the author of the *Nāmakaumudī* explains, "The word *kṛṣṇa* primarily signifies 'black like the *tamāla* tree', 'he who was suckled by Yaśodā', and 'the supreme *brahman*'."[3]

1. The reference is to Bh.P. 1/7/5, discussed by Jīva in sections 32-45.
2. *śravaṇarūpayā* : The devotional practice of listening to the scriptures is specified by Jīva on account of the phrase from this verse, *yasyāṃ vai śrūyamāṇānām* ("If one but hears this *Bhāgavata*").
3. The verse referred to here is quoted in full by Jīva in his *Kṛṣṇasandarbha*, and also appears in C. C. (a. 7/82); it is attributed to Lakṣmīdhara, and reads as follows:

tamālaśyāmalatviṣi śrīyaśodāstanandhaye /
kṛṣṇanāmno rūḍhir iti sarvaśāstravinirṇayaḥ //

48) atha tasyaiva prayojanasya brahmānandānubhavād api paramatvam anubhūtavān / yatas tādṛśaṃ śukam api tadānandavaiśiṣṭyalambhanāya tām adhyāpayāmāsety āha sa saṃhitām iti / kṛtvānukramya ceti prathamataḥ svayaṃ saṃkṣepeṇa kṛtvā paścāt tu śrīnāradopadeśād anukrameṇa vivṛtyetyarthaḥ / ata eva śrīmadbhāgavataṃ bhāratānantaraṃ yad atra śrūyate yac cānyatrāṣṭādaśapurāṇānantaraṃ bhāratam iti tad dvayam api samāhitaṃ syāt / brahmānandānubhavanimagnatvāt nivṛttiniratam sarvato nivṛttau niratam tatrāvyabhicāriṇam apītyarthaḥ //

48) Now, Vyāsa realized that this *prayojana* (i.e. love of God) was superior even to the experience of the bliss of *brahman*,

and so taught the *Bhāgavata* to Śuka, who was accustomed to remaining absorbed in the bliss of *brahman*, so that he might realize the superiority of the bliss of *bhagavat*. Thus is it described by Sūta in Bh.P. 1/7/8.

Here, the phrase "after composing and arranging" indicates that Vyāsa first composed the *Bhāgavata* himself, in an abbreviated form, and later, according to the instructions of Nārada, expanded it serially. Thus, the statements which are found in the *Bhāgavata* to the effect that the *Bhāgavata* is later than the *Mahābhārata*, and the statements found elsewhere[1] that the *Mahābhārata* is later than the eighteen Purāṇas can both be regarded as true.

(Śuka is described here as) "engaged in a life of renunciation" since he remained absorbed in the experience of the bliss of *brahman*; he was in all respects engaged in a life of renunciation and did not swerve from the ideal.

1. According to both B. D. and R. M., the reference here is to the following verse, found in both the *Skanda* and *Matsya Purāṇas* :

aṣṭādaśapurāṇāni kṛtvā satyavatīsutaḥ /
cakre bhāratam ākhyānaṃ vedārthair upabṛṃhitam //

"Vyāsa composed the epic, *Mahābhārata*, fortified with the meanings of the Vedas, after composing the eighteen Purāṇas." (Sk.P., *Prabhāsa Khaṇḍa* 2/94)

49) tam etaṃ śrīvedavyāsasya samādhijātānubhavaṃ śrīśaunakapraśnottaratvena viśadayan sarvātmārāmānubhavena sahetukaṃ saṃvādayati ātmārāmāś ceti / nirgranthā vidhiniṣedhātītā nirgatāhaṅkāragranthayo vā / ahaitukīṃ phalānusandhirahitām / atra sarvākṣepaparihārārtham āha itthambhūta ātmārāmāṇām apy ākarṣaṇasvabhāvo guṇo yasya sa iti / tam evārthaṃ śrīśukasyāpy anubhavena saṃvādayati harer guṇeti / śrīvyāsadevād yatkiñcicchrutena guṇena pūrvam ākṣiptā matir yasya saḥ / paścād adhyagād mahad vistīrṇam api / tataś ca tatsaṃkathāsauhārdena nityaṃ viṣṇujanāḥ priyā yasya tathābhūto vā teṣāṃ priyo vā svayam abhavad ityarthaḥ / ayaṃ bhāvaḥ brahmavaivartānusāreṇa pūrvaṃ tāvad ayaṃ garbham ārabhya śrīkṛṣṇasya svairitayā māyānivārakatvaṃ jñātavān / tataḥ svaniyojanayā śrīvyāsadevenānītasya tasyāntardarśanāt tannivāraṇe sati kṛtārthaṃ manyatayā svayam ekāntam eva gatavān / tatra śrīvedavyāsas tu taṃ vaśīkartuṃ tadananyasādhanaṃ śrībhāgavatam eva jñātvā tadguṇātiśayaprakāśama-

yāṃs tadīyapadyaviśeṣān kathañcic chrāvayitvā tena tam ākṣiptamatiṃ kṛtvā tad eva pūrṇaṃ tam adhyāpayāmāseti śrībhāgavatamahimātiśayaḥ proktaḥ / tad evaṃ darśitaṃ vaktuḥ śrīśukasya vedavyāsasya ca samānahṛdayam / tasmād vaktur hṛdayānurūpam eva sarvatra tātparyaṃ paryālocanīyaṃ nānyathā / yad yat tadanyathā paryālocanaṃ tatra tatra kupathagāmitaiveti niṣṭaṅkitam / 1/7 śrīsūtaḥ //

49) Sūta[1] uttered the verse, Bh.P. 1/7/10, in response to Śaunaka's question,[2] thereby explaining both the nature of the aforementioned experience of Vyāsa, born of *samādhi*,[3] as well as the basis for it, in terms of the common experience of all those who rejoice in the self alone.

Here, the word *nirgranthā* ("free from ties") means either "beyond all injunctions and prohibitions" or "free from the bonds of egoism". *Ahaituki* ("motiveless") means "not seeking any results". In order to remove any doubt, he explains, "The nature of Hari is such that even those who rejoice in the Self alone feel an attraction for him".

This same fact is related in Bh.P. 1/7/11 by explaining Śuka's own experience. Śuka had earlier had his heart captivated by what little he had heard of Hari's nature from Vyāsa. Later he studied the *Bhāgavata*, despite its great length. Thereafter his nature became such that the devotees of Viṣṇu became dear to him, due to the friendship which grew out of daily discourses with him about *bhagavat*. Or (the expression *viṣṇujanapriyaḥ*) may mean that Śuka had himself become dear to them.

The idea is this : According to the accounts of the *Brahmavaivarta Purāṇa*, even prior to this, while still lying in his mother's womb,[4] Śuka realized that Kṛṣṇa was capable of subduing *māyā* at will. Thus, according to Śuka's own orders, Vyāsa brought Kṛṣṇa there, who revealed himself to Śuka (still lying in his mother's womb). Being thus freed from the bonds of *māyā*, and considering his goal of life accomplished, Śuka (took birth) and retired to a secluded spot. Now, Vyāsa realized that the *Bhāgavata* was the only effective means to captivate him, and so somehow managed to have him hear a few selected portions of the *Bhāgavata*, in which the greatness of Hari's nature is particularly evident. By this means, Vyāsa captivated Śuka's heart, and taught him the whole of the *Bhāgavata*. Thus (the example of Śuka) also speaks of the extreme greatness of the *Bhāgavata*.

It is thereby demonstrated that Śuka, the narrator of the *Bhāgavata*, and Vyāsa shared the same sentiments (with regard to the *Bhāgavata*). Therefore, in every instance, the significance of this work must be evaluated in accordance with the understanding of its narrator, Śuka, and not otherwise. Whatever interpretations are found to be contrary to this should be considered mere deviations from the proper path.

1. *śrīsūtaḥ* : The name of Sūta, together with the figures 1/7, marks the end of Jīva's comments on Bh.P. 1/7/4-11, begun in section 30.

2. In Bh.P. 1/7/9, the verse immediately preceding the two verses under discussion here, Śaunaka asks Sūta why a sage such as Śuka, well-established in the life of renunciation, would study such a lengthy text as the *Bhāgavata*. Sūta's initial reply is a general statement regarding the ability of Hari to capture the hearts of such sages. His second reply describes the specific case of Śuka. (Cf. section 30 for the translation of these three verses.)

3. *samādhijātānubhavam*: R. M. describes this experience as the realization that (love of) Kṛṣṇa is superior even to the bliss of *brahman* (*brahmānandād apy adhikatayā kṛṣṇaviṣayakam*).

4. B. D. notes that in the *Mahābhārata*, Śuka is described as not having been born from a womb, and as taking a wife and having a daughter. B. D. explains the differences in these accounts as concerning different *kalpas*. (*bhārate tv ayonijātaḥ kathyate dāragrahaṇaṃ kanyāsantatiś ceti / tad etat sarvaṃ kalpabhedena saṃgamanīyam*/)

50) atha krameṇa vistaratas tathaiva tātparyaṃ nirṇetuṃ sambandhābhidheyaprayojaneṣu prathamaṃ yasya vācyavācakatāsambandhīdaṃ śāstraṃ tad eva dharmaḥ projjhitakaitavaḥ ityādipadye sāmānyākāratas tāvad āha vedyaṃ vāstavam atra vastu iti / ṭīkā ca atra śrīmati sundare bhāgavate vāstavaṃ paramārthabhūtaṃ vastu vedyaṃ na tu vaiśeṣikādivad dravyaguṇādirūpam ity eṣā / 1/1 śrīvedavyāsaḥ //

50) Now, in order to determine the significance of the *Bhāgavata* in the manner just indicated,[1] the *sambandha*, *abhidheya*, and *prayojana* will be ascertained, one after the other, and in detail,[2] in these six *sandarbhas*. The first of these (i.e. the *Tattvasandarbha*) will deal with the *sambandha*, or the relationship between the principle being taught and the medium through which it is taught. The substance of this relationship is described by Vyāsa in a general manner in Bh.P. 1/1/2 with the

phrase *vedyaṃ vāstavam atra vastu* ("The absolute reality is to be discovered in the *Bhāgavata*..."). According to the commentary of Śrīdhara: "Here, in this beautiful *Bhāgavata*, the absolute reality, i.e. *vastu* in the highest sense, is to be discovered, and not *vastu* in the sense of substance or attribute, as interpreted by the Vaiśeṣikas etc."[3]

1. *tathaiva* : B. D. explains, "in accordance with the understanding of Śuka and Vyāsa." (*śrīśukādihṛdayānusāreṇa*)

2. *vistarataḥ* : As B. D. explains Jīva has briefly described these three categories in the preceding sections. He now begins his detailed description, starting with the *sambandha*, the subject matter proper to the *Tattvasandarbha*. (*saṃkṣepeṇoktaṃ sambandhādikaṃ vistareṇa darśayitum upakramate...*/)

3. *vaiśeṣikādivat*: B. D. understands this as a reference to the Nyāya system of Gautama as well. (*kaṇādagautamoktaśāstravat*)

51 atha kiṃsvarūpaṃ tad vastutattvam ity atrāha

vadanti tat tattvavidas tattvaṃ yaj jñānam advayam /iti/

jñānaṃ cidekarūpam / advayatvaṃ cāsya svayaṃsiddhatādṛśātādṛśatattvāntarābhāvāt svaśaktyekasahāyatvāt paramāśrayaṃ taṃ vinā tāsām asiddhatvāc ca / tattvam iti paramapuruṣārthatādyotanayā paramasukharūpatvaṃ tasya bodhyate / ata eva tasya nityatvaṃ ca darśitam / 1/2 śrīsūtaḥ //

51 Then, in reply to the question, "What is the nature of this principle of reality (*tattva*)?", Sūta states: "The knowers of reality declare non-dual consciousness to be reality."[1] (Bh.P. 1/2/11)

Here, *jñāna* ("consciousness") means "having pure consciousness as its essential nature". This consciousness is termed *advaya* ("non-dual") for the reasons that there exists no other self-existent *tattva*, either similar or dissimilar;[2] it represents the sole support for its *śaktis*; and without this consciousness as their ultimate substratum, these *śaktis* could not exist.

Since the term *tattva* indicates the highest goal of life, this consciousness is understood to be of the nature of supreme bliss. Consequently it is also shown to be eternal.[3]

1. The second line of this verse, which forms the basis for the following three *sandarbhas*, reads as follows:

brahmeti paramātmeti bhagavān iti śabdyate //

"(That *tattva*) is designated *brahman*, *paramātman* and *bhagavat*."

2. *tādṛśātādṛśa* : According to B. D., *jīvas* are meant by "similar *tattvas*", and the insentient principles, *prakṛti* and time, by "dissimilar *tattvas*".

3. B. D. explains that the eternal nature of the *tattva* is based on the fact that it is self-existent. (*svayaṃsiddhatvena vyākhyānān nityaṃ tad ityarthaḥ*/)

R. M. comments that the words *brahman*, *jñāna* and *ānanda* indicate that *brahman* possesses knowledge and bliss as his essential attributes, since it is not possible for words with such different connotations to be identified with one and the same entity. (*brahmapadajñānapadānandapadānāṃ sāmānādhikaraṇyānupapattyā jñānapadānandapadayoḥ svābhāvikajñānavatsvābhāvikānandavatparatvāvagamāt* /)

52) nanu nīlapītādyākāraṃ kṣaṇikam eva jñānaṃ dṛṣṭaṃ tat punar advayaṃ nityaṃ jñānaṃ kathaṃ lakṣyate yan niṣṭham idaṃ śāstram ity atrāha

sarvavedāntasāraṃ yad brahmātmaikyatvalakṣaṇam /
vastv advitīyaṃ tan niṣṭhaṃ kaivalyaikaprayojanam // iti /

satyaṃ jñānam anantaṃ brahma iti yasya svarūpam uktaṃ yenāśrutaṃ śrutaṃ bhavati iti yadvijñānena sarvavijñānaṃ pratijñātaṃ sad eva saumyedam agra āsīt ityādinā nikhilajagadekakāraṇatā tad aikṣata bahu syām ityanena satyasaṅkalpatā ca yasya pratipāditā tena brahmaṇā svarūpaśaktibhyāṃ sarvabṛhattamena sārdham anena jīvenātmanā iti tadīyoktāv idantānirdeśena tato bhinnatve 'py ātmatānirdeśena tadātmāṃśaviśeṣatvena labdhasya bādarāyaṇasamādhidṛṣṭayukter atyabhinnatārahitasya jīvātmano yad ekatvaṃ tat tvam asi ityādau jñātā tadaṃśabhūtacidrūpatvena samānākāratā tad eva lakṣaṇaṃ prathamato jñāne sādhakatamaṃ yasya tathābhūtaṃ yat sarvavedāntasāram advitīyaṃ vastu tan niṣṭhaṃ tad ekaviṣayam idaṃ śrībhāgavatam iti prāktanapadyasthenānuṣaṅgaḥ / yathā janmaprabhṛti kaścid gṛhaguhāvaruddhaḥ sūryaṃ vividiṣuḥ kathañcid gavākṣapatitaṃ sūryāṃśukaṇaṃ darśayitvā kenacid upadiśyate eṣa sa iti etat tadaṃśajyotiḥsamānākāratayā tan mahājyotir maṇḍalam anusandhīyatām ityarthas tadvat / jīvasya tathā tadaṃśatvaṃ ca tadacintyaśaktiviśeṣasiddhatvenaiva paramātmasandarbhe sthāpayiṣyāmaḥ / tadetajjīvādilakṣaṇāṃśaviśiṣṭatayaivopaniṣadas tasya sāṃśatvam api kvacid upadiśanti / niraṃśatvopadeśikā śrutis tu kevalatanniṣṭhā / atra kaivalyaikaprayojanam iti caturthapādaś ca kaivalyapadasya śuddhatvamātravacanatvena śuddhatvasya ca śuddhabhaktitvena paryavasānena prītisandarbhe vyākhyāsyate / 12/13 śrīsūtaḥ //

52) But consciousness is seen to be absolutely momentary, taking the form of a blue object (one moment) and a yellow object (the next). How can such a consciousness be characterized as non-dual and eternal, as the *Bhāgavata* is intent on doing?

To this Sūta replies: "The *Bhāgavata*[1] has for its subject matter that non-dual reality which forms the essence of all the Upaniṣads, and is characterized by the oneness of *ātman* and *brahman*; its sole purpose is to bring about the attainment of *kaivalya*." (Bh.P. 12/13/12)

That is, this *Bhāgavata* has for its *niṣṭhā*, i.e. its sole concern, that non-dual reality which forms the essence of all the Upaniṣads. Its primary and most efficacious teaching is characterized as oneness between the *jīva* and *brahman*. This oneness is understood,[2] in such statements as *tat tvam asi* ("You are That," Ch.U. 6/8/7), to be an identity of form, since the *jīva*, being a portion of *brahman*, shares his conscious nature. Due to his nature and power,[3] *brahman* is the most extensive of all. He is that whose essential nature has been described by the words *satyaṃ jñānam anantaṃ brahma* ("*Brahman* is truth, knowledge, and infinity," Tai.U. 2/1/1); by knowing whom, all is said to be known: *yenāśrutaṃ śrutaṃ bhavati* ("...by learning about whom, the unheard becomes heard..." Ch.U. 6/1/3); who is declared to be the single cause of the universe: *sad eva saumyedam agra āsīt* ("In the beginning, my boy, this was being alone," Ch.U. 6/2/1); and who has been described as being able to create by a mere wish: *tad aikṣata bahu syām* ("He looked about and thought, 'May I be many,' " Ch.U. 6/2/3). That the *jīva* is not absolutely non-different from *brahman* has been established by arguments based on Vyāsa's vision in *samādhi*. Still, he is one with *brahman* in that he represents a particular portion of him. This is demonstrated by the phrase, *anena jīvenātmanā* ("by this living self", Ch. U. 6/3/2), in which the employment of the pronoun *idam* ("this") implies difference from *brahman* while the use of the word *ātman* ("self") indicates inclusion within *brahman*.[4]

The idea is this: Suppose someone who has been confined to a dark room from his birth wishes to know the nature of the sun. Then, someone points out to him a tiny ray of light which has somehow managed to peep through a small hole, and instructs him as follows: "This is that (sun). Seek to realize the sun as a great sphere of light, identical in nature with this ray of light, which is but a particle of that sun." We will demonstrate in the *Paramātmasandarbha* that the *jīva* similarly represents a portion of the *paramātman*, owing his very existence to a particular aspect of his unthinkable power. Therefore, the Upaniṣads teach in places that *brahman* possesses parts, but only in the sense that he is qualified by these parts, characterized as "*jīva*" etc. The Śruti texts, on the other hand, which indicate *brahman*, to be partless are concerned only with his absolute aspect.

The fourth *pāda* of this verse, *kaivalyaikaprayojanam* ("its sole purpose is to bring about the attainment of *kaivalya*"), will be analyzed in the *Prītisandarbha* by taking *kaivalya* to mean "purity" alone, and by showing "purity" to be synonymous with "pure bhakti".

1. *śrībhāgavatam iti prāktanapadyasthenānuṣaṅgaḥ* : This phrase, occurring at the end of the following sentence, indicates that the subject of the verse under discussion (Bh.P. 12/13/12), "the *Bhāgavata*", is taken from the earlier verse (Bh.P. 12/13/9). The four verses, 12/13/9-12, actually represent a single sentence in which the various characteristics of the *Bhāgavata* are described.

2. *jñātā* : Although R. M. vouches for the correctness of this reading, B. D. accepts the reading, *jātyā,* which would indicate a generic identity between *jīva* and *brahman*. The implications of this reading are not significantly different from those of the reading adopted here, since the idea of generic identity is also conveyed by the expression *samānākāratā* found in the same line.

3. *svarūpaśaktibhyām* : R. M. defines *svarūpa* as meaning "knowledge, bliss, etc.", and *śakti* as meaning "*māyā*, the material cause of the universe etc.". (*svarūpaṃ jñānasukhādi śaktir jagadupādānamāyādi tābhyām*|)

4. The full line reads: *seyaṃ devataikṣata hantāham imās tisro devatā anena jīvenātmanānupraviśya nāmarūpe vyākaravāṇi* | "That divine being looked about and thought, 'Let me enter these three *devatās* (fire, water and earth) through this living self, and manifest names and forms.'" (Ch. U. 6/3/2)

53) tatra yadi tvampadārthasya jīvātmano jñānatvaṃ nityatvaṃ ca prathamato vicāragocaraḥ syāt tadaiva tatpadārthasya tādṛśatvaṃ subodhaṃ syād iti tad bodhayitum anyārthaś ca parāmarśaḥ iti nyāyena jīvātmanas tadrūpatvam āha |

nātmā jajāna na mariṣyati naidhate 'sau
na kṣīyate savanavid vyabhicāriṇāṃ hi |
sarvatra śaśvad anapāyy upalabdhimātraṃ
prāṇo yathendriyabalena vikalpitaṃ sat ||

ātmā śuddho jīvaḥ na jajāna na jātaḥ janmābhāvād eva

tadanantarāstitālakṣaṇo vikāro 'pi nāsti / naidhate na vardhate vṛddhyābhāvād eva vipariṇāmo 'pi nirastaḥ / hi yasmāt / vyabhicāriṇām āgamāpāyināṃ bālayuvādidehānāṃ devamanuṣyādyākāradehānāṃ vā / savanavit tattatkāladraṣṭā / na hy avasthāvatāṃ draṣṭā tadavastho bhavatītyarthaḥ / niravasthaḥ ko 'sau ātmā / ata āha upalabdhimātraṃ jñānaikarūpam / kathambhūtam / sarvatra dehe śaśvat sarvadā anuvartamānam iti / nanu nīlajñānaṃ naṣṭaṃ pītajñānaṃ jātam iti pratīter na jñānasyānapāyitvam / tatrāha indriyabaleneti / sad eva jñānam ekam indriyabalena vividhaṃ kalpitam / nīlādyākārā vṛttaya eva jāyante naśyanti ca na jñānam iti bhāvaḥ / ayam āgamāpāyatadbādhabhedena prathamas tarkaḥ/ draṣṭṛdṛśyabhedena dvitīyo 'pi tarko jñeyaḥ / vyabhicāriṣv avasthitasyāvyabhicāre dṛṣṭāntaḥ yatheti //

53) And here, only if the conscious and eternal nature of the *jīva* first comes to mind in connection with the word *tvam*, will his similarity with the being signified by the word *tat* be easily comprehended. Therefore, in accordance with Br.S. 1/3/20, *anyārthaś ca parāmarśaḥ* ("The reference to the *jīva* has a different meaning"),[1] Pippalāyana utters the following words to King Nimi, showing the conscious and eternal nature of the *jīva*, in order to enlighten him about *brahman*: "The *ātman* was not born, nor will it die; it neither increases nor decreases, since it is the witness of the changes which occur in all ephemeral things. Just as *prāṇa* is conceived of as manifold on account of the senses, so is the *ātman*, though eternal, everywhere unchanging, pure awareness, conceived of as many." (Bh.P. 11/3/38)

That is, "the *ātman*", i.e. the pure *jīva*,[2] "was not born". Since it has no birth, it is likewise free from the modification classified as *astitā* ("existence") which immediately follows birth. "It does not increase." Since it is free from increase, the modification known as *vipariṇāma* ("transformation") is likewise ruled out.[3] The particle *hi* introduces the reason: "It is the *savanavit*", i.e. the witness of the different phases of time, "of all ephemeral things", i.e. of all things having a beginning and an end, whether bodies in the stages of childhood, youth, etc., or bodies in the form of gods, mortals, etc. The idea is that the observer of things subject to certain states is not itself subject to those states.

What is this unconditioned *ātman*? He replies, *upalabdhimātram*, i.e. he whose nature is consciousness alone. What is it like? It exists "everywhere", i.e. in every body, "eternally", i.e. at all times. But we see that consciousness of a blue object disappears, and that of a yellow object arises. Doesn't this prove the changing nature of consciousness? To this he replies, *indriyabalena* ("on account of the senses").[4] Consciousness, which is existence itself, is one; it is conceived of as manifold on account of the senses. It is the mental modifications alone, in the form of blue objects etc., which appear and disappear, not consciousness. This is what is meant.

The first argument[5] is based on the distinction between that which is subject to origination and annihilation, and that which is free from them.[6] The second argument is to be understood in terms of the distinction between the seer and the seen. The phrase "just as *prāṇa*" represents an illustration of something which does not swerve from its own state, even in the midst of things which are themselves changing.

1. *anyārthaś ca parāmarśaḥ*: According to B. D., this *sūtra* refers to the *daharavidyā* portion of the *Chāndogya Upaniṣad* (8/1/1), which describes the meditation on *paramātman* in the form of the small space within the heart. Here the body of the worshipper is thought of as the "city of *brahman*", and the *dahara*, or "small space", as *paramātman*. The worshipper is instructed to meditate on *paramātman*, residing in his heart. Later, however, in Ch.U. 8/12/13, there is a description of the "serene one" (*samprasādaḥ*), who rises from the body, reaches the highest light, and assumes his own real nature. B. D. identifies the "serene one" as the *jīva*, who has acquired wisdom, and the "highest light" as *puruṣottama*. Now the question arises, "Why, in the midst of this teaching concerning the meditation on *paramātman*, is there reference to the *jīva*?" The reply is given in the *sūtra*: "The reference to *jīva* has a different meaning." That is, it is meant to lead to knowledge of *paramātman*, since the *jīva* realizes his own true nature when *paramātman* is attained. (*daharavidyā chāndogye paṭhyate...| atropāsakasya śarīraṃ brahmapuraṃ tatra hṛtpuṇḍarīkastho daharaḥ paramātmā dhyeyaḥ kathyate...| tadvākyamadhye sa eṣa samprasādo 'smāc charīrāt samutthāya paraṃ jyotir upasampadya svena rūpeṇābhiniṣpadyate sa uttamaḥ puruṣaḥ iti vākyaṃ paṭhitam | atra samprasādo labdhavijñāno jīvas tena yat paraṃ jyotir upapannaṃ sa eva puruṣottama ityarthaḥ | tatra jīvaparāmarśo 'nyārthaḥ | yaṃ prāpya jīvaḥ svasvarūpeṇābhiniṣpadyate sa paramātmeti paramātmajñānārtha ityarthaḥ |*)

2. *śuddho jīvaḥ* : While Jīva understands the term *ātman* to refer to the pure *jīva*, and invokes the authority of the *Brahmasūtra* to explain why the *jīva* is referred to in terms befitting *brahman*, Śrīdhara interprets the term *ātman* in this verse to indicate *brahman* directly. Apart from this important difference,

the remaining portion of Jīva's commentary on this verse is a virtual word-for-word repetition of Śrīdhara's commentary.

3. As B. D. explains, the six kinds of modifications, enumerated by Yāska in his *Nirukta* (1/2), are alluded to here, four explicitly (birth, increase, decay, and death) and two by implication (existence and transformation). (*jāyate 'sti vardhate vipariṇamate 'pakṣīyate naśyati ceti bhāvavikārāḥ ṣaṭ paṭhitāḥ...* /)

4. *indriyabalena* : B. D. writes that consciousness assumes the shape of its object by proceeding through the senses, and is indicated by the term *vṛtti*. It is the *vṛtti* alone, taking the form of blue objects etc., which perishes with the disappearance of the blue object etc. (*tasyendriyapraṇālyā nīlādiniṣṭhā yā viṣayatā vṛttipadavācyā saiva nīlādyapagame naśyatīti* /)

5. *tarkaḥ* : R. M.'s commentary on the first argument indicates that the distinction established here is between the body and the *ātman*. (Cf. f.n. 6 below.)

6. *āgamāpāyatadbādhabhedena* : Although this reading is not found in available manuscripts, it is vouched for by R. M. in his commentary. The reading found in most editions, *āgamāpāyitadavadhibhedena*, conveys basically the same meaning, and is also possible here. However, the same expression is found in verse form in section 55, where the latter reading is ruled out on metrical considerations, as having one too many syllables. (Cf. Jīva: 1967: 125-26 for further arguments in favor of this reading.)

R. M. interprets this first argument to mean that the body possesses the characteristics of coming into being and passing away, while the *ātman* lacks such characteristics. (*dehasyāgamāpāyadharmaḥ* / *ātmanaś ca tadbādhaḥ* / *tadabhāva iti* /)

54) dṛṣṭāntaṃ vivṛṇvann indriyādilayena nirvikārātmopalabdhiṃ darśayati

aṇḍeṣu peśiṣu taruṣv aviniściteṣu
prāṇo hi jīvam upadhāvati tatra tatra /
sanne yad indriyagaṇe 'hami ca prasupte
kūṭastha āśayam ṛte tadanusmṛtir naḥ //

aṇḍeṣu aṇḍajeṣu / peśiṣu jarāyujeṣu / taruṣu udbhijjeṣu / aviniściteṣu svedajeṣu / upadhāvati anuvartate / evaṃ dṛṣṭānte nirvikāratvaṃ pradarśya dārṣṭāntike 'pi darśayati / katham / tadaivātmā savikāra iva pratīyate yadā jāgare indriyagaṇaḥ yadā ca svapne tatsaṃskāravān ahaṅkāraḥ yadā tu prasuptaṃ tadā tasmin prasupta indriyagaṇe sanne līne ahami ahaṅkāre ca sanne līne kūṭastho nirvikāra ātmā / kutaḥ / āśayam ṛte liṅgaśarīram upādhiṃ vinā vikārahetor upādher abhāvād ityarthaḥ/ nanv ahaṅkāraparyantasya sarvasya laye śūnyam evāvaśiṣyate kva tadā kūṭastha ātmā / ata āha tadanusmṛtir naḥ tasyākhaṇḍātmanaḥ suṣuptisākṣiṇaḥ smṛtiḥ naḥ asmākaṃ jāgraddraṣṭṝṇāṃ jāyate etāvantaṃ kālaṃ sukham aham asvāpsaṃ na kiñcid avediṣam iti / ato 'nanubhūtasya tasyāsmaraṇād asty eva suṣuptau tādṛgātmānubhavaḥ viṣayasambandhābhāvāc ca na spaṣṭa iti bhāvaḥ / ataḥ svaprakāśamātravastunaḥ sūryādeḥ prakāśavad upalabdhimātrasyāpy ātmana upalabdhiḥ svāśraye 'sty evety āyātam / tathā ca śrutiḥ yad vai tan na paśyati paśyan vai draṣṭavyān na paśyati na hi draṣṭur dṛṣṭer viparilopo vidyate iti //

54) Pippalāyana further develops this metaphor, and shows how, with the merging of the senses, the unchanging *ātman* is realized: "For *prāṇa* follows the *jīva* wherever he may go, whether in eggs, fetuses, trees, or indeterminate creatures. When the senses and 'I'-consciousness have merged in deep sleep, then the immovable *ātman* is free from its dwelling place, and (upon waking) we remember that." (Bh.P. 11/3/39) Here, *aṇḍeṣu* refers to creatures born from eggs, *peśiṣu* to those born from wombs, *taruṣu* to those born from sprouts, and *aviniściteṣu* to those born from moisture. The verb *upadhāvati* means "follows".

Having thus shown the changeless nature (of *prāṇa*) in the illustration, he goes on to show the changeless nature (of the *ātman*) in the illustrated portion of this analogy. How is that ? The *ātman* appears to be changing when the senses are functioning in the waking state, or when the sense of "I", made up of impressions from the waking state, functions in the dream state. When, however, one is in deep sleep, his senses and "I"-consciousness both merged, then the *ātman* remains *kūṭastha*, i.e. unchanging. In what way ? *Āśayam ṛte*, i.e. free from its limiting adjunct, the subtle body. The idea is that it is unchanging since it lacks *upādhis*, which are the cause of change.

But when everything, including even the sense of "I", becomes merged, only a void remains. Where is this changeless *ātman* then ? To this he replies: "We remember that." "We", i.e. the waking perceivers, remember that indivisible *ātman*, the witness of the state of deep sleep,[1] and say (upon waking): "I slept soundly for a long time. I wasn't aware of anything." The experience of the *ātman* in deep sleep is such since there can be no memory of that which has not been experienced; it is hazy due to the absence of any connection with sense objects. This is the idea. It therefore follows that the *ātman*, which is pure awareness itself, possesses the power of knowing, which is grounded in itself, just as self-luminous objects, like the sun etc., possess the power of illumination.[2] As stated in Śruti: "And when (in deep sleep), he does not see, still he sees, though he does not see objects of sight,[3] for there can be no severing of sight from the seer..." (Bṛ.U. 4/3/23)

This is the third argument, based on the distinction between the categories of "witness" and "objects witnessed". The fourth argument is understood in terms of the categories, "the sufferer" and "the repository of love".

1. *akhaṇḍātmanaḥ suṣuptisākṣiṇaḥ* : Up until this point, Jīva's commentary is a virtual word-for-word replica of Śrīdhara's. Here, however, Śrīdhara writes, "(We remember) the witness of deep sleep, in the form of bliss, devoid of any particular awareness of sights, sensations,... etc" (*tasya darśana-sparśanādiviśeṣajñānaśūnyasya sukhātmanaḥ suṣuptisākṣiṇaḥ...*/) The interpretation offered by Jīva, that one remembers the *ātman* upon waking, is one which an Advaitin like Śrīdhara would never accept since it contradicts the basic tenet that the knower (the *ātman*) can never be known. The oft-quoted line cited by Śrīdhara describing the experience of deep sleep is meant only to show that the *ātman* does not cease to exist in the state of deep sleep, as demonstrated by the fact that upon waking there is the memory of a vague feeling of joy (*sukham*) and the passage of time (*etāvantaṃ kālam*).

B. D. explains that the *ātman* is indivisible because of its atomic nature. (*akhaṇḍātmana iti aṇurūpatvād vibhāgānarhasyetyarthaḥ*/)

R. M. interprets the witness of the deep sleep state to be *brahman*, on account of whom the *jīva* experiences his own bliss during the state of deep sleep. (*suṣuptisākṣiṇaḥ suṣuptidaśāyāṃ jīvaṃ svasukham anubhāvayitur brahmaṇaḥ* /)

2. This conclusion concerning the dual nature of the *ātman* as both knower and knowledge is not found in Śrīdhara's commentary, which continues with the quotation from Śruti.

3. *draṣṭavyān* : Jīva quotes Bṛ.U.4/3/23 as found in Śrīdhara's commentary, where the word *draṣṭavyān* occurs in place of the pronoun *tān*, the commonly accepted reading. B. D. explains the implications of this verse as follows: "The statement that the self-conscious agent does not see in the state of deep sleep is based on the fact that there are no visible objects in deep sleep, and not on the fact that the seer is absent." (*tad ātmacaitanyaṃ kartṛ suṣuptau na paśyati yad ucyate tat khalu draṣṭavyaviṣayābhāvād eva na tu draṣṭṛtvābhāvād ityarthaḥ* /)

55) tad uktam

anvayavyatirekākhyas tarkaḥ syāc caturātmakaḥ /
āgamāpāyatadbādhabhedena prathamo mataḥ //
draṣṭṛdṛśyavibhāgena dvitīyo 'pi matas tathā /
sākṣisākṣyavibhāgena tṛtīyaḥ sammataḥ satām //

duḥkhipremāspadatvena caturthaḥ sukhabodhakaḥ /
11/3 iti śrīpippalāyano nimim //

55) Therefore it is said:[1] "This reasoning is known as '*anvayavyatireka*' ('positive and negative concomitance')[2] and is of four kinds. The first argument is based on the distinction between that which is subject to origination and annihilation, and that which is free from them;[3] the second is based on the distinction between the seer and the seen. The third is considered by the wise to turn on the distinction between the witness and the objects witnessed, while the fourth convincing argument rests on the distinction between the sufferer and the repository of love."

1. *tad uktam* : The verses which follow this introduction represent Jīva's own metrical rendering of the four arguments delineated in the two previous sections, based on Bh.P. 11/3/38-39.

2. *anvayavyatirekākhyas tarkaḥ* : B. D. interprets the word *tarka* ("reasoning") to mean *anumāna* ("inference"), "one of the branches of *tarka*" (*tarkaśabdena tarkāṅgakam anumānaṃ bodhyam* /). The particular type of *anumāna* employed by Jīva, *anvayavyatireka*, makes use of both positive and negative proofs to demonstrate the nature of the *ātman* as being contrary to that of the body, and vice versa. B. D. writes, "The *ātman* is distinct from the body since the body is evanescent, objective, the witnessed object, and the locus of suffering." (*āgamāpāyino dṛśyāt sākṣyād duḥkhāspadāc ca dehāder ātmā bhidyate* /)

3. Cf. section 53, f. n. 6 for the discussion on the reading of this compound adopted here.

56) evambhūtānāṃ jīvānāṃ cinmātraṃ yat svarūpaṃ tayaivākṛtyā tadaṃśitvena ca tadabhinnaṃ yat tattvaṃ tad atra vācyam iti vyaṣṭinirdeśadvārā proktam / tad eva hy āśrayasaṃjñakaṃ mahāpurāṇalakṣaṇarūpaiḥ sargādibhir arthaiḥ samaṣṭinirdeśadvārāpi lakṣyata ity atrāha dvābhyām

atra sargo visargaś ca sthānaṃ poṣaṇam ūtayaḥ /
manvantareśānukathā nirodho muktir āśrayaḥ //
daśamasya viśuddhyarthaṃ navānām iha lakṣaṇam /
varṇayanti mahātmānaḥ śrutenārthena cāñjasā //

manvantarāṇi ceśānukathāś ca manvantareśānukathāḥ / atra sargādayo daśārthā lakṣyanta ityarthaḥ / tatra ca daśamasya viśuddhyarthaṃ tattvajñānārthaṃ navānāṃ lakṣaṇaṃ svarūpaṃ varṇayanti / nanv atra naivaṃ pratīyate / ata aha śrutena śrutyā kaṇṭhoktyaiva stutyādisthāneṣu añjasā sākṣād varṇayanti arthena tātparyavṛttyā ca tattadākhyāneṣu //

56) The *tattva* which forms the subject matter of the *Bhāgavata* is the principle of non-difference between the *jīva*, whose nature has just been described,[1] and *brahman*, based on the fact that the *jīva* is, by nature, pure consciousness and a portion of *brahman*; this has been described from the *vyaṣṭi*, or individual, point of view. The same *tattva* is also described from the *samaṣṭi*, or aggregate, point of view,[2] by means of the categories which form the characteristics of Mahāpurāṇas, such as *sarga* etc.; it is then termed *āśraya*, the ultimate ground of existence. These categories are enumerated by Śuka in the following two verses: "We find in the *Bhāgavata* the categories: 1) *sarga*, 2) *visarga*, 3) *sthāna*, 4) *poṣaṇa*, 5) *ūti*, 6) *manvantara*, 7) *īśānukathā*, 8) *nirodha*, 9) *mukti*, and 10) *āśraya*. The great souls describe the characteristics of the first nine, either directly, with the aid of Śruti, or by explaining their significance (indirectly) in order to clarify the meaning of the tenth." (Bh.P. 2/10/1-2)

Here, *manvantareśānukathāḥ* is a *dvandva* compound meaning "*manvantaras* and *īśānukathās*". The idea is that these ten topics, *sarga* etc., are described here. And of these ten, they describe the *lakṣaṇa*, i.e. the nature, of the first nine, "in order to clarify the meaning of the tenth", i.e. in order to bring about an understanding of the true nature (*tattva*) of the tenth. But this is not at all evident in this verse.[3] To clear this up, Śuka replies, "They describe them *śrutena*, i.e. by means of Śruti (texts) uttered in eulogistic passages etc., *añjasā*, i.e. directly, and also *arthena*, i.e. by demonstrating their significance through a variety of legends."

1. *evambhūtānām* : B. D. takes this as a reference to sections 53-55, wherein the *jīva* was described as similar in nature to *īśvara*, and the investigation into the nature of the *jīva* was undertaken so as to lead to an understanding of the nature of *īśvara*. (*īśvarajñānārthaṃ jīvasvarūpajñānaṃ nirṇītam / atha tatsādṛśyeneśvarasvarūpaṃ nirṇetuṃ pūrvoktaṃ yojayati evambhūtānām ityādinā /*)

2. *vyaṣṭinirdeśadvārā...samaṣṭinirdeśadvārā* : B. D. explains the distinction between these two points of view as follows: "The *samaṣṭi* is the aggregate; the *vyaṣṭi* is a single instance of that. *Brahman*, possessed of *śaktis*, such as the *jīva* etc., is the *samaṣṭi*, while the *jīva* is the *vyaṣṭi*. (*samudāyaḥ samaṣṭiḥ tadekadeśas tu vyaṣṭir ityarthaḥ / jīvādiśaktimad brahma samaṣṭiḥ jīvas tu vyaṣṭiḥ /*)

3. Although Jīva closely follows the commentary of Śrīdhara in this and

the following sections, he has failed to record certain remarks, leaving the sense of the commentary somewhat unclear. The portion immediately preceding this seemingly inappropriate interjection reads as follows: "The ten topics, *sarga* etc., are described here. But won't a difference in topics cause a rift in the text? To this he replies, '(They describe) the nature of the nine in order to clarify the meaning of the tenth, i.e. *āśraya*.' And since only one (of the ten) is considered to be predominant, no blame can be attached." (...*sargādayo 'tra daśārthā lakṣyante | nanv evam arthabhedāc chāstrabhedaḥ syāt tatrāha | daśamasyāśrayasya viśuddhyarthaṃ navānāṃ lakṣaṇaṃ svarūpam | ekasyaiva prādhānyān nāyaṃ doṣa ityarthaḥ |*) The remaining portion of Jīva's commentary here is more or less identical with Śrīdhara's.

57) tam eva daśamaṃ vispaṣṭayituṃ teṣāṃ daśānāṃ vyutpādikāṃ saptaślokīm āha

bhūtamātrendriyadhiyāṃ janma sarga udāhṛtaḥ /
brahmaṇo guṇavaiṣamyād visargaḥ pauruṣaḥ smṛtaḥ //
bhūtāni khādīni mātrāṇi ca śabdādīni indriyāṇi ca / dhīśabdena mahadahaṅkārau / guṇānāṃ vaiṣamyāt pariṇāmāt / brahmaṇaḥ parameśvarāt kartur bhūtādīnāṃ janma sargaḥ / puruṣo vairājo brahmā tatkṛtaḥ pauruṣaḥ carācarasargo visarga ityarthaḥ /
sthitir vaikuṇṭhavijayaḥ poṣaṇaṃ tadanugrahaḥ /
manvantarāṇi saddharma ūtayaḥ karmavāsanāḥ //
avatārānucaritaṃ hareś cāsyānuvartinām /
puṃsām īśakathāḥ proktā nānākhyānopabṛṃhitāḥ //
vaikuṇṭhasya bhagavato vijayaḥ sṛṣṭānāṃ tattanmaryādāpālanenotkarṣaḥ sthitiḥ sthānam / tataḥ sthiteṣu svabhakteṣu tasyānugrahaḥ poṣaṇam / manvantarāṇi tattanmanvantarasthitānāṃ manvādīnāṃ tadanugṛhītānāṃ satāṃ caritāni tāny eva dharmas tadupāsanākhyaḥ saddharmaḥ / tatraiva sthitau nānākarmavāsanā ūtayaḥ / sthitāv eva harer avatārānucaritam asyānuvartināṃ ca kathā īśānukathāḥ proktā ityarthaḥ /
nirodho 'syānuśayanam ātmanaḥ saha śaktibhiḥ /
muktir hitvānyathārūpaṃ svarūpeṇa vyavasthitiḥ //
sthityanantaraṃ cātmano jīvasya śaktibhiḥ svopādhibhiḥ sahāsya harer anuśayanaṃ hariśayanānugatatvena śayanaṃ nirodha ityarthaḥ / tatra hareḥ śayanaṃ prapañcaṃ prati dṛṣṭinimīlanaṃ jīvānāṃ śayanaṃ tatra laya iti jñeyam / tatraiva nirodhe 'nyathārūpam avidyādhyastam ajñatvādikaṃ hitvā svarūpeṇa vyavasthitir muktiḥ //

57) In order to clarify the meaning of the tenth topic alone, Śuka utters the following seven verses, explaining the significance

of all ten : "The origination of the elements, sense objects, sense organs, and intellect, due to the disturbance of the equilibrium of the *guṇas* by Brahmā is known as *sarga*. The gross creation produced by the *puruṣa* is called *visarga*." (Bh.P. 2/10/3)

Here, the term *bhūta* refers to the elements, ether etc.; *mātra* signifies sense objects, such as sound etc. *Indriya* ("sense organs") represents the third element of this compound, and the term *dhī* indicates that *mahat* and *ahaṅkāra* are also to be included. "Due to the disturbance of the equilibrium of the *guṇas*" means "due to the transformation of the *guṇas*". This origination of the elements etc. "from Brahmā", i.e. from the creator, *parameśvara*, is what is known as *sarga*. The *puruṣa* is Brahmā, born from Virāj; what is created by him is known as *pauruṣa*. This *pauruṣa* creation of the moving and the unmoving is known as *visarga*. This is the idea.

"*Sthiti* signifies the triumph of Vaikuṇṭha (i.e. Viṣṇu); *poṣaṇa* indicates his grace; *manvantara* stands for the virtuous conduct of the holy; and *ūti*, for the subtle impressions from past actions. The descriptions of the deeds of the *avatāras* of Hari and his associates, supplemented by various legends, are known as *īśakathā*." (Bh.P. 2/10/4-5)

Here, *sthiti*, or *sthāna*, signifies the "triumph", i.e. excellence, "of Vaikuṇṭha", i.e. of *bhagavat*, in maintaining the different fixed limits for creatures. *Poṣaṇa* indicates the grace of *bhagavat* on his devotees dwelling within this period of maintenance. *Manvantara* refers to the lives of virtuous individuals, such as Manu etc., who have received the grace of *bhagavat*, and who dwell within the different *manvantaras*. Their lives are themselves considered *dharma*; reverence for the lives of these virtuous individuals is known as *saddharma*. *Ūti* stands for the impressions formed by the various activities performed during the period of maintenance. The stories of the deeds of the *avatāras* of Hari and his followers during the period of maintenance are called *īśānukathā*. This is the idea.

"*Nirodha* signifies the coming to rest of the *jīva*, together with his *śaktis*, in consequence of the cosmic sleep[1] of Hari. *Mukti* indicates the abandonment of what is foreign to one's own nature, and the establishment in one's own true nature."[2] (Bh.P. 2/10/6)

That is, following the period of maintenance, "the *ātman*", i.e. the *jīva*, comes to a state of rest "together with his *śaktis*", i.e.

with his own limiting adjuncts, as a consequence of "his", i.e. Hari's, rest; this is what is known as *nirodha*. Here, the "rest of Hari" (*śayana*) signifies a closing of the eyes from the manifest universe, while the "rest of the *jīva*" signifies the merging of the *jīvas* in the state of *nirodha*. *Mukti* indicates the steady dwelling in one's own true nature, in the condition of *nirodha*,[3] by abandoning all that is foreign to one's own nature, i.e. ignorance etc., superimposed by *avidyā*.

1. *anuśayanam* : Śrīdhara reads this as two words, *anu* and *śayanam*, and explains, "after the cosmic sleep of Hari". (*harer yoganidrām anu paścāt...*)

2. *svarūpeṇa* : Śrīdhara writes, "as identical with *brahman*". (*svarūpeṇa brahmatayā*) According to B. D., the true nature of the *jīva* is "characterized by the eight qualities, freedom from sin etc." (*svarūpeṇāpahatapāpmatvādiguṇāṣṭakaviśiṣṭena jīvasvarūpeṇa...* /) The reference is to the eight characteristics of the *ātman*, enumerated in the *daharavidyā* section of the Ch. U. (8/1/5): freedom from sin, old age, death, sorrow, hunger, and thirst, desiring what is real, and imagining what is real.

3. *tatraiva nirodhe* : It should be noted that Śrīdhara does not restrict *mukti* to the period after the death of the body. Aside from this additional phrase, Jīva's explanation of *mukti* is virtually identical with Śrīdhara's. B. D., like Jīva, describes *mukti* as a condition after death. He writes, "The state of *mukti* is characterized by freedom from rebirth and dwelling in the presence of *bhagavat*." (*vyavasthitir viśiṣṭā punarāvṛttiśūnyā bhagavatsannidhau sthitir muktir ityarthaḥ* /)

58) ābhāsaś ca nirodhaś ca yato 'sty adhyavasīyate /
sa āśrayaḥ paraṃ brahma paramātmeti śabdyate //

ābhāsaḥ sṛṣṭiḥ nirodho layaś ca yato bhavati adhyavasīyata upalabhyate jīvānāṃ jñānendriyeṣu prakāśate ca sa brahmeti paramātmeti prasiddha āśrayaḥ kathyate / iti śabdaḥ prakārārthaḥ tena bhagavān iti ca / asya vivṛtir agre vidheyā //

58) "That is the *āśraya*, from which come[1] the origin and dissolution of the universe, and by virtue of which[2] it is perceived; it is designated the supreme *brahman* and *paramātman*." (Bh. P. 2/10/7)

That is, he who is well-known under the designations *brahman* and *paramātman*, from whom come the *ābhāsa*, i.e. the origin, and the *nirodha*, i.e. the dissolution (of the universe), and because of whom it *adhyavasīyate*, i.e. is perceived, or shines, through the sense organs of *jīvas*, he is known as the *āśraya*. Since the particle *iti* indicates variety, *bhagavat* is also to be understood as one of his designations. A further explanation (of this topic) is given below.

1. *asti* : R.M. interprets the verb *asti* ("is") to mean *tiṣṭhati* ("exists"), and thus explains that the *āśraya* is also the ground for the universe during the period of maintenance. (*astīty asya tiṣṭhatītyarthaḥ / yataḥ sthitir iti paryavasitam /*)

2. *yataḥ* : R. M. explains that the pronoun *yataḥ* is to be construed with the second half of this line as well as the first. (*adhyavasīyate ity atrāpi yata ity asyānvayaḥ /*)

59) sthitau ca tatrāśrayasvarūpam aparokṣānubhavena vyaṣṭidvārāpi spaṣṭaṃ darśayitum adhyātmādivibhāgam āha

yo 'dhyātmiko 'yaṃ puruṣaḥ so 'sāv evādhidaivikaḥ /
yas tatrobhayavicchedaḥ puruṣo hy ādhibhautikaḥ //
ekam ekatarābhāve yadā nopalabhāmahe /
tritayaṃ tatra yo veda sa ātmā svāśrayāśrayaḥ //

yo 'yam ādhyātmikaḥ puruṣaś cakṣurādikaraṇābhimānī draṣṭā jivaḥ sa evādhidaivikaś cakṣurādyadhiṣṭhātā sūryādiḥ / dehasṛṣṭeḥ pūrvaṃ karaṇānām adhiṣṭhānābhāvenākṣamatayā karaṇaprakāśakartṛtvābhimānitatsahāyayor ubhayor api tayor vṛttibhedānudayena jīvatvamātrāviśeṣāt / tataś cobhayaḥ karaṇābhimānitadadhiṣṭhātṛdevatārūpo dvirūpo vicchedo yasmāt sa ādhibhautikaś cakṣurgolakādyupalakṣito dṛśyo dehaḥ puruṣa iti puruṣasya jīvasyopādhiḥ / sa vā eṣa puruṣo 'nnarasamayaḥ ityādiśruteḥ //

59) In order to clearly demonstrate the nature of the *āśraya* during the period of maintenance, from the *vyaṣṭi* point of view as well, that is, in terms of one's own immediate experience, Śuka explains the distinction between the categories, *adhyātma* etc., in the following two verses: "He who is the *ādhyātmika puruṣa* is verily the *ādhidaivika puruṣa*. The *puruṣa* who is responsible for the division of these two is verily the *ādhibhautika puruṣa*. In the absence of any one of these three, we do not perceive the others. Then, he who knows all three is the *ātman* (i.e. the *jīva*), who is himself grounded in him (i.e. in *parmātman*) who has no *āśraya* other than himself."[1] (Bh.P. 2/10/8-9)

That is, he who is the *ādhyātmika puruṣa*, the *jīva*, or perceiver, who identifies himself with the sense organs, such as the eyes etc., is also the *ādhidaivika puruṣa*, the presiding deity of the eye setc., such as Sūrya (the sun) etc. Prior to the creation of the body, there exists no dwelling place for the sense organs, which are thus rendered impotent. Consequently, no distinct modifications arise within either (the *ādhyātmika puruṣa*), who considers himself to be the illuminator of the senses, or his ally (the *ādhidaivika puruṣa*). As a result, both remain indistinguishable from the pure *jīva*. Then, on account of the *ādhibhautika puruṣa*, i.e. the visible body, endowed with eyeballs etc., the other two *puruṣas* are divided, and assume their respective forms, the one identifying himself with the senses, and the other as the presiding deity of the senses. The *ādhibhautika puruṣa* (i.e. the physical body) is referred to as a *puruṣa* (literally, a "person") insofar as it represents the limiting adjunct of the *puruṣa*, or *jīva*. This usage is justified by the following Śruti text: "This *puruṣa* (i.e. the physical person) is the embodiment of the essence of food." (Tai.U. 2/1/1)

1. The translation of this final line is based on Jīva's commentary presented in the following section. A more natural reading of this line, and the one accepted by Śrīdhara, would be, "Then, he who knows all three is the *ātman*, who has no *āśraya* other than himself." Despite Jīva's departure from Śrīdhara's interpretation of the final line, his remarks on the first of these two verses are virtually identical with those of Śrīdhara.

60) ekam ekatarābhāva ity eṣām anyonyasāpekṣasiddhatvenānāśrayatvaṃ darśayati / tathā hi dṛśyaṃ vinā tatpratītyanumeyaṃ karaṇaṃ na sidhyati nāpi draṣṭā na ca tadvinā karaṇapravṛttyanumeyas tadadhiṣṭhātā sūryādiḥ na ca taṃ vinā dṛśyam ity ekatarasyābhāva ekaṃ nopalabhāmahe / tatra tadā tat tritayam ālocanātmakena pratyayena yo veda sākṣitayā paśyati sa paramātmā āśrayaḥ / teṣāṃ api parasparam āśrayatvam astīti tadvyavacchedārthaṃ viśeṣaṇaṃ svāśrayo 'nanyāśrayaḥ / sa cāsāv anyeṣāṃ āśrayaś ceti / tatrāṃśāṃśinoḥ śuddhajīvaparamātmanor abhedāṃśasvīkāreṇaivāśraya uktaḥ/ ataḥ paro 'pi manute 'nartham iti

jāgratsvapnasuṣuptaṃ ca guṇato buddhivṛttayaḥ /
tāsāṃ vilakṣaṇo jīvaḥ sākṣitvena vivakṣitaḥ //

iti śuddho vicaṣṭe hy aviśuddhakartuḥ ityādy uktasya sākṣisaṃjñinaḥ śuddhajīvasyāśrayatvaṃ na śaṅkanīyam / athavā nanv ādhyātmikādīnām apy āśrayatvam asty eva / satyaṃ tathāpi parasparāśrayatvān na tatrāśrayatākaivalyam iti te tv āśraya-śabdena mukhyatayā nocyanta ity āha tritayam iti / sa ātmā sākṣī jīvas tu yaḥ svāśrayo 'nanyāśrayaḥ paramātmā sa evāśrayo yasya tathābhūta iti / vakṣyate ca haṃsaguhyastave

sarvaṃ pumān veda guṇāṃś ca tajjño
na veda sarvajñam anantam īḍe / iti

tasmāt ābhāsaś ca ityādinoktaḥ paramātmaivāśraya iti /2/10 śrīśukaḥ //

60) The second of these two verses (i.e. Bh.P. 2/10/9) reveals the fact that none of these (three *puruṣas*) can be considered the *āśraya*,[1] since they are all mutually dependent. That is, in the absence of the visible object, it is not possible to establish the existence of either the sense organ, whose existence is inferred from the perception of the object, or the seer. And in the absence of either the sense organ or the seer, it is not possible to establish the existence of the presiding deities of the senses, such as Sūrya (the sun) etc., whose existence is inferred from the functioning of the sense organs. Furthermore, without the presiding deity, the sense organs cannot function; and in the absence of the senses, the existence of the visible object cannot be established. Thus, in the absence of any one of these, we do not perceive the others. Then, he who "knows" these three, i.e. perceives them as the witness through a reflective cognition, he, i.e. *paramātman*, is the *āśraya*. The qualifier *svāśraya*, i.e. "having no *āśraya* other than itself", is meant to distinguish *paramātman* from the other three, which also function as *āśrayas*, each being the *āśraya* for the others. And (in addition to being its own *āśraya*), the *paramātman* is also the *āśraya* for the others.[2]

The term *āśraya* is used here only with reference to that aspect of the pure *jiva*, or "part", which is identical with the *paramātman*, or "whole". Thus, there should be no hesitation in considering the pure *jiva*, known as the "witness" and characterized in the following verses, to be the *āśraya*: "...though beyond the three *guṇas*, he considers himself to be composed of the three *guṇas*, and consequently comes to grief" (Bh.P. 1/7/5); "The states of waking, dream, and dreamless sleep are all modifications of the intellect based on the *guṇas*. The *jiva*, being their witness, is considered distinct from them"

(Bh.P. 11/13/27); and "...the pure (witness) observes the modifications of the mind, the impure agent" (Bh.P. 5/11/12).

But then,[3] shouldn't the *ādhyātmika puruṣa* and the others also be considered *āśrayas*?[4] True, but since they are mutually dependent, they cannot be considered *āśrayas* in any absolute sense; therefore, the term *āśraya* should not be applied to them in its primary sense. This is the significance of the phrase, "In the absense of any one of these three, we do not perceive the others."

Then why not consider the witness alone to be the *āśraya*? To this Śuka replies, "Then he who knows all three is the *ātman*..." This *ātman* is the *jīva*, or witness. But he who represents his own *āśraya*, i.e. has no *āśraya* other than himself, is *paramātman*. It is he who is the *āśraya* for the witnessing *jīva*. As stated in the *Haṃsaguhyastava*, "Man knows all, including the *guṇas*; but knowing all that, he still does not know the all-knowing, infinite (*paramātman*). My salutations to that (*paramātman*)" (Bh.P. 6/4/25). Therefore, the *paramātman* alone is declared to be the *āśraya* in the *Bhāgavata* verse which defines the term (Bh.P. 2/10/7).[5]

1. *anyonyasāpekṣasiddhatvenānāśrayatvam* : All available editions of T. S. read either ...*siddhatve nānāśrayatvam* or ...*siddhatve nānātmatvam*. However, both B. D. and R. M. are agreed that the final member of the first compound is the instrumental *siddhatvena*, after which B. D. reads *anāśrayatvam* and R. M., *anātmatvam*. (B. D.: *sāpekṣatvena siddhes teṣām āśrayatvaṃ nāsti*...; R. M.: *anyasāpekṣyānupapattimūlakasiddhitvena anātmatvam*...) The sentence in which this phrase occurs is identical with the opening sentence of Śrīdhara's commentary on this verse, with the exception that the reading found there is ...*siddhitve nānātmatvam*; and it is perhaps on the strength of this that the editors of T. S. have chosen the readings mentioned above, rather than follow the commentaries of B. D. and R. M.

2. This entire first paragraph is a literal reproduction of the first half of Śrīdhara's commentary on Bh.P. 2/10/9. The paragraphs which follow this represent Jīva's own interpretation, and bear no resemblance to the remaining portion of Śrīdhara's commentary on this verse.

3. *athavā* : In the preceding paragraph, Jīva had qualified the interpretation of Śrīdhara by maintaining that the witness is not *paramātman*, but the pure *jīva* who, as a *śakti* of *paramātman*, constitutes a portion of him. Jīva is forced into this interpretation, since an admission that *paramātman* directly functions as the witness of the mind and senses is tantamount to admitting the identity of the *jīva* and *paramātman*. However, once Jīva has identified the

witness with the pure *jīva*, who is dependent on *paramātman*, he can no longer interpret the expression *svāśrayāśrayaḥ* as meaning "having no *āśraya* other than himself". Thus, as B.D. explains, "dissatisfied, Jīva offers a second interpretation, introduced by the word *athavā*." (*asantoṣād vyākhyāntaram athaveti* /)

4. The idea is that if the *jīva*, though dependent on *paramātman*, can be considered an *āśraya*, why not consider the three *puruṣas* to be *āśrayas* as well?

5. *ābhāsaś ca* : The reference is to the verse cited in section 58, in which the *āśraya* is designated *paramātman* and the supreme *brahman*, and not by terms indicating the *jīva*.

61) asya śrībhāgavatasya mahāpurāṇatvavyañjakalakṣaṇaṃ prakārāntareṇa ca vadann api tasyaivāśrayatvam āha dvayena

sargo 'syātha visargaś ca vṛttī rakṣāntarāṇi ca /
vaṃśo vaṃśānucaritaṃ saṃsthā hetur apāśrayaḥ //
daśabhir lakṣaṇair yuktaṃ purāṇaṃ tadvido viduḥ /
kecit pañcavidhaṃ brahman mahadalpavyavasthayā //

antarāṇī manvantarāṇi / pañcavidham

sargaś ca pratisargaś ca vaṃśo manvantarāṇi ca /
vaṃśānucaritaṃ ceti purāṇaṃ pañcalakṣaṇam //

iti kecid vadanti / sa ca matabhedo mahadalpavyavasthayā mahāpurāṇam alpapurāṇam iti bhinnādhikaraṇatvena / yady api viṣṇupurāṇādāv api daśāpi tāni lakṣyante tathāpi pañcānām eva prādhānyenoktatvād alpatvam / atra daśānām arthānāṃ skandheṣu yathākramaṃ praveśo na vivakṣitaḥ teṣāṃ dvādaśasaṅkhyatvāt / dvitīyaskandhoktānāṃ teṣāṃ tṛtīyādiṣu yathāsaṅkhyaṃ na samāveśaḥ nirodhādīnāṃ daśamādiṣv aṣṭamavarjam anyeṣām apy anyeṣu yathoktalakṣaṇatayā samāveśanāśakyatvād eva / tad uktaṃ śrīsvāmibhir eva

daśame kṛṣṇasatkīrtivitānāyopavarṇyate /
dharmaglāninimittas tu nirodho duṣṭabhūbhujām //
prākṛtādicaturdhā yo nirodhaḥ sa tu varṇitaḥ / iti ato

'tra skandhe śrīkṛṣṇarūpasyāśrayasyaiva varṇanaprādhānyaṃ tair vivakṣitam / uktaṃ ca svayam eva

daśame daśamaṃ lakṣyam āśritāśrayavigraham / iti

evam anyatrāpy unneyam / ataḥ prāyaśaḥ sarve 'rthāḥ sarveṣv eva skandheṣu gauṇatvena vā mukhyatvena vā nirūpyanta ity eva teṣām abhimatam / śrutenārthena cāñjasā ity atra ca tathaiva pratipannaṃ sarvatra tattatsambhavāt / tataś ca prathamadvitīyayor api mahāpurāṇatāyāṃ praveśaḥ syāt / tasmāt kramo na gṛhītaḥ //

61) Sūta also declares (*paramātman*)[1] alone to be the *āśraya*, in the following two verses, though enumerating the characteristics which indicate the *Bhāgavata* to be a Mahāpurāṇa in a different fashion[2] : "The knowers of Purāṇas understand a Purāṇa to have the following ten characteristics:

1) *sarga*, 2) *visarga*, 3) *vṛtti*, 4) *rakṣā*, 5) *antara*, 6) *vaṃśa*, 7) *vaṃśānucarita*, 8) *saṃsthā*, 9) *hetu*, and 10) *apāśraya*. Some, O Brāhmaṇa, consider the characteristics to be fivefold based on a distinction between major and minor." (Bh.P. 12/7/9-10)

Here, *antarāṇi* signifies *manvantaras*. Some consider the characteristics of Purāṇas to be fivefold by citing the following verse: "*Sarga*, *pratisarga*, *vaṃśa*, *manvantara*, and *vaṃśānucarita* are the five characteristics of a Purāṇa."[3] This difference of opinion is "based on a distinction between major and minor", i.e. based on the fact that major and minor Purāṇas each have their own distinctive topics. Even though all ten topics are described in such Purāṇas as the *Viṣṇu* etc., still, since only five are principally discussed, they are considered minor.[4]

This is not to say that these ten topics can be found one after the other in the subsequent *skandhas* of the *Bhāgavata*, for the *Bhāgavata* contains twelve such *skandhas*.[5] Nor can the characteristics enumerated in the second *skandha* be found one after the other in *skandhas* three through twelve, since it is not possible to find the topics *nirodha*, *mukti*, and *āśraya* in *skandhas* ten, eleven, and twelve; the same is also true regarding the other characteristics and *skandhas*, with the exception of *skandha* eight (which deals with the topic *manvantara*).[6] Therefore, Śrīdhara himself states: "The destruction (*nirodha*) of the wicked kings, necessitated by a decline in righteousness, is described in *skandha* ten, in order to spread the fame of Kṛṣṇa. The four kinds of *nirodha*, *prākṛta* etc.,[7] have already been described." Thus, Śrīdhara considers the tenth *skandha* to be chiefly concerned with describing the *āśraya* alone, in the form of Kṛṣṇa. As he himself says: "The tenth topic (*āśraya*), in the form of him (i.e. Kṛṣṇa) who is the refuge for all who seek shelter with him, is the aim of the tenth *skandha*." And the same conclusion can be reached with regard to the other *skandhas* as well. Thus, according to Śrīdhara, virtually every topic is described either directly or indirectly, in every *skandha*. This same idea is indicated by the phrase, "(The first nine topics are described) either directly, with the aid of Śruti, or by explaining their significance (indirectly),"[8] since one or the other of these methods is met with throughout the *Bhāgavata*. Thus, the first and second *skandhas* are also to be considered as partaking of the nature of a Mahāpurāṇa. Therefore, we do not accept the idea that the ten topics are dealt with in successive chapters.

1. *tasyaiva* : R. M. understands the pronoun *tasya* to indicate *brahman*. (*tasyaiveti brahmaṇa evetyarthaḥ* /)

2. *prakārāntareṇa* : B. D. explains that in some cases the names alone are different, while in some places the topics themselves are different. (*kvacin nāmāntaratvād arthāntaratvāc cetyarthaḥ* /) Despite these differences, however, Jīva still maintains that the two lists indicate the same characteristics, as we shall see in the following two sections.

3. This verse is found, with minor variations, in the following Purāṇas: *Agni* 1/14, *Garuḍa* 1/2/27, *Kūrma* 1/1/12, *Matsya* 53/64, *Śiva* 1/41, *Vāyu* 4/10/11, *Viṣṇu* 3/6/25, etc. (Cf. Tagare: 1976: xviii.)

4. *viṣṇupurāṇādau...alpatvam* : The distinction between Mahāpurāṇas and Alpapurāṇas is apparently not found in other Purāṇas, and does not seem to correspond to the well-known distinction between Mahāpurāṇas and Upapurāṇas. The *Viṣṇu Purāṇa*, for example, is traditionally considered to be a Mahāpurāṇa in the latter sense; and as it is one of the most highly respected of Purāṇas by the Gauḍīya Vaiṣṇavas, it is unlikely that any slight is intended here by calling it an "Alpapurāṇa".

5. B. D. writes, "Some thick-headed people arrange these ten topics in order from the third *skandha* onward..." (*etāni daśalakṣaṇāni kecit tṛtīyādiṣu krameṇa sthūladhiyo yojayanti* .../) It may be noted that among those who accept a chapter-by-chapter distribution of these ten topics are Vopadeva, Vallabha, Vīrarāghava, Vijayadhvaja, and Śrīdhara himself. (Cf. Tagare : 1976: xxiii-xxxiii.)

6. Jīva elaborates on this idea in S. S., explaining that *sarga* is directly described in *skandhas* two and three, *visarga* in two, three, and four, *vṛtti* in seven and eleven, *rakṣā* in all the *skandhas*, *manvantara* in *skandha* eight, *vaṃśa* and *vaṃśānucarita* in four and nine, *saṃsthā* in eleven and twelve, *hetu* in three and eleven, and *āśraya* in ten.

7. Cf. section 63 for an enumeration and discussion of the four kinds of *nirodha*.

8. This is the final line of Bh.P. 2/10/2, cited earlier in section 56.

62) atha sargādīnāṃ lakṣaṇam āha
avyākṛtaguṇakṣobhān mahatas trivṛto 'hamaḥ /
bhūtamātrendriyārthānāṃ sambhavaḥ sarga ucyate //
pradhānaguṇakṣobhān mahān tasmāt triguṇo 'haṅkāraḥ tasmād bhūtamātrāṇāṃ bhūtasūkṣmāṇām indriyāṇāṃ ca sthūlabhūtānaṃ ca tadupalakṣitataddevatānāṃ ca sambhavaḥ sargaḥ / kāraṇasṛṣṭiḥ sarga ityarthaḥ /
puruṣānugṛhītānām eteṣāṃ vāsanāmayaḥ /
visargo 'yaṃ samāhāro bījād bījaṃ carācaram //
puruṣaḥ paramātmā / eteṣāṃ mahadādīnāṃ jīvasya pūrvakarmavāsanāpradhāno 'yaṃ samāhāraḥ kāryabhūtaś carācaraprāṇirūpo bījād bījam iva pravāhāpanno visarga ucyate/ vyaṣṭisṛṣṭir visarga ityarthaḥ / anenotir apy uktā /
vṛttir bhūtāni bhūtānāṃ carāṇām acarāṇi ca /
kṛtā svena nṛṇāṃ tatra kāmāc codanayāpi vā //
carāṇāṃ bhūtānāṃ sāmānyato 'carāṇi cakārāc carāṇi ca kāmād vṛttiḥ / tatra tu nṛṇāṃ svena svabhāvena kāmāc codanayāpi vā yā niyatā vṛttir jīvikā kṛtā sā vṛttir ucyata ityarthaḥ /
rakṣācyutāvatārehā viśvasyānuyuge yuge /
tiryaṅmartyarṣideveṣu hanyante yais trayīdviṣaḥ //
yair avatāraiḥ / aneneśakathā sthānaṃ poṣaṇaṃ ceti trayam uktam /
manvantaraṃ manur devā manuputrāḥ sureśvarāḥ /
ṛṣayo 'ṃśāvatārāś ca hareḥ ṣaḍvidham ucyate //
manvādyācaraṇakathanena saddharma evātra vivakṣita ityarthaḥ / tataś ca prāktanagranthenaikārthyam /
rājñāṃ brahmaprasūtānāṃ vaṃśas traikāliko 'nvayaḥ /
vaṃśyānucaritaṃ teṣāṃ vṛttaṃ vaṃśadharāś ca ye //
teṣāṃ rājñāṃ ye ca vaṃśadharās teṣāṃ vṛttaṃ vaṃśyānucaritam //

62) Sūta then describes the characteristics of *sarga* etc.: "The origination of *mahat* from a disturbance of the *guṇas* of the unmanifest (*prakṛti*), of the three-fold 'I'-consciousness, and of the subtle elements, senses, and sense objects is called *sarga*." (Bh.P. 12/7/11)

That is, *mahat* originates from a disturbance of the *guṇas* of *prakṛti*; from *mahat* comes *ahaṅkāra*, composed of the three *guṇas*; from *ahaṅkāra* arise the *bhūtamātras*, or subtle elements, the senses, and the gross elements, along with their respective presiding deities. This process of origination is termed *sarga*. That is to say, *sarga* indicates causal creation.

"The assembling of these (elements of creation), with the aid of the *puruṣa*, based on the stored-up impressions (of *jīvas*), is called *visarga*. It is the creation of all moving and unmoving beings, and proceeds like one seed growing out of another." (Bh.P. 12/7/12)

Here, the *puruṣa* stands for *paramātman*. The assembling of these elements of creation, i.e. *mahat* etc., is based primarily on the stored-up impressions from past actions of the *jīva*. It represents the effect in the form of living beings, both moving and unmoving. This unbroken cycle, like one seed arising from another, is called *visarga*; that is, it is the creation of the particular. The category *ūti* ("the subtle impressions from past actions") is also indicated by this verse.

"Unmoving beings constitute the *vṛtti*, or means of subsistence, for moving beings. The means of subsistence for men is accomplished naturally, out of desire, or in accordance with scriptural injunction." (Bh.P. 12/7/13)

That is, unmoving beings generally constitute the means of subsistence for moving beings, based on desire. The conjunction *ca* in this verse indicates that moving beings are also to be understood (as constituting the means of subsistence for other moving beings). The regulated *vṛtti* of men, however, performed to maintain their livelihood, is carried out "naturally", i.e. based on their own nature, either out of desire, or according to scriptural injunction; this is what is known as *vṛtti*.

"*Rakṣā* ('protection of the universe') indicates the exploits of the *avatāras* of Acyuta (i.e. Viṣṇu), who come age after age, among animals, mortals, *ṛṣis*, and *devas*, and who destroy the enemies of the Vedas." (Bh.P. 12/7/14)

Here, the pronoun *yaiḥ* indicates that it is the *avatāras* who destroy the enemies of the Vedas.[1] The three categories, *īśakathā* ("stories of the *avatāras*"), *sthāna* ("maintenance of the universe"), and *poṣaṇa* ("the grace of *bhagavat* on his devotees") are also indicated by this verse.

"*Manvantara* is said to contain six elements: the Manu, the *devas*, the rulers of the *devas*, the *ṛṣis*, and the partial *avatāras* of Hari." (Bh.P. 12/7/15)

Since the descriptions of the deeds of Manu etc. are indicated by the term *saddharma*, this characterization (of the category *manvantara*) is identical with the earlier one. (Bh.P. 2/4/10)

"The dynastic succession, past, present, and future, of the kings fathered by Brahmā is known as *vaṃśa*. The descriptions of the lives of their descendants is known as *vaṃśānucarita*." (Bh.P. 12/7/6)

Here, "of their (descendants)" means "of the descendants of the kings". It is the description of the lives of these descendants which is known as *vaṃśānucarita*.

1. Due to the construction of this sentence, the pronoun *yaiḥ* could also be construed with the compound *tiryaṅmartyarṣideveṣu*, indicating that it is the animals, mortals, etc. who destroy the enemies of the Vedas. It is to avoid such a confusion that Jīva makes this comment.

It may be noted that while Jīva's interpretations of the *Bhāgavata* verses (12/7/9-19) in this and the following section closely follow the commentary of Śrīdhara, the attempt to reconcile this list of topics with the earlier one (Bh.P. 2/10/1-7), given in sections 56-58, is Jīva's own contribution, and is not found in Śrīdhara's commentary.

63) naimittikaḥ prākṛtiko nitya ātyantiko layaḥ /
samstheti kavibhiḥ proktaś caturdhāsya svabhāvataḥ // asya parameśvarasya / svabhāvataḥ śaktitaḥ / ātyantika ity anena muktir apy atra praveśitā /

hetur jivo 'sya sargāder avidyākarmakārakaḥ /
yaṃ cānuśayinaṃ prāhur avyākṛtam utāpare //
hetur nimittam / asya viśvasya / yato 'yam avidyayā karmakārakaḥ / yam eva hetuṃ kecic caitanyaprādhānyenānuśayinaṃ prāhuḥ apara upādhiprādhānyenāvyākṛtam iti /

vyatirekānvayau yasya jāgratsvapnasuṣuptiṣu /
māyāmayeṣu tad brahma jīvavṛttiṣv apāśrayaḥ //
śrībādarāyaṇasamādhilabdhārthavirodhād atra ca jīvaśuddhasvarūpam evāśrayatvena na vyākhyāyate kintv ayam evārthaḥ jāgradādiṣv avasthāsu māyāmayeṣu māyāśaktikalpiteṣu mahadādidravyeṣu ca kevalasvarūpeṇa vyatirekaḥ paramasākṣitayānvayaś ca yasya tad brahma ca jīvānāṃ vṛttiṣu śuddhasvarūpatayā sopādhitayā ca vartaneṣu sthitiṣv apāśrayaḥ sarvam atyatikramyāśraya ityarthaḥ / apa ity etat khalu varjane varjanaṃ cātikrame paryavasyatīti / tad evam apāśrayābhivyaktidvārabhūtaṃ hetuśabdavyapadiṣṭasya jīvasya śuddhasvarūpajñānam āha dvābhyām

padārtheṣu yathā dravyaṃ tanmātraṃ rūpanāmasu /
bījādipañcatāntāsu hy avasthāsu yutāyutam //
virameta yadā cittaṃ hitvā vṛttitrayaṃ svayam /
yogena vā tadātmānaṃ vedehāyā nivartate //
rūpanāmātmakeṣu padārtheṣu ghaṭādiṣu yathā dravyaṃ pṛthivyādi yutam ayutaṃ ca bhavati kāryadṛṣṭiṃ vināpy upalambhāt tathā tanmātraṃ śuddhaṃ jīvacaitanyamātraṃ vastu garbhādhānādipañcatāntāsu navasv apy avasthāsv avidyayā yutaṃ svatas tv ayutam iti śuddham ātmānam itthaṃ jñātvā nirviṇṇaḥ sann apāśrayānusandhānayogyo bhavatīty āha virameteti / vṛttitrayaṃ jāgratsvapnasuṣuptirūpam / ātmānaṃ paramātmānam / svayaṃ vāmadevāder iva māyāmayatvānusandhānena devahūtyāder ivānuṣṭhitena yogena vā/tataś cehāyās tadanuśīlanavyatiriktaceṣṭāyāḥ /12/7 śrīsūtaḥ / uddiṣṭaḥ sambandhaḥ//

63) "*Saṃsthā*, or dissolution, is declared by the wise to result from the essential power (of *parameśvara*), and to be of four kinds: *naimittika* (causal), *prākṛta* (natural), *nitya* (necessary), and *ātyantika* (final)." (Bh.P. 12/7/17)

Here, the pronoun *asya* indicates *parameśvara*, and the term *svabhāvataḥ* means "due to his *śakti*".[1] The mention of *ātyantika*, or final dissolution, indicates that *mukti* is also included here.

"The *jīva* performs actions out of ignorance, and is thus the *hetu*, or cause, of the creation etc. of the universe. Some call that *anuśayin*, while others call it *avyākṛta*." (Bh.P. 12/7/18)

Here, the term *hetu* indicates the occasional cause; *asya* means "of the universe". The compound *avidyākarmakārakaḥ* provides the reason: "since he performs actions out of ignorance". Some refer to this *hetu* as *anuśayin*,[2] emphasizing the conscious aspect, while others call it *avyākṛta*,[3] emphasizing its association with *upādhis*.

"That *brahman*, who is both associated with and distinct from the states of waking, dream, and deep sleep as well as the products of *māyā*, serves as the *apāśraya*, or ground, for the functions of the *jīva*." (Bh.P. 12/7/19)[4]

The pure form of the *jīva* is not explained here to be the *āśraya*, since that would contradict Vyāsa's experience in *samādhi*. Rather, the idea is this: *Brahman*, in his pure form, is distinct from the states of waking etc., as well as from the products of *māyā*, such as *mahat* etc., which are conceived through the power of *māyā*; in his role as the supreme witness, he is associated with them. That is to say, though the *apāśraya* is the ground (*āśraya*) for the functions of the *jīvas*, both in its pure form, and in its qualified form, as dwelling in the midst of these functions, it is all-transcending. This is indicated by the preverb *apa* (in *apāśraya*) which indicates "abandonment", which is itself synonymous with "transcendence".

Therefore, Sūta, in the following two verses, speaks of the pure conscious nature of the *jīva*, designated by the term *hetu*, as a means to revealing the true nature of the *apāśraya*: "Just as a substance is both associated with and distinct from the objects which it constitutes, made up of names and forms, so is the reality[5] both associated with and distinct from the various stages of life, beginning with inception and ending with death. When one withdraws the mind and goes beyond the three states (waking, dreaming, and deep sleep), either on his own, or with the aid of yoga, he realizes the *ātman*, and refrains from endeavors." (Bh.P. 12/7/20-21)

That is, just as a substance, such as earth etc., is associated with objects, such as jars etc., and is also distinct from them when viewed without regard for its effect, so also the *tanmātra*, i.e. the reality, or pure consciousness of the *jīva*, is associated, through *avidyā*, with the nine stages of life, beginning with inception and ending with death, and yet is, in itself, unassociated.

Having realized the pure *ātman* to be such, one becomes indifferent and qualified to inquire into the nature of the *apāśraya*. This is explained by Sūta in the second of these two verses (Bh. P. 12/7/21). Here, the "three states" are those of waking, dreaming and deep sleep; the term *ātman* signifies *paramātman*. The expression "on his own" means "by inquiring into the illusory nature of things, as did Vāmadeva etc.", and "through yoga" means "through the practices of yoga, performed by Devahūti etc." "Refraining from all endeavors" means "from all endeavors other than the pursuit of *paramātman*".

Thus has the *sambandha* been indicated.[6]

1. *asya svabhāvataḥ* : Śrīdhara interprets the pronoun *asya* to mean "of the universe", and *svabhāvataḥ* to mean "due to *māyā*". He thus understands this phrase as indicating either that the four kinds of dissolution have sprung from *māyā*, or that the universe, which is subject to these four kinds of dissolution,

has sprung from *māyā*. (*asya viśvasya/ svabhāvato māyāto niṣpannasya/ yad vā māyāto yaś caturvidho laya iti* /)

2. *anuśayin* : B. D. characterizes the *anuśayin* as the *jīva* who has already experienced his residual *karman*. (*bhuktaśiṣṭakarmaviśiṣṭo jīvo 'nuśayīty ucyate* /) However, since the term *anuśayana* had been used earlier (Bh.P. 2/1/6, section 57) to indicate the condition of the *jīva* during dissolution, due to the cosmic sleep of Hari, and not due to the exhaustion of his own *karman*, it seems more likely that the *anuśayin* here refers to the *jīva* with *karman* left to experience, and on account of whom a new cycle of creation begins. This interpretation is further justified by the expression *avidyākarmakārakaḥ*, since the effects of actions performed out of ignorance must necessarily be experienced at some later date.

3. *avyākṛtam* : The mention of the unmanifest *prakṛti* (*avyākṛta*) is perhaps a reference to the system of Sāṅkhya. Jīva's attempt to reconcile the two views mentioned in this verse by explaining them as representing different standpoints is taken directly from Śrīdhara's commentary.

4. According to Śrīdhara, the functions of the *jīva* are the three states of consciousness, *viśva*, *taijasa*, and *prājña*, through which *brahman* functions as the *jīva* during the conditions of waking, dreaming, and deep sleep respectively. *Brahman* is associated with these states, which are themselves the product of *māyā*, in his role as the witness. When, however, the *jīva* attains the state of *samādhi*, he is distinct from them. (*jāgradādiṣv avasthāsu jīvatayā vartata iti jīvavṛttayo viśvataijasaprājñās teṣu māyāmayeṣu sākṣitayānvayaḥ samādhyādau ca vyatireko yasya tad brahman*.../)

5. *tanmātram* : Śrīdhara reads *sanmātram*, and glosses *sattāmātram*, i.e. "pure existence". He also explains that the first line of this verse presents two distinct illustrations showing the relationship between the *apāśraya* and phenomenal existence. He writes, "Just as substance is both associated with and unassociated with objects, and pure existence both associated with and unassociated with names and forms, so is the *apāśraya* both associated with and unassociated with the stages of life from inception to death." (*padārtheṣu ghaṭādiṣu dravyaṃ mṛdādiṣu yathā yutam anvitam ayutaṃ ca*.../ *rūpanāmasu ca sanmātraṃ sattāmātraṃ yathā* / *evam* ...*dehāvasthāsu yutam ayutaṃ ca yat tad apāśraya iti*//)

6. *uddiṣṭaḥ sambandhaḥ* : Jīva writes in S. S. that only a general introduction has been given of the *sambandha*, or ultimate principle. (*sambandhinaḥ paramatattvasya diṅmātram eva darśitamitya rthaḥ* //) Jīva's treatment of the *sambandha* is continued in the three *sandarbhas* which follow this: the *Bhagavatsandarbha*, *Paramātmasandarbha*, and *Kṛṣṇasandarbha*.

iti kaliyugapāvanasvabhajanavibhajanaprayojanāvataraśrī-śrībhagavatkṛṣṇacaitanyadevacaraṇānucaraviśvavaiṣṇavarāja-sabhāsabhājanabhājanaśrīrūpasanātanānuśāsanabhāratīgarbh eśrībhāgavatasandarbhe tattvasandarbho nāma prathamaḥ sandarbhaḥ //

Here ends the first volume of the *Bhāgavatasandarbha*, entitled *Tattvasandarbha*, written according to the teachings[1] of Rūpa and Sanātana, the objects of veneration in the assemblies of all great Vaiṣṇavas, and the companions of the holy Bhagavān Kṛṣṇa Caitanya, the purifier of the Kali Yuga, who incarnated in order to bestow the boon of his own worship.

1. *anuśāsana* : Jīva explains that this may be taken either in the sense of "teachings" or "command". (*anuśāsanam ājñā śikṣā vā*)

CONCLUSION

Having examined both the historical setting in which the *Tattvasandarbha* and commentaries were written, as well as the ideas found in the texts themselves, we are now in a position to examine the following questions: 1) the relationship between the life and teachings of Caitanya as presented in the orthodox biographies, and the philosophical and sectarian views of Jīva, Baladeva, and Rādhāmohana; 2) the role which the latter three authors have played in the sectarian development of the Gauḍīya Vaiṣṇava school; and 3) the extent to which the present-day movement reflects the sentiments and ideology of its founder, Caitanya.

It is no secret that Caitanya's most important biographer, Kṛṣṇadāsa Kavirāja, relied heavily on the writings of the Vṛndāvana Gosvāmins for the philosophical portions of the *Caitanya Caritāmṛta*. The Kavirāja's justification for almost literally putting the words of the Gosvāmins in Caitanya's mouth no doubt stemmed from his belief that the writings of the Gosvāmins represented, if not the direct teachings of Caitanya, then at least his sentiments and beliefs. While Kṛṣṇadāsa was perhaps justified in making this assumption with regard to Rūpa and Sanātana, both of whom had close personal contact with Caitanya, the case of Jīva, who probably never met Caitanya, is somewhat different. Still, when we examine the *Caitanya Caritāmṛta* together with Jīva's *Tattvasandarbha*, it becomes clear that Kṛṣṇadāsa has borrowed heavily from the latter work as well in presenting the teachings of Caitanya. Consequently, as many scholars are quick to point out, it is virtually impossible to reach any definite conclusions from such portions regarding the exact relationship between the teachings of Caitanya and the views of Jīva. We would only suggest that those passages from the *Caitanya Caritāmṛta* which are obviously based on the works of the Gosvāmins, Jīva in particular, and which imply that Caitanya had a well-defined philosophical system in mind be viewed with extreme caution.

In further considering the relationship between Jīva and

Caitanya, we should first point out that Jīva himself nowhere claims to be presenting either the teachings or views of Caitanya. In the opening sections of the *Tattvasandarbha*, Jīva cites Gopāla Bhaṭṭa as the original author of the text, who himself relied on the writings of such Vaiṣṇava *ācāryas* as Śrīdhara, Rāmānuja, and Madhva; and at the conclusion of the work, Jīva states that the *Tattvasandarbha* was written according to the teachings of Rūpa and Sanātana. Nevertheless, both the initial *maṅgala* verse to Caitanya and the reference to him in the colophon of the *Tattvasandarbha* give the clear impression that Jīva considered his views to be representative of the general tradition initiated by Caitanya, and it seems reasonable to expect to find at least a basic consistency between the doctrines of Jīva and those of Caitanya.

While the lengthy philosophical portions of the *Caitanya Caritāmṛta* cannot be relied upon for such a comparison, other types of evidence are, however, available to us. We have tried to demonstrate in the first chapter of this study the reliability of the accounts indicating Caitanya's great love for the *Bhāgavata Purāṇa*, his respect for Śrīdhara's commentary, and his lack of interest in traditional Vedānta. If one accepts these as Caitanya's actual views, it must be admitted that at least the conception of the *Tattvasandarbha* is consistent with the teachings of Caitanya. When we examine the contents of this work, however, it becomes clear that Jīva was not nearly as happy with Śrīdhara's commentary as was Caitanya, and it seems likely that Jīva's claims to follow Śrīdhara represent more a concession to Caitanya's beliefs than a personal preference on his own part. In actual fact, Jīva follows Śrīdhara on only the most minor points, ignoring all of his Advaitic interpretations on the plea that they are "non-Vaiṣṇava" and were meant merely to entice the Advaitins to study the *Bhāgavata*. As we have seen in T. S. 60, Jīva even goes so far as to quote portions of Śrīdhara's commentary only to refute his interpretation in subsequent paragraphs. Jīva's claim to follow the natural sense of the *Bhāgavata* in such cases is also not justified since he often resorts to unlikely interpretations of terms or analyses of compounds to establish his own views.

Despite Jīva's claims to rely on the ideas of earlier Vaiṣṇava teachers, his Acintyabhedābhedavāda, or doctrine of unthinkable unity within difference, actually represents an original contribution to Indian thought. Though in many respects similar to the systems of Bhāskara and Nimbārka, Jīva's Acintyabhedābhedavāda is based almost entirely on a few key verses from the *Bhāgavata* and *Viṣṇu Purāṇas* regarding the threefold *śakti* doctrine and the triple designation of reality as *brahman*, *paramātman*, and *bhagavat*. The identity of *bhagavat* with Kṛṣṇa, and the glorification of Rādhā as Kṛṣṇa's principal *śakti* also represent some of its chief features.

However, while Jīva bases the whole of his *Bhāgavatasandarbha* on a series of verses from the *Bhāgavata*, it is questionable whether his doctrines actually represent the true spirit of this text. As instances to the contrary, we mention the following facts: the belief that Kṛṣṇa is the source of all *avatāras* is found in but a single verse of the *Bhāgavata*, and contradicted numerous times throughout the text; the name of Rādhā, whose worship alongside of Kṛṣṇa is an indispensable feature of Gauḍīya Vaiṣṇava worship, is nowhere found in the *Bhāgavata*; and the famous verse designating the supreme truth as *brahman*, *paramātman*, and *bhagavat* gives no indication that a hierarchy is meant within which *bhagavat* occupies the highest position. Furthermore, though the *Bhāgavata* undoubtedly embodies a variety of philosophical viewpoints, there can be no question that the doctrine of Advaita represents one of its keynotes, beautifully harmonized with the devotional undertones of the text, a fact which is clearly brought out in the commentary of Śrīdhara. Thus, considering the harsh criticism which Caitanya leveled against Vallabha for contradicting Śrīdhara's commentary and interpreting the *Bhāgavata* from his own point of view, one may legitimately wonder whether Caitanya would have been any more pleased with Jīva's nominal regard for Śrīdhara and his original interpretations of the *Bhāgavata*.

Caitanya's attitude towards the other religious and philosophical traditions of India are, like his own philosophical views, not easily discernible from the biographies. On the one hand, Kṛṣṇadāsa portrays Caitanya as almost hostile towards both the Advaitins and the Mādhvas, and intent on converting others to his own beliefs. On the other hand, we find Caitanya reverently entering Śiva temples, and expressing joy that one of his companions, a devotee of Rāma, refused to take initiation with a Kṛṣṇa mantra. Caitanya's primary considerations seem to have been sincerity and devotion, and his criticism of other sects was generally directed towards those which lacked these, whether they be the Tattvavādins of Uḍipī or the Advaitins of Banaras. It thus appears likely that Caitanya's attitude towards the other religious traditions of India was one of liberality, and that the narrowness which is sometimes seen in the *Caitanya Caritāmṛta* should be attributed rather to the sectarian enthusiasm of Kṛṣṇadāsa than to Caitanya.

Regarding Caitanya's own *sampradāya*, Kṛṣṇadāsa and the other biographers, with the exception of Kavi Karṇapūra, have very little to say. Caitanya is generally spoken of as formally belonging to the Advaitic Bhāratī Sampradāya of his *sannyāsa* guru, Keśava, although the affiliation is never taken very seriously. The real tradition which Caitanya is said to represent is normally traced through his mantra guru to Mādhavendra; and despite the various traditions linking Mādhavendra to the Mādhva Sampradāya, Kṛṣṇadāsa makes no mention of Mādhavendra's spiritual lineage. It seems safe to assume that Kṛṣṇadāsa was opposed to the idea that Mādhavendra was a Mādhva *sannyāsin*, and it is possible that the unflattering account of the Mādhvas in Uḍipī was the direct result of Kṛṣṇadāsa's unhappiness with this tradition.

Jīva, on the other hand, exhibits a noticeably less caustic attitude towards both Śaṅkara and Madhva, although, like Kṛṣṇadāsa, he is also not specific about Caitanya's own *sampradāya*. Aside from a single statement in *Sarvasaṃvādinī* crediting Caitanya with initiating his own *sampradāya*, there is nothing in the texts studied here to indicate that Jīva was concerned with the question at all. Jīva echoes Kṛṣṇadāsa's belief that the Caitanya tradition began with Caitanya's *paramaguru*, Mādhavendra, referring to a "Mādhava Sampradāya" in his *Vaiṣṇavavandanā*. There is, however, no mention of Mādhavendra's own sectarian affiliation in the works of Jīva. It seems likely from certain remarks in the *Tattvasandarbha* (cf. T. S. 28, f. n. 6) that Jīva was not even aware of the tradition linking Mādhavendra to the Mādhva Sampradāya at the time he wrote that work, probably indicating that it was composed prior to Karṇapūra's *Gauragaṇoddeśadīpikā*.

Baladeva's claims regarding Mādhavendra's sectarian ties

were thus based on a tradition which neither Caitanya nor Jīva seem to have recognized, and which Kṛṣṇadāsa probably knew of, but repudiated. As we have tried to show, the line of gurus tracing Caitanya to the Mādhva Sampradāya, though of uncertain origin, questionable accuracy, and contrary to the customary practice of tracing a *sannyāsin's sampradāya* through his *sannyāsa* guru, should not be credited to Baladeva; more than likely it dates back at least to the middle of the 16th century with Karṇapūra's *Gauragaṇoddeśadīpikā.* The real significance of Baladeva's declaration of Mādhva affiliation lies in the fact that it gave a legitimacy to this tradition which it otherwise might not have had, and in this respect marks a real turning point in the history of the Gauḍīya Vaiṣṇava movement.

The most radical aspect of Baladeva's writings is not, however, his attempt to demonstrate the formal affiliation of the Gauḍīya Vaiṣṇava school to the Mādhva Sampradāya, but rather his interpretation of the school's doctrines from a Mādhva point of view, and his attempt to show that both Caitanya and Jīva recognized their indebtedness to the teachings of Madhva. As we have seen, Baladeva rarely misses an opportunity in his *Tattvasandarbha* commentary to cite Madhva as Jīva's source of inspiration. From a philosophical point of view, Baladeva places considerably more emphasis on the dualistic side of Jīva's writings, and displays a hostility towards the views of Śaṅkara which is uncharacteristic of Jīva, who himself cites Śaṅkara as an authority several times in his *Sarvasaṃvādinī.* In tone, Baladeva is more polemical than conciliatory, and closer in temperament to the later Mādhva authors than to Jīva and the other Gosvāmins.

Given the radical nature of Baladeva's writings, certain questions naturally arise: How did the works of Baladeva come to be accepted by the Gauḍīya Vaiṣṇava community as representative and authoritative statements of their philosophical position ? What initial opposition, if any, was there to the views of Baladeva ? How have subsequent generations of Gauḍīya Vaiṣṇavas reacted to the sectarian and philosophical developments initiated by Baladeva?

In order to answer the first of these questions, it is necessary to return to the historical circumstances surrounding the dispute in Jaipur. Considering the variety of opinions on the part of modern historians regarding Baladeva's motives for writing his *Govindabhāṣya* while in Jaipur, and the actual significance that work had on the resolution of the dispute, it seems safe to assume that Baladeva's contemporaries in Vṛndāvana were also somewhat confused by his actions in Jaipur. More than likely, their main concern was the happy resolution of the dispute, allowing the Gauḍīya Vaiṣṇavas of Jaipur, and probably of Vṛndāvana as well, to continue their mode of worship and, in the case of some, their means of livelihood; how Baladeva settled the dispute, what his actual motives were, and what implications they held for future generations of Gauḍīya Vaiṣṇavas were probably secondary considerations. As mentioned earlier, the belief that Caitanya had at least a formal connection with the Mādhva Sampradāya was something which Viśvanātha himself accepted, and thus was probably not as controversial as it otherwise might have been. Furthermore, those who might have objected to the affiliation of the Gauḍīya Vaiṣṇava school with the Mādhva Sampradāya could always comfort themselves with the belief that Baladeva was merely relying on this tradition as a convenient expedient to settle affairs in Jaipur.

In addition, despite the long-standing tradition in opposition to *Brahmasūtra* commentaries, initiated presumably by Caitanya himself, it seems clear that the absence of such a work was at least partly responsible for the questionable status of the Gauḍīya Vaiṣṇava school, and that Baladeva's *Govindabhāṣya* was a much appreciated addition to the school's literature. It is also likely that relatively few Gauḍīya Vaiṣṇavas would have studied such a long and difficult work, and one wonders how many were actually aware of the shift in position towards the dualism of Madhva which the *Govindabhāṣya* represented.

While there were thus several compelling reasons for the Gauḍīya Vaiṣṇavas of Vṛndāvana and Jaipur to welcome the writings of Baladeva, the situation in Bengal may have been quite different. For one thing, the Bengali Vaiṣṇavas did not face the same kinds of sectarian difficulties as their counterparts in Vṛndāvana and Jaipur, and questions of recognition by other Vaiṣṇava sects of North India probably held little interest for them. Also, the Gauḍīya Vaiṣṇavas of Bengal had, from the beginning, placed greater emphasis on the divinity and worship of Caitanya than did the Vṛndāvana community under the Gosvāmins, and it is likely that they would have had a greater objection to attempts at undermining the independence of the Caitanya tradition.

Baladeva's attempt to affiliate the Gauḍīya Vaiṣṇavas with the Mādhva Sampradāya and his interpretation of the doctrines of Jīva from a Mādhva point of view were probably the chief factors in Rādhāmohana's decision to compose his own *Tattvasandarbha* commentary, which, we may speculate, was at least partially representative of the Bengali point of view. An examination of Rādhāmohana's commentary reveals a strong belief in the independence of the Caitanya tradition, as well as a desire to show the superiority of Jīva's philosophical position over that of the other Vaiṣṇava *ācāryas*, including Madhva. In attitude, Rādhāmohana is much closer to Jīva than is Baladeva, exhibiting a non-polemical style and much greater respect for Śaṅkara. Rādhāmohana also relies on Śrīdhara's *Bhāgavata* commentary to a larger extent than does Baladeva, who seldom, if ever, refers to it.

If the popularity of their respective commentaries on the *Tattvasandarbha* is any indication of the relative success of their endeavors, Baladeva clearly emerges the victor over Rādhāmohana. Nearly all of the editions of the *Tattvasandarbha* are accompanied by Baladeva's commentary, and the Bengali translators and editors rely heavily on Baladeva's interpretations for their translations or summaries. As a result of this practice, readers of the Bengali versions of the *Tattvasandarbha* often come away with the impression that Jīva was more of a dualist and pro-Madhva than is actually the case.

On the other hand, Baladeva's *Govindabhāṣya*, though generally recognized as the official Gauḍīya Vaiṣṇava commentary on the *Brahmasūtra*, does not seem to have attained the same place of importance within the Gauḍīya Vaiṣṇava community as have the works of Jīva, primarily the *Tattvasandarbha*, or the writings of the other Gosvāmins. This fact is clearly seen in Rāmmohan Roy's *Gosvāmīr Sahita Vicāra*, written in 1818 in response to a letter from an unnamed Gauḍīya Vaiṣṇava Gosvāmin. Though the original letter is not given, it is clear from Rāmmohan's reply that the Gosvāmin had based his arguments almost exclusively on Jīva's *Tattvasandarbha*, arguing strongly for the authority of the *Bhāgavata Purāṇa* and its function as the only legitimate commentary on the *Brahmasūtra*.

Unfortunately, the issue of sectarian affiliation remains unsettled to this day. The dispute has, however, taken on an interesting dimension not present in the earlier phases of the movement. According to Joseph O'Connell (1970:291), the Gauḍīya Mission (Sārasvata Gauḍīya Āsana and Mission), one of the most active champions of Mādhva affiliation and the chief publisher of the works of Baladeva, has initiated a new order of *sannyāsins* within the Gauḍīya Vaiṣṇava movement who follow the traditions of the Mādhva Sampradāya. This order of *sannyāsins*, introduced by Bhaktivinod Ṭhākur and Bhaktisiddhānta Sarasvatī, serves the dual purpose of undermining the authority and power of the hereditary gurus of the various Gosvāmin lines and offering a respectable alternative to the loosely organized and not highly regarded order of Gauḍīya Vaiṣṇava ascetics known as "Vairāgīs". The *sannyāsins* of this order, though claiming affiliation with the Brahma Sampradāya of Madhva, apparently maintain a certain degree of independence from the Mādhvas, referring to their own order as the "Brahma-Mādhva-Gauḍīya-Vaiṣṇava Sampradāya". This designation, however, could be the result of either a real or anticipated objection to the legitimacy of their order on the part of the Mādhvas, who generally are not anxious to recognize any association with the Gauḍīya Vaiṣṇavas.

It is also interesting to note that Bhaktīvedānta Swāmī, founder of the International Society for Krishna Consciousness (ISKCON), traces his spiritual lineage through Bhaktisiddhānta Sarasvatī and Bhaktivinod Ṭhākur; and while it is difficult to say how anxious the Gauḍīya Mission is to acknowledge its common heritage with ISKCON, it is significant that the latter organization, which exhibits such a sectarian attitude towards other religious movements, should have its roots in a tradition directly traceable to the views of Baladeva.

It thus seems clear that much of what goes on today under the designation "Gauḍīya Vaiṣṇavism" bears only a vague resemblance to the life and teachings of Caitanya. This is not surprising when we consider that nearly 450 years have elapsed since the death of Caitanya and that he himself left behind no written account of his teachings. The forces which have helped to shape the growth and development of the Gauḍīya Vaiṣṇava movement in new directions are numerous: the zealous biographers, whose sectarian enthusiasm was not always matched by their discrimination; the scholastic Gosvāmins who sought to categorize the different stages of devotion and to explain them with the help of subtle metaphysical models; the iconoclastic Nityānanda and his son Vīrabhadra who tried to apply to society the ideal of equality and brotherhood which Caitanya saw in the community of devotees; and many more.

But of all those who helped shape the growth of the movement, perhaps none exerted as powerful an influence or changed the direction of the movement as profoundly as did Baladeva. The effects of Baladeva's activities and writings are seen not only in isolated segments of the Gauḍīya Vaiṣṇava community, such as the Gauḍīya Mission, which actively support the belief of Mādhva affiliation, but also in the renewed interest within the school in Vedānta and the teachings of Madhva. Baladeva also gave the Gauḍīya Vaiṣṇavas a sense of pride and legitimacy with his *Govindabhāṣya*, raising their status to a position equal to that of the other Vaiṣṇava *sampradāyas* in the eyes of many. And despite what one might think of the accuracy of his claims regarding the teachings and sectarian affiliation of Caitanya, it must be admitted that Baladeva was almost single-handedly responsible for defending the legitimacy of the Gauḍīya Vaiṣṇava school at a time when its very existence was in jeopardy. On the other hand, Baladeva brought to the school a polemical attitude, directed chiefly against the Advaitins, which, though present in the biographies, is inconsistent with Caitanya's own reverence for Śrīdhara, and absent in the writings of the Gosvāmins.

The *Tattvasandarbha* commentaries of Baladeva and Rādhāmohana represent, in a sense, two forces which, though contrary in many respects, exist side by side in the present-day Gauḍīya Vaiṣṇava movement. Jīva's *Tattvasandarbha* is still probably the most widely read philosophical work within the school; the *Bhāgavata* is the most authoritative scripture; the biographies the most popular literature; and the life of Caitanya the driving force behind the movement. At the same time, however, Baladeva's *Govindabhāṣya* and other writings are accepted as authoritative statements of Gauḍīya Vaiṣṇava doctrine, despite the important differences which exist between his philosophical views and Jīva's. As a result of the influence of Baladeva's writings and activities, today, many Gauḍīya Vaiṣṇavas who have not taken sides on the issue of sectarian allegiance, as well as non-Vaiṣṇavas who are only slightly familiar with the movement, unquestioningly associate the name of Madhva with that of Caitanya, and consider the Gauḍīya Vaiṣṇavas to be, like the Mādhvas, pure dualists, without having the least knowledge of the complex set of factors which gave rise to this tradition.

GLOSSARY

abhidheya: the means to be employed in order to attain the goal of life, *preman*, or love of God; characterized as devotional practices such as those taught in Bh.P. 7/5/23 (listening to the scriptures, singing the praises of the Lord, etc.), also known as *vaidhibhakti* or *sādhanabhakti*; cf. T. S. 9.

Acintyabhedābhedavāda: the doctrine of unthinkable unity within difference, used to describe the relationship between *bhagavat*, on the one hand, and *jīvas* and the universe, on the other, emphasizing the supra-logical nature of this relationship; cf. T. S. 43.

ādhibhautika puruṣa : the aspect of a person derived from the five elements, i.e. the physical body.

ādhidaivika puruṣa : the presiding deities of the senses which allow them to function, such as the sun presiding over the sense of sight.

ādhyātmika puruṣa : the indwelling spirit, the perceiver who identifies himself with the sense organs.

Advaitavāda : the doctrine of non-dualism, chief exponent of which was Śaṅkarācārya; the belief that *brahman* alone is real, the phenomenal universe illusory, and that the *jīva* is none other than *brahman*; also known simply as Advaita, not to be confused with Advaitācārya (similarly known as Advaita), one of Caitanya's close associates from his boyhood in Navadvīpa.

antaraṅgaśakti : the internal, or essential, power of *bhagavat* ; also known as *svarūpaśakti*, and consisting of three aspects: *sandhinī* (existence), *saṃvit* (knowledge), and *hlādinī* (bliss).

anubandhas : certain topics which are traditionally dealt with in philosophical works such as T. S. and generally stated in the preliminary portion of the text; cf. *abhidheya*, *prayojana*, and *sambandha*; cf. also T. S. 9.

āśraya : the supreme reality as the ground for phenomenal existence ; from the individual, or *vyaṣṭi*, point of view, the ground for living beings, and from the aggregate, or *samaṣṭi*, point of view, the source of the origin, maintenance, and dissolution of the universe; the tenth and most important characteristic of a Mahāpurāṇa, ultimately identical with *bhagavat*, or Kṛṣṇa; cf. T. S. 56, 59-60.

ātman : the Self, considered in Advaita Vedānta to be identical with *brahman*; the individual self, considered by the Gauḍīya Vaiṣṇavas to be a portion of *brahman* and more commonly referred to as *jīvātman* or *jīva*.

avatāra : a partial manifestation of *bhagavat*, emanating from *paramātman* and appearing in the mortal world to fulfill a special need; classified according to time of manifestation and/or function, there are 22 *līlāvatāras*, 14 *manvantarāvatāras*, 4 *yugāvatāras*, 3 *guṇāvatāras*, 3 *puruṣāvatāras*, and numerous minor *avatāras* ; also classified according to the degree of power which they manifest, there are *vilāsāvatāras*, *vaibhavas*, *āveśas*, etc.; cf. T. S. 8, f.ns. 2-8.

avidyā : primal ignorance, often identified with *māyā*, but used more often in the individual, or *vyaṣṭi*, context as referring to the false identification of the *jīva* with his physical and mental adjuncts.

bahiraṅgaśakti : the external power of *bhagavat*, responsible for the creation, maintenance, and dissolution of the universe; also known as *māyāśakti*, a derivative and subordinate form of the *svarūpaśakti*, which resides in *paramātman* and has no effect on the essential nature of *bhagavat*.

bhagavat : the highest conception of the supreme; the embodiment of bliss and the repository of all auspicious attributes; identified with Kṛṣṇa and attainable through the path of *bhakti*.

bhakti : devotion to *bhagavat*, or Kṛṣṇa; the means to the realization of *preman*; in the preliminary stages, termed *vaidhibhakti* or *sādhanabhakti*, and in the mature stage, when spontaneous and passionate, termed *rāgabhakti* or *rucibhakti*.

brahman : the unqualified aspect of *bhagavat*, seen as pure, undifferentiated consciousness; a partial and, hence, lower conception of the supreme, realizable by followers of the path of *jñāna*, or knowledge; cf. T. S. 8.

brahmacarya : the first of the four traditional *āśramas*, or stages of life, that of a student observing the vow of continence; preliminary monastic vows, followed by the final vows of *sannyāsa*.

cicchakti : the power of consciousness (*cit*); one of the essential powers of *bhagavat*, corresponding to the *saṃvicchakti*, cf. *antaraṅgaśakti*.

guruparamparā: spiritual lineage, traced successively from guru to disciple; in the Vaiṣṇava *sampradāyas*, originating with *bhagavat* and passed on through Śrī, Brahmā, Haṃsa, or Rudra; normally traced through the mantra guru for householders, and the *sannyāsa* guru for *sannyāsins*.

īśvara : a term more commonly used by the Advaitins, but roughly equivalent to the Gauḍīya Vaiṣṇava concept of *paramātman*, special emphasis being placed on the function of controlling *māyā*; also the name of Caitanya's mantra guru, Īśvara Purī.

jīva: the individual soul, generically identical with *bhagavat*, but quantitatively distinct; they are atomic in nature, i.e. innumerable, indivisible, infinitesimal, and discrete.

jīvaśakti : cf. *taṭasthaśakti*.

jñāna : wisdom; the path followed by seekers after the unconditioned *brahman*.

Kṛṣṇa: the ultimate source of all *avatāras*, identified with *bhagavat* himself; possessing a non-phenomenal body, he eternally sports with Rādhā and other companions in his own supernatural abode.

līlā : the divine sport of *bhagavat* in his human form, often used to refer to Kṛṣṇa's sport among the gopīs of Vṛndāvana.

māyā : the power of illusion; both the material and efficient cause of the universe; hides the true nature of reality and makes it appear to be what it is not through its two powers, the *āvaraṇaśakti* and the *vikṣepaśakti*.

māyāśakti : the external power of *bhagavat* which gives rise to the phenomenal universe; also known as the *bahiraṅgaśakti*.

Māyāvāda : a term used by Kṛṣṇadāsa Kavirāja to refer (somewhat disparagingly) to the philosophy of Advaitavāda, special emphasis being given to the belief in the illusory nature of the universe and individual souls; followers of this doctrine are referred to as Māyāvādins.

mokṣa : cf. *mukti*.

mukti: final emancipation, according to the Advaitins attainable while still living, but held by the *Gauḍīya* Vaiṣṇavas to be achieved after physical death of five kinds: *sālokya*, *sārṣṭi*, *sārūpya*, *sāmīpya*, and *sāyujya*; cf. Ch. I, f.n. 11.

pañcabhāva: five attitudes which an aspirant may assume in relationship to the Lord: *śānta* (the serene attitude), *dāsya* (the attitude of a servant to his master), *sākhya* (that of a friend to a friend), *vātsalya* (that of a parent for a child), and *mādhurya* (that of a lover for her beloved); each succeeding attitude is said to be superior to and to include the preceding ones, culminating in *mādhurya*.

paramātman : the supreme reality as the ground for the universe and living beings; the source of all *avatāras*, and the indweller of all beings; realizable by those following the path of yoga; cf. T. S. 8.

Paricchedavāda : the doctrine of division which maintains that just as indivisible space appears to be divided by objects such as jars etc., without really being divided, so does *brahman*, indivisible consciousness, appear to be divided by the body and mind of *jīvas*; cf. T. S. 36-39.

pramāṇa : the means of acquiring certain knowledge, principal of which are: *śabda* (valid testimony or revelation), *pratyakṣa* (sense-perception), and *anumāna* (inference); Vedānta accepts also: *upamāna* (analogy), *abhāva* or *anupalabdhi* (proof from non-existence or non-perception), and *arthāpatti* (inference from circumstance); Jīva also accepts: ārṣa (statements of *devas* and *ṛṣis*), sambhava (probability), *aitihya* (traditional knowledge), and *ceṣṭā* (gesture); cf. T.S. 9.

Pratibimbavāda : the doctrine of reflection which maintains that just as the one sun appears to be many when reflected in various receptacles of water, and to move when the water moves etc., so does the one *brahman* appear to be many when reflected in the minds of *jīvas*, and to take on the characteristics of the *jīvas*; cf. T. S. 36-39.

prayojana : the aim of life, also termed *sādhya*, and identified by Jīva to be *preman*, or love of God.

preman : love of God; realizable by followers of the path of *bhakti* and considered to be the highest goal of life.

puruṣa : the supreme "person", more or less identical with *paramātman*; having three manifestations: 1) Saṅkarṣaṇa—the ruler of *prakṛti*, 2) Pradyumna—the source of the various *avatāras*, and 3) Aniruddha— the inner controller (Cf. T. S. 8, f.n. 4) ; also used to denote *bhagavat* himself, when prefixed by *parama* or *pūrṇa* etc. (cf. T. S. 30); also used to denote the three elements necessary for perception: 1) *ādhyātmika puruṣa* (the perceiver), 2) *ādhidaivika puruṣa* (the medium), and 3) *ādhibhautika puruṣa* (the sense object) (cf. T.S.59, 60).

puruṣārtha : the aim of human existence; generally considered to be four in number : 1) *kāma* (gratification of desires), 2) *artha* (acquisition of wealth), 3) *dharma* (discharge of duties), and 4) *mokṣa* (final emancipation); Gauḍīya Vaiṣṇavas include *preman*, love of God, as the fifth and highest aim of life.

rāgabhakti : cf. *bhakti.*

rasa : religious sentiments corresponding to the five *bhāvas*, or spiritual attitudes assumed by a devotee.

rucibhakti : cf. *bhakti.*

śabda : valid testimony or revelation; in the latter sense restricted to Śruti, or revealed scriptures, which in Vedānta means the Vedas, but is expanded to include Itihāsa and Purāṇas by the Gauḍīya Vaiṣṇavas.

sādhana : spiritual practices; cf. *abhidheya.*

sādhya : the goal of spiritual practices; cf. *prayojana.*

śakti: the power associated with *bhagavat*, said to be threefold depending upon whether it is internal, external, or peripheral; cf. *antaraṅgaśakti, bahiraṅgaśakti* and *taṭasthaśakti.*

Śaktipariṇāmavāda : the doctrine that the universe and living beings represent a transformation of the power residing in *paramātman.*

samādhi : profound concentration of mind wherein the individual becomes absorbed in the object of his contemplation; used in the Bh.P. to describe Vyāsa's state of mind when the *Bhāgavata* was revealed to him; cf. Ch. V, f.n. 7.

samaṣṭi : the aggregate, i.e. *Prakṛti*, grounded in *Paramātman.*

sambandha : the object of inquiry which forms the subject matter of a particular text; in T. S., it refers to the fact that Kṛṣṇa is the ultimate subject matter of the *Bhāgavata Purāṇa*, and that one of the purposes of T. S. is to elucidate this fact.

sampradāya : a religious tradition handed down through an unbroken line of teachers; according to the orthodox Vaiṣṇava view, there are four *sampradāyas*, named after their original founders, Śrī, Brahmā, Rudra, and Haṃsa (Sanakādi), and established through Rāmānuja, Madhva, Viṣṇusvāmin, and Nimbārka respectively; also used to refer to the ten orders of the Śaṅkara Daśanāmin monastic institution; in a looser sense, used to denote any religious movement or school.

sannyāsa: renunciation of the world, normally indicating membership in the monastic order of the initiating monk, or *sannyāsin*.

svarūpaśakti : cf. *antaraṅgaśakti*.

taṭasthaśakti : the peripheral power of *bhagavat*, responsible for the manifestation of *jīvas*, who occupy a position just on the borderline between *bhagavat* and *prakṛti*; also known as *jīvaśakti*.

tattva : the supreme truth or principle of reality; described as non-dual consciousness, and denoted variously as *brahman*, *paramātman*, and *bhagavat*; ultimately identical with Kṛṣṇa (cf. T. S. 9, 51) ; also used in the sense of ontological category, as in Baladeva's discussion of the five *tattvas* (cf. T.S. 34, f.n. 1).

Tattvavāda : the term used in C. C. to describe the philosophy of Madhva; literally "the doctrine of ontological categories".

upādhi : limiting adjuncts, the identification with which results in a mistaken notion of reality; in the case of the *jīva*, the body-mind complex which makes him identify with his lower self and not, as the Gauḍīya Vaiṣṇavas hold, with the Lord, of which he is a part.

Vedānta: one of the six orthodox schools of Indian philosophy, based on the authority of the Upaniṣads and the teachings of the Upaniṣads, *Bhagavadgītā*, and *Brahmasūtra*.

viśeṣa : that quality within objects which causes a distinction to appear between substance and attribute—in the example of the ocean, between the water and the waves—when, in reality, none exists; employed to explain how *brahman*, though essentially existence, knowledge, and bliss itself, appears to be the possessor of these qualities; a concept peculiar to the Mādhvas, but employed by Baladeva to give a rational explanation to Jīva's supralogical concept of *acintyaśakti* (the unthinkable power of *bhagavat*).

Vivartavāda : the Advaitic doctrine of illusory creation which maintains that the universe is merely a false reading of the absolute due to the veiling power of māyā, just as in the dark a rope is mistakenly taken to be a snake.

vyaṣṭi : the individual, i.e. the *jīva,* grounded in *Paramātman.*

BIBLIOGRAPHY

Baladeva Vidyābhūṣaṇa. 1927. *Siddhāntaratna.* Banaras: Sanskrit College.

——— 1968. *Govindabhāṣya.* Calcutta: Śrī Sārasvata Gauḍīya Āsana and Mission.

Betty, L. Stafford. 1978. *Vādirāja's Refutation of Śaṅkara's Non-dualism.* Delhi: Motilal Banarsidass.

Bhaktisiddhānta Sarasvatī. 1973. *Śrī Brahma Saṃhitā.* Madras: Sree Gaudiya Math.

Bhaktiśrīrūpasiddhānta. 1970. *Īśā Upaniṣad* (with commentaries of Madhva and Baladeva). Calcutta: Śrī Sārasvata Gauḍīya Āsana and Mission.

Caṭṭopādhyāya, Gītā. 1972. *Bhāgavata of Bāṅglā Sāhitya.* Calcutta: Kavi and Kavitā.

Chakravarti, Janardan. 1975. *Bengal Vaiṣṇavism and Śrī Chaitanya.* Calcutta: The Asiatic Society.

Chakravarti, Sudhindra Chandra. 1969. *Philosophical Foundation of Bengal Vaiṣṇavism.* Calcutta: Academic Publ.

Colebrooke, T. E. 1873. *Miscellaneous Essays, by H. T. Colebrooke, with Life of the Author,* Vol. I. London: Trübner and Co.

Dās, Haridās. 1956. *Śrī Śrī Gauḍīya Vaiṣṇava Abhidhāna.* Navadvīpa: Haribol Kuṭīr.

Das, Sambidananda. 1972. *Sri Chaitanya Mahaprabhu.* Madras: Sree Gaudiya Math.

Dasgupta, Surendranath. 1949. *A History of Indian Philosophy,* Vol. IV. Cambridge: University Press.

De, Sushil Kumar. 1961. *Early History of the Vaiṣṇava Faith and Movement in Bengal.* Calcutta: Firma K. L. Mukhopadhyay.

——— 1974. *Bengal's Contribution to Sanskrit Literature.* New Delhi: Today and Tomorrow's Printers and Publ.

Farquhar, J. N. 1967. *An Outline of the Religious Literature of India.* Delhi: Motilal Banarsidass.

Gambhīrānanda, Swami. 1972. *Eight Upaniṣads,* Vol. I. Calcutta: Advaita Ashrama.

——— 1977. *Brahma-sūtra Bhāṣya of Śaṅkarācārya.* Calcutta: Advaita Ashrama.

Gokulanātha. 1931. *Do Sau Bāvan Vaiṣṇava kī Vārtā*. Bombay: Gaṅgāviṣṇu Śrīkṛṣṇadāsa.

——— 1970. *Caurāsī Vaiṣṇavan kī Vārtā*. Mathurā: Śrīgovardhan Granthamālā Kāryālaya.

Gosvāmī, Śaraṇavihārī. 1966. *Kṛṣṇabhakti-kāvya Meṅ Sakhībhāva*. Banaras: Chowkhamba Vidyabhawan.

Growse, F. S. 1978. *Mathurā: A District Memoir*. Ahmedabad: The New Order Book Co.

Haig, Wolseley. 1937. *The Cambridge History of India*, Vol. IV. New York: The Macmillan Company.

Hardy, Friedhelm. 1974. "Mādhavendra Purī: A Link Between Bengal Vaiṣṇavism and South Indian *Bhakti*." London: JRAS.

Haynes, Richard. 1974. *Svāmī Haridās and the Haridāsī Sampradāy*. Doctoral Dissertation: University of Pennsylvania.

Jīva Gosvāmin. 1919. *Tattvasandarbha*. Calcutta: Sacīndramohana Ghoṣa.

——— 1938. *Tattvasandarbha*. Calcutta: Bani Press.

——— 1951. *Tattvasandarbha*. Calcutta: Haridās Śarma.

——— 1953. *Sarvasaṃvādinī*. Calcutta. Haridās Śarma.

——— 1957. *Tattvasandarbha*. Vārāṇasī. Acyutagranthamālā.

——— 1967. *Tattvasandarbha*. Calcutta: Jadavpur University.

Kane, P. V. 1930. *History of Dharmaśāstra*, Vol. I. Poona: Bhandarkar Oriental Research Institute.

Kennedy, Melville T. 1925. *The Caitanya Movement*. London: Oxford University Press.

Kṛṣṇadāsa Kavirāja. 1963. *Caitanya Caritāmṛta*. Calcutta: Sādhanā Prakāśanī.

——— 1977. *Caitanya Caritāmṛta*. Khaḍagpur: Śrī Caitanya Āśrama Press.

Līlāsuka and Prabodhānanda. 1978. *Sri Krishna Karṇāmritam and Chaitanya Chandrāmritam*. Madras: Sree Gaudiya Math.

Mādhava Vidyāraṇya. 1978. *Śaṅkara Digvijaya*. Madras: Sri Ramakrishna Math.

Mādhavānanda, Swami. 1975. *Bṛhadāraṇyaka Upaniṣad with the Commentary of Śaṅkarācārya*. Calcutta: Advaita Ashrama.

Madhva. 1971. *Sarvamūlagranthāḥ*, Vol. II. Uḍipī: Akhila Bhārata Mādhva Mahāmaṇḍala.

Mahadevan, T. M. P. 1938. *The Philosophy of Advaita*. London: Luzac and Co.

Mahanamabrata Brahmachari. 1974. *Vaiṣṇava Vedānta*. Calcutta: Das Gupta and Co. Ltd.

Majumdar, A. K. 1969. *Caitanya: His Life and Doctrine*. Bombay: Bharatiya Vidya Bhavan.

Majumdar, Biman Bihari. 1959. *Caitanyacariter Upādāna*. Calcutta: University of Calcutta.

Mishra, Umesh. 1966. *History of Indian Philosophy*, Vol. II. Allahabad: Tirabhukti Publ.

Mukherjee, Dilip Kumar. 1970. *Chaitanya*. New Delhi: National Book Trust, India.

Mukherjee, Prabhat. 1940. *The History of Medieval Vaishnavism in Orissa*. Calcutta: R. Chatterjee.

Nābhādāsa. 1962. *Bhaktamālā*. Lucknow: Tejkumāra Press.

Nikhilananda, Swami. 1974. *Vedāntasāra of Sadānanda*. Calcutta: Advaita Ashrama.

O'Connell, Joseph T. 1970. *Social Implications of the Gauḍīya Vaiṣṇava Movement*. Doctoral Dissertation: Harvard.

Olivelle, Patrick. 1977. *Vāsudevāśrama Yatidharma Prakāśa: A Treatise on World Renunciation*. Vienna: E. J. Brill.

Pal, Bipinchandra. 1962. *Bengal Vaishnavism*. Calcutta: Yugayatri Prakashak Ltd.

Pansikar, Wasudev Laxman Śāstrī. 1978. *Bhagavadgītā* (with commentaries of Śaṅkara, Śrīdhara, etc.). New Delhi: Munshiram Manoharlal Publ.

Parekh, Bhai Manilal C. 1969. *Shri Vallabhacharya, Life, Teachings and Movement*. Rajkot: Shri Bhagavata Dharma Mission.

Rādhādāmodara. 1930. *Vedāntasyamantaka*. Lahore: Motilal Banarsidass.

Raghunathan, N. 1976. *Śrīmad-Bhāgavatam*, Vol. I. Madras: Vighneswara Publ. House.

Rāmmohan Roy. 1815. *Rāmamohanagranthāvalī*. Calcutta: Vaṅgīya Sāhitya Pariṣat.

Raychaudhuri, Tapan. 1966. *Bengal under Akbar and Jahangir*. Delhi: Munshiram Manoharlal.

Roy, Ashim Kumar. 1978. *History of the Jaipur City*. New Delhi: Manohar.

Śaṅkara. 1964. *Ten Principal Upaniṣads with Śāṅkarabhāṣya*. Delhi: Motilal Banarsidass.

Sarkar, Jadunath. 1932. *Chaitanya's Life and Teaching*. Calcutta: B. C. Sarkar and Sons.

Śarmā, Gopīlāl. 1967. *Caurāsī Vaiṣṇavan kī Padyātmaka Vārtā.* Jaipur: Śrī Puṣṭi Mārgīya Vaiṣṇava Maṇḍala.

Śāstrī, Pāṇḍeya Rāmateja. 1962. *Bhāgavata Purāṇa* (with Śrīdhara's commentary). Banaras: Paṇḍita Pustakālaya.

Sen, Dinesh Chandra. 1917a. *Chaitanya and His Companions.* Calcutta: University of Calcutta.

——— 1917b. *The Vaisnava Literature of Mediaeval Bengal.* Calcutta: University of Calcutta.

——— 1922. *Chaitanya and his Age.* Calcutta: University of Calcutta.

Shah, Jethalal G. 1969. *Shri Vallabhacharya, His Philosophy and Religion.* Nadiad: The Pushtimargiya Pustakalaya.

Sharma, B. N. K. 1960. *A History of the Dvaita School of Vedānta and its Literature,* Vol. I. Bombay: Bookseller's Publ. Co.

——— 1961a. *A History of the Dvaita School of Vedānta and its Literature,* Vol. II. Bombay: Bookseller's Publ. Co.

——— 1961b. *Śrī Madhva's Teachings in his own Words.* Bombay: Bharatiya Vidya Bhavan.

——— 1962. *Philosophy of Śrī Madhvācārya.* Bombay: Bharatiya Vidya Bhavan.

Sharma, M. L. 1969. *History of the Jaipur State.* Jaipur: The Rajasthan Institute of Historical Research.

Sinha, Jadunath. 1976. *The Philosophy and Religion of Chaitanya and His Followers.* Calcutta: Sinha Publ. House Ltd.

Swāhānanda, Swāmī. 1975. *Chāndogya Upaniṣad.* Madras: Sri Ramakrishna Math.

Tagare, Ganesh Vasudeo. 1976. *The Bhāgavata Purāṇa.* Delhi: Motilal Banarsidass.

van Buitenen, J.A.B. 1968. *Pravargya.* Poona: Deccan College.

van Gulik, R. H. 1935. *Hayagrīva, the Mantrayānic Aspect of Horse-cult in China and Japan.* Leiden: E. J. Brill.

Vasu, Śrīśa Chandra. 1912. *The Vedānta-sūtras of Bādarāyaṇa with the Commentary of Baladeva.* Allahabad: Indian Press.

Vireswarananda, Swami. 1964. *Srimad-Bhagavad-Gita* (with Srīdhara's commentary). Madras: Sri Ramakrishna Math.

Vishnu Puri. 1979. *Bhakti Ratnavali or A Necklace of Devotional Gems.* Madras: Sri Ramakrishna Math.

Vṛndāvanadāsa. 1967. *Caitanya Bhāgavata.* Calcutta: Sādhanā Prakāśanī.

Wilson, H. H. 1976. *Religious Sects of the Hindus,* Vol. I. New Delhi: Asian Publication Services.

INDEX

abhāva, 73
Abhedavāda, 140
abhidheya, 58, 60, 63, 73, 125, 131, 132, 143-45, 150
Acintyabhedābhedavāda, 39, 40, 49, 60, 180, 181
Acyutānanda Dāsa, 34-35
Acyutapreksa, 114
Adel, 19, 35
ādhibhautika puruṣa, 165-66, 168
ādhidaivika puruṣa, 165-66, 168
adhikāra, 74
ādhyātmika puruṣa, 165-66, 168
Advaita (vāda), 9, 16, 22, 40, 110, 181-82
Advaitācārya (Advaita), 4, 12, 24, 30, 32, 39, 51, 53, 67, 122
Advaitasiddhi, 22
Agni, 104, 106
Agni Purāṇa, 84, 89, 94, 95, 101, 103, 105, 107, 108, 171
Agra, xii
ahaṅkāra, 71, 163, 172
aitihya, 73
ajñāna, 135
ākhyāna, 82, 83,89
Akṣobhya, 30-31
Alpapurāṇa, 171
Ambarīṣa, 95
Amer, 43
Aniruddha, 70
antaraṅgaśakti, 72
anubandha, 58, 64, 73, 74
anumāna, 40, 73-74, 160
Anupama, 21
anupalabdhi, 73-74
anuśayin, 175, 177
apāśraya, 170, 176-77
Appayya Dīkṣita, 63
ārṣa, 73
artha, 19, 73
arthāpatti, 73
āśraya, 60, 161-62, 164-65, 167-71, 175-77
Aśvins, 94, 96
Atharvaveda, 78-80, 81, 84
ātman, 136, 153, 155-57, 158, 159, 164-65, 168, 176
Aurangzib, 44
āvaraṇaśakti, 132
avatāra, 13, 39, 53, 59, 65-66, 70, 71, 12, 110, 163, 173, 181
avidyā, 135, 139, 140, 164, 176
avyākṛta, 175, 177

Bādarāyaṇa, 30
bahiraṅgaśakti, 72, 128
Baladeva Vidyābhūṣaṇa, xiii, xiv-xvi, 18; association with Mādhvas, 25; initiation with Rādhādāmodara, 25-26; the Jaipur incident, 26-29, 42-47; the *guruparamparā*, 30-38; his philosophy, 39-42; writing of *Govindabhāṣya*, 42-47; list of writings, 47-48; 51, 54, 62; T. S. commentary, 65-178; 182-85, 187-88
Baleśvara, 25
Benares, 8, 13, 19, 22, 182
Bhagavadgītā, 17, 19, 46, 48, 49, 74, 90, 95, 120, 131
bhagavat, 9, 13, 40, 52-53, 58, 65, 69-70, 71-72, 75, 82, 98-100, 103, 106, 107, 113, 120-21, 128-29, 131, 133-34, 140, 144-45, 147, 149, 163, 165, 173, 181
Bhāgavata Purāṇa, xiii, 14-17, 20, 22, 38, 41, 48, 49, 52, 53, 57-59, 63-64, 69, 71, 73, 79, 89, 90; origin and authority of, 91-108; commentaries on, 109-10; its role in *Bhāgavatasandarbha*, 111-123; import of, 124-150; in connection with *sambandha* etc., 150-61; in connection with *āśraya* and ten characteristics, 161-77; 180-81, 185-87
Bhāgavatas, 17, 52
Bhāgavatasandarbha, xiii, xv, 25, 42, 57-58; editions of, 61; 69, 71, 113, 119, 177
Bhāgavatatatparya, 113, 121
Bhāgavatī Saṃhitā, 127
Bhagavatsandarbha, 58, 177
bhakti, xi, xiii, 5, 9, 12, 15, 17, 20, 51, 72, 73, 107, 110, 127-28, 141, 144-46
Bhaktijñānabrahmayoga, 34
Bhaktirasāmṛtasindhu, xii
Bhaktiratnākara, 21, 23-24, 33
Bhaktiratnāvalī, 16, 109
Bhaktisandarbha, 58
Bhaktisiddhānta Sarasvatī, 186
Bhaktivedanta Swami, 186
Bhaktivinod Ṭhākur, xiv, 25, 26, 186
bhaktiyoga, 127-29, 144-46
Bhāmatī, 75
Bharatatātparya, 113, 121

Bhāratī Sampradāya, 7-8, 11, 17, 19, 24, 123, 182
Bhāskara, 52, 98, 181
Bhaviṣya Purāṇa, 80, 89
bhrama, 74
Brahmā, 14, 30, 34, 53, 64,70, 79, 85, 87, 92, 97, 114, 123, 163
brahmacarya, 7-8
Brahmaloka, 79, 80
Brahma-Madhva-Gauḍīya Sampradāya, 186
brahman, 7, 18, 39, 40, 51-53, 69-70, 71-72, 75-76, 90, 104-05, 107, 126, 130, 135-37, 139-43, 147-48, 150, 152-56, 161, 164, 171, 175, 177, 181
Brāhmaṇas, 82
Brahmaṇya (Brahma Tīrtha), 30, 121, 123
Brahma Purāṇa, 79-80, 89
Brahma Saṃhitā, 10
Brahma Sampradāya, xiii, 47, 49, 53, 76, 122, 186
Brahmasūtra (*Sūtras*), xiii, 9, 13, 22, 46, 49, 53, 59, 75-76, 85, 90, 91, 97, 121, 122, 141-42, 155, 156, 185-86
Brahmatarka, 121, 123
Brahmavaivarta Purāṇa, 125, 149
Bṛhadāraṇyaka Upaniṣad, 78, 80, 89, 158, 159
Buddhism, 111

Caitanya, xi, xii, xiv-xvi; biographies of, 1-3; early years, 3-4; mantra initiation, 4; *sannyāsa*, 5-8; meeting with Sārvabhauma, 8-9; South India pilgrimage, 9-12; meeting with Tattvavādins, 11-12; North India pilgrimage, 13-15; meeting with Prakāśānanda, 13-14; meeting with Vallabha, 14-15; relationship to Śrīdhara, 15-17; 30-31, 34, 39, 48, 53, 57, 65-68, 93, 114, 121, 122, 178-88
Caitanya Bhāgavata, 2, 32
Caitanyacandrodaya, 7
Caitanya Caritāmṛta, 3, 13, 20, 21, 36, 49, 63, 65, 71, 72, 93, 147, 179, 180, 182
Caitanyacaritāmṛtamahākāvya, 1, 6
Caṇḍīdāsa, 16
Catuḥślokī, 14
Caturvargacintāmaṇi, 103, 109
Caturvedaśikhā, 121
caturvyūha, 70
Caurāsi Vaiṣṇavan kī Vārtā, 37
ceṣṭā, 73
Chakravarti, Janardan, xiv
Chakravarti, Sudhindra, xv
Chāndogya Upaniṣad, 80, 153, 156, 164
cicchakti, 129
Cilkāhrada, 25
Citsukha, 113
Colebrooke, H. T., 51

Dadhīci, 94, 96
daharavidyā, 156, 164
Dāmodara Svarūpa, 1, 7-8, 12
Darśanas, 78
Dās, Haridās, 27, 41, 51
Dayānidhi, 30-31
De, S. K., xv, 2, 12, 15, 16, 17, 18, 19, 22, 23, 30, 33, 63
Devahūti, 176
dharma, 19, 73, 91, 92, 94, 103, 110, 117, 118, 163
Dimock, Edward, xiv
Do Sau Bāvan Vaiṣṇava kī Vārtā, 35, 36
Draviḍa, 119, 120
Dvaitādvaitavāda, 52
Dvāpara Yuga, 65-66, 82, 87
Dvārakāmāhātmya, 95

Ekādaśītattva, 54
Ekajīvavāda, 140

Farquhar, J. N., xiv, 45

Gadādhara, 67
Galta (Valley), 27-29, 43
Garuḍa Purāṇa, 59, 63, 89, 97, 99, 121, 171
gāthā, 82-83
Gauragaṇatattvasvarūpacandrikā, 33, 38
Gauragaṇoddeśadīpikā, 1, 33, 37, 44, 182, 183
Gaurīdāsa Paṇḍit, 48
Gautama, 87, 95, 151
Gayā, 4
Gāyatrī, 14, 59, 91-95, 97, 100, 103-108
Ghosh, Dulal Chandra, 22
Gītagovinda, 16
Gokulanātha, 35-37
Gopāla Bhaṭṭa, xii, xiii, 57, 63, 68, 180
Gopālaguru, 33-34
Gopāla Maṭha, 34
Gopī, 5, 16, 52, 110
Gopīnātha, 8, 36
Gosvāmins, xii, xiii, 1, 3, 17, 23, 24, 37, 38, 48, 51, 53, 54, 68, 134, 179, 185, 186
Gosvāmir Sahita Vicāra, 63, 185-86
Goswami, Sitanath, 62, 78, 108, 122, 132
Govardhananātha temple, 35

Govinda, 27-28, 36, 39, 44, 46
Govinda (Caitanya's companion), 67
Govindabhāṣya, xiv, xv, 25; its composition, 26-29; the *guruparamparā*, 30-38; 41, 42, 45-46, 47-48, 54, 134, 184, 185, 187, 188
Govindadāsa, 9-10, 12
Govindadeva temple (in Vṛndāvana), 24; (in Jaipur), 27, 43, 44
Govindāṣṭaka, 110
Growse, F. S., 43
guṇas, 53, 70, 89, 90, 127, 131, 133, 134, 163, 167, 168, 172
guṇāvatāra, 70
Gupta, Murāri, 1, 6, 12
guruparamparā, xv, 1, 28, 29-38, 42, 43, 45, 46, 48, 122, 123, 183-85

Haṃsa Sampradāya, 45
Hardy, Friedhelm, xiv, 20
Haribhaktivilāsa, xii, 63
Haridāsī sect, 43, 45-46
Hayagrīva, 94-96
Haynes, Richard, 43, 49
Hemādri, 103, 109
hetu, 170, 171, 175, 176
Himagopāla temple, 36
Hiraṇyakaśipu, 95
hlādinīśakti, 72
Hṛdaya Caitanya, 48

Indra, 96, 133
īśānukathā (*īśakathā*), 161, 163, 173
ISKCON, 186
īśvara, 9, 14, 104, 128, 130, 132, 134, 135, 137-39, 140, 143, 161
Īśvara Purī, 4, 10, 16, 17, 18, 30-32, 122, 123
Itihāsa, 58-59; authority of, 77-123

Jagannātha temple, 8, 12, 34, 36
Jaipur, 25, 26-29, 38, 42-44, 46-47, 54, 184
Jai Singh, 43-44, 45
Janamejaya, 98
Jāt rebellion, 43
Jayadeva, 16
Jayadharma, 30, 123
Jayadhvaja (Jaya Tīrtha), 30, 123
Jīva Gosvāmin, xii, xiii, xv, xvi, 9, 10, 14, 16; date of birth, 21; education, 22; debate with Vallabha, 22-23; contribution to movement and writings, 23; 48, 51-53; his T. S. (summary), 57-64, (text), 65-178; 179-88
jīva, 7, 9, 40, 51, 52, 70, 127, 131-44, 152, 153-56, 158-59, 161, 163-69, 173, 175-77
jīvaśakti, 40, 72
jñāna, 12, 17, 72, 151
Jñānasindhu, 30-31

Kaḍacā, 7, 9-10, 12
kaivalya, 153-54
kāla, 49, 154
Kāli, 10
Kali Yuga, 30, 65-66, 67, 78, 87, 101, 109, 110, 111, 117, 178
kalpa, 89, 90, 150
kāma, 19, 73
Kaṇāda, 78
Kane, P. V., 51
Karabhājana, 65-66
karaṇāpāṭava, 74
Kāraṇasamudra, 71
karman, 11, 12, 89, 134, 177
Karṇapūra, Kavi, 1, 6, 7, 12, 18, 33-34, 37, 49, 123, 182-83
Kaṭha Upaniṣad, 69, 84, 85
Katwa, 5
Kaustubha, 66
Kāvya, 118
Kena Upaniṣad, 133
Kennedy, Melville, xiv, 24
Keśava Bhāratī, 5-8, 11, 17, 32, 34, 55, 122, 182
Kramasandarbha, 15, 92, 99, 119
Kṛṣṇa, xii, 5, 10, 11, 27, 39, 45, 58, 60, 65-67, 70, 71-72, 73, 84, 110, 116, 117, 124, 125, 126, 129, 146-47, 149, 150, 170, 171, 181, 182
Kṛṣṇadāsa (Caitanya's attendant), 9
Kṛṣṇadāsa Kavirāja 2, 3, 5, 7, 9-13, 15, 17, 19, 36, 49, 71, 72, 179, 182, 183
Kṛṣṇadāsa Sārvabhauma, 27
Kṛśṇagaṇoddeśadīpikā, 49
Kṛṣṇakarṇāmṛta, 10
Kṛṣṇalīlāmṛta, 4
Kṛṣṇasandarbha, 58, 71, 147, 177
Kṛta Yuga, 66, 87
Kumārila, 98
Kūrma Purāṇa, 89, 171

Lakṣmī, 52, 123
Lakṣmīdhara, 147
Lakṣmīpati, 30-32
Lalitamādhava, xii
līlā, 141-42
līlāvatāra, 70, 96, 133
Liṅga Purāṇa, 89

Mādhava, 30-31
Mādhavendra Purī, 4, 7, 16, 17, 18,

20; his *sampradāya*, 30-32, 34, 35, 38; his association with Vṛndāvana temple, 35-36; 55, 122, 123, 182
Madhusūdana, 22
Madhva, xiii, 11, 12, 22, 25, 28-29, 30, 34, 39-42, 45, 48, 52-53, 55, 57, 59, 63, 64, 67, 68, 75, 111, 113, 114, 121-23, 180, 182-88
Mādhva Sampradāya, xiii-xv, 12, 18, 25-27, 29, 32, 35, 37-39, 45, 46, 49, 51, 76, 114, 122-23, 181, 182-88
Madhyandina Śruti, 78
Mahābhārata, 59, 76, 77, 80, 82, 85, 87, 97-99, 103, 106, 113, 121, 148, 150
Mahanama Brahmachari, 21
Mahānidhi, 30
Mahāpurāṇa, 60, 161, 170, 171
Mahāsaṃhitā, 121
mahat, 71, 163, 172-73, 175
mahāvākya, 6-7, 75
Majumdar, A. K., xv, 6, 8, 18, 19, 22, 28-29, 30, 37, 41, 45, 122
Majumdar, B. B., xv, 18, 32-33, 49
Manu, 173
Manu Smṛti, 77-78, 85
manvantara, 161, 163, 170-71, 173-74
manvantarāvatāra, 70
Mathurā, 68
Matsya Purāṇa, 82, 89, 90-92, 95, 110, 117, 148, 171
māyā, 9, 60, 69, 70, 125, 127, 129-36, 139-41, 143, 145, 149, 154, 175-77
māyāśakti, 40, 72
Māyāvāda, 13, 51, 52, 59, 67, 111
Māyāvādin, 7, 11, 51
mokṣa, 19, 73
Mukherjee, Prabhat, 34-35, 36
Muktāphala, 109, 118
mukti, 11, 19, 161, 163-64, 170, 175
Mūla Maṭha, 31
Mysore, 25

Nāmakaumudī, 147
Nārada, 14, 34, 64, 101, 114, 115, 116, 117, 118, 128, 148
Nārada Purāṇa, 87, 89
Narahari Cakravartin, 24
Nārāyaṇa, 28, 34, 45, 52, 53, 64, 69, 70, 71, 87, 96, 98
Narottama, 23
Navadvīpa, xi, 1, 3-5, 16, 22, 26
Navya Nyāya, xi, 8
Nayanānanda, 48
Nimāi, see Caitanya
Nimbārka, 30, 43, 45, 49, 181
Nimi, 65, 155
nirodha, 161, 163-64, 170-71
Nirukta, 157
Nityānanda, 2, 5, 12, 22, 23, 24, 30, 39, 48, 67, 187
Nityānandadāsa, 23
Nityasvarūpa Brahmacārī, 53, 61-62
Nṛhari (Narahari), 30-31
Nyāya, 22, 143, 151
Nyāyasūtra, 54

O'Connell, Joseph, xiv, 186
om, 14
Orissa, 25, 34

Padmakota, 10
Padmanābha, 30-31, 34
Padma Purāṇa, 30, 39, 49, 71, 85, 89, 111, 128
pañcabhāva, 39
Pāṇini Sūtra, 104
paramātman, 40, 58, 70, 71-72, 104, 128, 130, 142, 151, 154, 156, 164, 167, 168-69, 170, 173, 176, 181
Paramātmasandarbha, 58, 106, 154, 177
Paramavyoman, 69, 70-71
parameśvara, 131, 132, 134, 137, 163, 175
Parāśara, 86, 87
Parekh, M. C., 35
Paricchedavāda, 60, 136-41
Parikṣit, 83, 115, 116, 118, 126
paurāṇika pramāṇas, 41
Pippalāyana, 155, 158
poṣaṇa, 161, 163, 173
Pradhāna, 71
pradhāna, 85
Pradyumna, 70
Prahlāda, 95
prājña, 177
Prakāśānanda, 13-14, 93
prakṛti, 40, 52-53, 70, 71, 85, 129, 140, 152, 172, 177
pramāda, 74
pramāṇa, 40-42, 58; discussion in T. S., 73-123
Prameyaratnāvalī, xv, 30, 33, 39, 42, 45, 73-74
prāṇa, 155-56, 158
prasthānatraya, 46, 49
Pratāpa Rudra, 34
prātibhāsika, 139
Pratibimbavāda, 60, 136-40
pratyakṣa, 40, 73-74, 75-76
Pravargya ceremony, 95, 96
Prayāga, 13, 21
prayojana, 58, 60, 63, 73, 74, 125, 131, 132, 144, 146, 147, 150
preman, 9, 19, 69, 71, 73, 127, 145-47
Premavilāsa, 21, 23
Prītisandarbha, 58, 154
Puṇyāraṇya, 112, 113

Purāṇa, 9, 53, 58-59, 63; authority of, 77-123
Purī, 8, 9, 12-13, 15, 17, 20, 34
Purīdāsa, 61-62
Purūravas, 80
puruṣa, 60, 69, 70, 105, 107, 127-30, 140, 141, 146-47, 163, 166, 167, 169, 173
puruṣārtha, 11, 71, 73
puruṣāvatāra, 70
Puruṣottama, 30, 87
Pūrva Mīmāṃsā, 22, 80

Rādhā, xii, 10, 27-28, 39, 45, 50, 72, 181
Rādhādāmodara, 25-26, 41-42, 48, 134
Rādhākānta Maṭha, 34
Rādhāmohana, xvi, 17, 51-55, 62,T. S. commentary, 65-178; 185-87
rāgabhakti, 72
Raghunandana, 54
Raghunātha Bhaṭṭa, xii
Raghunātha Dāsa, xii, xiii
Rājendra, 30
rakṣā, 170-71, 173
Rāma, 45, 181
Rāmānanda Rāya, 10, 66
Rāmānandins, xiii, 28-29, 44-45, 47
Rāmānuja, xiii, 22, 30, 41, 52, 57, 59-60, 63, 68, 75, 119, 180
Rāmāyaṇa, 106
Rāmkeli, 21
Rāmmohan Roy, 63, 185-86
rasa, xii, 10
Rasikānanda Murāri, 48
Remunā, 25, 36
Ṛgveda, 78-80, 84
Roy, A. K., 29, 43, 44
rucibhakti, 39
Rudra, 30, 87
Rudra Sampradāya, 37, 47
Rūpa, xii, 10, 13, 16, 21, 22, 27, 43, 44, 48, 57, 63, 68, 177, 179

śabda, 9, 40-41, 42, 58, 73-74, 75, 77, 79
Sadācārī Rājā, 26
Sadānanda, 74
sādhana, 11, 63, 72, 145, 146
sādhya, 11, 63
Śākta, xi
śakti, 9, 19, 39, 40, 52-53, 104, 129, 130, 133, 151, 154, 168, 175, 181
Śaktipariṇāmavāda, 9, 40, 41, 49
samādhi, 60, 63, 91, 127-28, 134, 143, 144, 149, 153, 175, 177
samaṣṭi, 60, 161
Sāmaveda, 78-80, 81, 84, 97, 101, 105
sambandha, 58, 60, 73, 74, 150-51, 176-77
sambhava, 73
saṃsthā, 170, 171, 175
Sanaka, 30
Sanakādi Sampradāya, 45
Sananda, 30
Sanātana (Gosvāmin), xii, xiii, 13, 21, 22-23, 57, 63, 68, 178, 179
Sanātana (Sanakādi), 30
Sanatkumāra, 30
Sandhyā rites, 108
Śaṅkara, 10, 13, 15, 16, 17, 18, 19, 22, 25, 40, 41, 48, 51-52, 53, 55, 59, 74, 75, 80, 98, 110, 112, 113, 121, 122, 132, 135, 136, 142, 182, 183, 185
Śāṅkara Sampradāya, 18, 19, 32
Saṅkarṣaṇa, 70
Sāṅkhya, 85, 177
saṅkīrtana, xi, xii, 4, 5, 8
Śāntipur, 4, 51
Sārasvata Gauḍīya Āsana and Mission (Gauḍīya Mission), 48, 186-87
Sārasvata Kalpa, 94, 105, 108
Sarasvatī, 89, 105, 108
Sarasvatī Sampradāya, 19
sarga, 161, 163, 170-73
Sarkar, Jadunath, xi, 21, 23
Sārvabhauma, Vāsudeva, 8-9, 10, 13, 19, 22
Sarvasaṃvādinī, xv, 22, 57, 62, 67, 74, 76, 85, 182, 183
Śatapatha Brāhmaṇa, 80
Ṣaṭsandarbha, see *Bhāgavatasandarbha*
Sātvata, 112, 113
Sātvatasaṃhitā, 127, 144
Satyavatī, 87
Śaunaka, 82, 104, 124, 127, 149, 150
Savitṛ, 107, 108
Sāvitrī, 105, 108
Sen, D. C., xv., 1, 10, 18, 20, 23, 36
Shah, J. G., 35, 36
Sharma, B.N.K., 12, 41, 63, 113, 123
Siddhāntaratna, 49-50
Sinha, Jadunath, 48
Sītā, 45
Śiva, 59, 70, 104, 110, 111, 181
Śiva Purāṇa, 84, 89, 171
Skanda Purāṇa, 79, 84, 85, 86, 87, 88, 89, 94, 95, 98, 101, 106, 108, 148
Smārta, 17, 52
Smṛti, 75, 85, 88, 143
Soma, 128
Sphoṭavāda, 75
Śrī, 30, 70, 119
Śrībhāṣya, 119
Śrīdhara, 14-17, 19, 20, 51, 52, 54, 57, 59, 62, 65, 66, 68, 82, 83, 92, 93, 95, 99, 106, 108, 119, 120, 124, 128,

130, 151, 156, 157, 159, 161, 162, 164, 166, 168, 170, 171, 174, 177, 180, 181, 185, 187
Śrīkṛṣṇabhāvanāmṛta, 42
Śrīkṛṣṇacaitanyacaritāmṛta, 1
Śrīnivāsa, 23
Śrīraṅgam, 68
Śrī Sampradāya, xiii, 26-27, 44, 47, 49
Śrīvāsa, 67
Śrīvatsa, 66
Śṛṅgeri, 10, 18
Śruti, 69, 76, 80, 112, 118, 121, 129, 133, 135, 137, 142, 143, 154, 159, 161, 166, 171
Stavamālā, 43
sthāna (*sthiti*), 161, 163, 173
śūdra, 78, 80, 85, 92, 103
Śuka, 66, 83, 95, 112, 114, 116, 117, 118, 124-26, 140, 148, 149, 150, 161, 162, 165, 168
Śukahṛdaya, 109, 141
Sūrya, 104, 166, 167
Sūta, 81, 82, 84, 85, 124, 127, 131, 140, 141, 144, 147, 148, 149, 150, 153, 170, 172, 176
svarūpaśakti, 72, 129, 130
Śyāmānanda, 23, 48
Śyāmasundara, 66

taijasa, 177
Taittirīya Upaniṣad, 69, 153
Tantrabhāgavata, 109, 121
taṭasthaśakti, 72
tattva, 42, 49, 58, 60, 134, 151, 161
Tattvasandarbha, xv, xvi, 9, 17, 51, 53-55; summary, 57-60; editions, 60-64; text, 65-178; 179, 180, 183, 185, 187
Tattvavādin, 11, 12, 121, 122, 182
Tīrtha Sampradāya, 19, 31
Tretā Yuga, 66, 87
Tvaṣṭṛ, 96

Uḍipī, 11, 12, 182
Ugraśravas, 85
Ujjvalanīlamaṇi, xii
upādhi, 131, 137, 139, 141, 142, 158, 175
upākhyāna, 82, 83
upamāna, 73, 74
Upaniṣad, 14, 41, 42, 46, 53, 58, 88, 98, 153
Upapurāṇa, 171
Urvaśī, 80
Uttara Todari, 44
ūti, 161, 163, 173

Vācaspati Miśra, 22, 75
vaidhībhakti, 39
vaidya, 96
Vaikuṇṭha, 11, 70, 105
Vairāgin, 24, 186
Vaiśeṣika, 151
Vaiṣṇavatoṣiṇī, xiii
Vaiṣṇavavandanā, 182
Vaiśya, 25
Vakreśvara Paṇḍit, 33-34
Vallabha, 14, 15, 19, 22, 24, 35-36, 38, 47, 171, 181
Vallabhācārins, xiii, 37, 47
Vallabha Sampradāya, 24, 35
Vāmadeva, 176
Vāmana Purāṇa, 89
vaṃśa, 170, 171, 174
vaṃśānucarita, 170, 171, 174
Varāha Purāṇa, 89
Varṇavāda, 75
Vasu, B. D., 122
Vāyu, 122
Vāyu Purāṇa, 81, 82, 171
Veda, 9, 14, 41, 42, 58-59, 75, 76, 77-88, 90, 91, 92, 97, 100, 101, 103, 105, 112, 121, 123, 173
Vedāṅga, 88
Vedānta, xiii, 13, 17, 22, 46, 48, 110, 121, 180
Vedāntasāra, 74, 132
Vedāntasyamantaka, 41-42, 134
vibhava (*vaibhava*), 70
Vidagdhamādhava, xii
vidyā, 135, 139
Vidyānagara, 10
Vidyānidhi, 30
Vidyāpati, 16
Vijayadhvaja, 92, 121, 123, 171
Vijaya Gopāla, 27
vikṣepaśakti, 132
vilāsa, 70
vipralipsā, 74
Vīrabhadra, 23, 24, 187
Virāj, 163
Virajā River, 71
Vīrarāghava, 171
visarga, 161, 163, 170, 171, 173
viṣaya, 73, 74
viśeṣa, 39-42
Viṣṇu, 40, 52, 59, 70, 95, 104, 105, 107, 149, 173
Viṣṇudharmottara Purāṇa, 65, 84, 100
Viṣṇupriyā, 4
Viṣṇu Purāṇa, 9, 17, 39, 82, 85, 86, 89, 120, 170, 171, 181
Viṣṇu Purī, 16, 20, 32
Viṣṇusvāmin, 30, 37, 47, 49
viśva, 177
Viśvambhara, 3; see Caitanya
Viśvanātha Cakravartin, 26-28, 33, 37, 38, 42, 47, 48, 184
Viśvarūpa, 96

Vivartavāda, 9
Vopadeva, 118, 171
Vṛndāvana, xii, xiii, 13, 21, 22, 23, 25, 26, 36, 38, 42-44, 47, 54, 71, 184, 185
Vṛndāvanadasa, 2, 5, 6, 8
Vṛtra, 91, 94, 96
vṛtti, 75, 157, 170, 171, 173
Vyañjulī vow, 95
Vyāsa, 13, 14, 34, 60, 63, 78, 80-82, 84-87, 90-91, 97-99, 112, 114-18, 121, 124, 126, 127, 129, 131, 133, 140, 141, 143, 145, 147-50, 153
Vyāsarāya Maṭha, 31, 35, 123
Vyāsa Tīrtha, 30-31, 121, 123
vyaṣṭi, 60, 161, 165
vyāvahārika, 138-39

Wilson, H. H., xiv, 49

yajña, 81
Yajurveda, 78-80, 81, 82, 83, 84, 85
Yāska, 157
Yaśodā, 110
Yoga, 63, 72, 145
yugāvatāra, 70

ERRATA

Page	Line	For	Read
12	5, 14, 17	Mādhva	Madhva
19	36	interyrtation	interpretation
34	21	Caitan-ya's	Caitanya's
45	2	Rāmānandans	Rāmānandins
63	8	*terms*	terms
63	33	Rāmanuja	Rāmānuja
85	36	*sūtas*	Sūtas
98	21	a'ter	after
106	5	*Purāṇas*	Purāṇas
136	38, 39, 40	*parıcchedavāda*	Paricchedavāda
136	40, 41	*pratıbımbavāda*	Pratibimbavāda
154	8	*brahman*, to be partless	*brahman* to be partless,
166	1	eye setc.,	eyes etc.,
177	40	...*garbh*	...*garbhe*
177	41	*eśrī*...	*śrī*...